Woodturning
A MANUAL OF TECHNIQUES

Hugh O'Neill

The Crowood Press

First published in 1989 by
The Crowood Press Ltd
Ramsbury, Marlborough
Wiltshire SN8 2HR

Paperback edition 1992
This impression 2001

British Library Cataloguing-in-Publication Data

A catalogue record for this book is available from the British Library.

ISBN 1 85223 723 6

Dedication
To the Committee and members of the Association of Woodturners of
Great Britain for their help, guidance and friendship.

Line-drawings by Terry Hunns
Photographs by Kevin O'Neill, Craft Supplies Ltd, and the author

Typeset by Action Typesetting Limited, Gloucester
Printed and bound in Great Britain by
The Bath Press, Bath

Contents

Introduction

If you are reading this book in bed, in those few quiet moments before sleep permeates the consciousness, then don't bother. Put the book down, go to sleep and dream of woodturning. You may learn more about the subject that way!

This book is not intended for 'just dipping into', nor is it for sitting down to and reading from cover to cover. I first had the idea of writing it some years ago when I did a review of some of the two-day woodturning courses that are offered in many parts of the country. Leaving apart the fact that some were good and a few were very poor, they all left me with one clear message. You are shown, and indeed try, many things over the two days. You return to your own workshop and try to put into practice some of the things you have learned. Initially you focus upon your own favourite form – it may be bowls, spindles or whatever. A week later you can really only remember about ten per cent of what you were taught. You have a vague idea about another twenty per cent of the basics, but can recall virtually nothing of the finer points that your instructor had passed on to you.

I thought then that what would be useful would be a book which first covers in detail the same ground as the courses, and then goes on into some of the more difficult things that you later have to work out for yourself – like turning natural edge work, equipping a workshop, thinking about design and so on. This book is intended as an adjunct to a short course, not a replacement for one. Equally I knew that beyond describing skills and recording the wrinkles, a little theory might show why we do things the way that we do. This would provide the sort of foundation upon which we all build technique and develop our own unique style. This is what I aim to do in this book.

The book has also been given a 'what happens next?' flavour. Once you have the basic course under your belt and can utilise most of the skills demonstrated, you will want to start to move forward. You are not an expert, nor are you quite ready for the expert advice presented on some of the major seminars.

You want to try some of the more difficult techniques like wet turning, natural edge pieces, and maybe hollow spheres. You wish to extend your knowledge of woods and how to use the materials that you can find without always having to go to the timber yard. So I have tried to fill the gap that occurs in the two or three years after the course.

Obviously the book will contain a lot of insights into what I do and the mistakes that I make. Hopefully, however, this is not a book about 'my way'. Where appropriate, and where known, I have referred to what other (and far more expert) turners do. Although some turners will try to tell you that 'this is the right way!' you only have to look at the variety of approaches followed and the ideas expounded by different master turners to know that there is no one way. It is what best suits you that really matters.

Over the years I have set myself up for criticism. It was in the *Woodworker* magazine that I first said that you can not learn woodturning from a book. I also said that photographs are usually a poor way of illustrating the skills of turning. So why are there photographs here? I have used sketches where they are needed and only used photographs where they do clearly illustrate a point. I still maintain that you can not learn turning from a book. We learn skills by doing and then letting the lessons permeate our subconscious.

Throughout the book there are exercises – these are meant to be tried as and when you read about them – not tomorrow or at the week-end when you are in the shed. You learn turning by getting 'hands-on' experience. The structure of the earlier parts of the book are based upon the idea of 'read a piece, then make a piece'.

Some may be surprised that the book does not start by looking at lathes. In fact I have put the chapter on choosing a lathe towards the end. I believe that the biggest mistake that you can make is to buy a lathe too soon. Such a purchase should not be considered until after you have done some turning.

You cannot know what to look for until you have tried various machines, and you can easily end up making an expensive mistake. Even more to the point, you cannot choose a suitable lathe until you know what sort of turning you are going to focus upon – and this will only crystallise after you have done some turning and tried various styles.

I started with a lathe attachment for a Black and Decker drill. It was given to me by a friend whose fence I had repaired (and I owe the lady in question a life-long debt of gratitude). As a lathe it was a good start because it was so bad! It very quickly showed me some of the things to avoid in my next lathe. It also became a challenge, presenting a never ending range of problems to be overcome. My second lathe, an Elu DB 180 was also not a deliberate choice made after careful consideration, but an unexpected bargain that I was offered. Despite its several faults and inadequacies, it soon paid for itself. It also showed me precisely what I wanted in my third lathe.

Now I use a massive old Wadkin RS which is marvellous, and it is supported by a Multico which was cheap and cheerful. Neither are perfect – perfection in lathes does not exist – everything is a compromise. Neither are they necessarily likely to suit you, your needs will probably be very different to mine, but they do suit me – at the moment! However, I already have plans for my next two!

So to get started beg, borrow, hire, or rent time on someone else's lathe. Go on a short course to a centre where you can try several lathes. Try the exercises in this book on a friend's lathe. Then sit back and think. Only then should you consider purchasing your own.

I have written this book with another theme in mind. I was a beginner when I first put a 'carpentry' chisel to wood forty-nine years ago at school. I was a beginner when I went on the two-day courses, I am a beginner now and I will be a beginner the next time I go into my workshop and on every occasion after that. I know that I will always have things to learn, ideas to try out, mistakes to make, and new skills to develop. Sometimes I put to one side all the short-cuts that I have been shown, and start again from basic principles; this way I unlearn some of the bad habits which come with familiarity. So this book is for beginners – novice beginners, five years experienced beginners; even, hopefully, a few hoary old pro-beginners.

Perhaps my biggest learning experience in recent times has been the writing of this book. It has made me think through what I do, and analyse all the whys and wherefores of every bit of technique that I use. Some aspects did not stand up to the examination – clearly they were bad habits that had crept in and become firmly established. So to every reader I have to say, 'Thank you! Thank you for making me a better turner.'

Finally, you may find there is some repetition in the contents. This is quite deliberate. We learn by rote, by practice, by analysis, by use, and by frequent recall. Nobody takes in everything the first time, so some key points of practice have been reiterated as a lead into considering some variations or related topic. There are also some things that we cannot remind ourselves of often enough. I know one turner of many years experience who, as he switches on the lathe for the first time each day, says, 'Remember to keep the bevel rubbing.'

So let's begin with a little 'hands-on'.

1 Getting Started

It is workshop time!

You will need a plane, a chisel, a mallet, a sharpening stone, a vice (or means of holding the wood), and some scraps of timber. A bit of old deal will do.

Start with the plane. Hopefully the cutting edge is a little dull from when the kid tried to smooth a bump off the concrete path. Set the blade to give a coarsish cut – the blade clearly showing below the shoe of the plane. Now take a cut along the grain of the piece of deal. With considerable effort you will produce a coarse, broken 'shaving'. The 'finished' surface of the wood is torn, and fibres have split away. With the plane in this condition we won't even try to make a pass across the end grain – it probably would not cut at all however hard you push.

Now give the iron a few rubs on the sharpening stone and then fix it back into the plane. This time set it fine – only the merest edge of the blade will be showing. In fact if it is set fine enough you will probably detect the blade edge more by feel than by sight. This time, as you make a pass along the wood, you will find that with very little effort you can produce a long, fine shaving and the surface of the wood will be smooth and polished.

Try also a pass across the end grain. You will not produce a shaving but rather fine 'sawdust'. Unless the blade was super-sharp the cut face may be flat, but it is likely to be 'pitted' where each fibre of the grain has been torn away from the

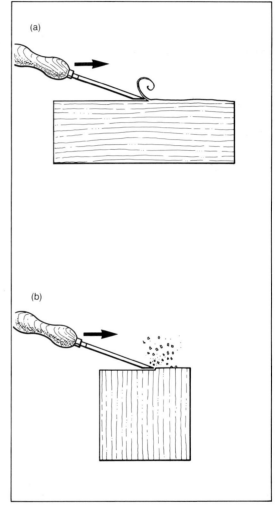

Cutting along and across grain. (a) Cutting along the grain, the chisel parts the long fibres from their neighbour. A flat bevel rubs on the cut timber and prevents the edge digging in deep. The result is a clean cut and fine shavings. (b) Working across the grain, the chisel slices off the ends of the grain which break away as 'sawdust'.

adjacent one. The corner may have broken away where the plane exited from the pass.

Yes, of course, you can remember all that from your early days of woodworking – probably from school. Nevertheless try it again now and as you do so tell yourself:

'One: blunt tools tear wood, and with the power and speed of a lathe the tearing is likely to be even greater than this.
Two: taking deep cuts also tears wood and requires much more effort.
Three: fine cuts are easy.
Four: fine cuts with sharp tools leave smooth finishes.
Five: a really fine planing cut with a sharp tool leaves a finish more "polished" than will the finest grade of sandpaper.'

And as you go off the edge on the end grain and the corner breaks away:

'And six. Wood that is unsupported and is cut across the grain, parts along the fibres and tears away.'

There is another little test that is worth doing to further illustrate this point. Take a clean paintbrush and stroke the ends of the bristles across the edge of a table. To start with, and through the middle of the stroke, the bristles will be bent back but will stay together as a mass. However as you get to the edge the remaining bristles will lodge on the table edge and will part right away from the mass. This is exactly what happens when you cut across end grain of a piece of wood. In fact it is worse. The fibres of the wood cannot bend as do the brush bristles; so they tear apart, break off, and leave the surface pitted.

In a nutshell what you have demon-

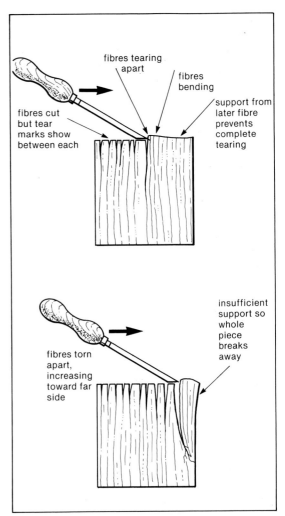

Cutting end grain – even with a fairly sharp chisel.

strated for yourself is a substantial part of the theory of tool choice and tool control in woodturning.

Of course there is a difference between a plane (and a carpentry chisel), and the lathe and its tools. Indeed there are two fundamental differences. First, with the plane there is the body and shoe plate to prevent the blade digging in or taking too deep a cut. The second difference is that you move the plane and keep the wood fixed. In essence, with the lathe it is the other way around. You move the wood and keep the tool (and the lathe) still – or at least you try to!

So let's see how we can emulate the plane when we are using tools without the assistance of the depth-controlling shoe plates. It is back to the workbench time!

This time use an ordinary chisel; you might as well start with it nice and sharp – we already know that 'blunt tools tear wood'. Try two things. First rest the bevel of the chisel on the surface of the piece of wood. Now, holding the chisel handle firmly with one hand and with the finger and thumb of the other gripping and steadying the blade, push the tool along the surface of the wood. Keep the bevel flat and rubbing on the surface of the wood and you will not take off a shaving but you will polish or 'burnish' the surface.

Take another pass. This time raise the handle of the chisel the merest fraction until the edge starts to cut into the wood. Now you do take off a fine shaving but, providing you keep the bevel rubbing behind the cutting edge, you will still burnish the wood. The chisel glides easily along, and passes through the wood quickly. If it doesn't then go and sharpen the tool!

The third pass is going to take much more effort. Increase the angle of the blade, push harder, and the chisel digs in, taking off a thick shaving and leaving a slightly rougher surface. The chisel pass was much slower. Too steep an angle or loss of control of the blade and you dig in and the pass stops.

Last exercise. Cut a small mortise into the wood – a rectangular hole. Keep the faces vertical. You will probably have to use a mallet. Note how the cut across the end grain leaves a clean polished face (if the chisel is sharp enough) whereas the cut made along the grain tends to break away long splinters. The chisel did not pass through the wood, but proceeded in a series of short jerks with each mallet blow.

So, what are the lessons here?

1 The chisel bevel should be kept in contact with the wood as it:
   (a) Controls the depth of cut (just like the shoe of the plane).
   (b) Leaves a clean cut and burnishes the surface of the wood.
2 Once the edge of the blade is unsupported by the bevel rubbing on the wood behind the cut, the edge digs in.
3 When cutting along the grain with a tool that is anything less than razor-sharp, then you tend to lift up and tear through the fibres rather than slice them.
4 In fine cuts the chisel moves much more quickly, whereas with coarser cuts chisel speed is lower and the effort required is greater.

Probably the only principle of turning that the exercises have not now demonstrated is that the corners of the edges of tools can catch on a rotating work piece and dig in.

If you always have these principles in mind, you will usually know what sort of tool to use to do different turning jobs. You can work out where to set the lathe tool rest, and even the speed at which the lathe should be run.

So let's take our first look at the lathe. A few moments ago we saw that the difference between the plane and the lathe was that with the former the tool moved and the wood remained still, whereas with the

9

lathe it is the opposite way round. It is both as simple as that, and yet as complicated.

The lathe takes the effort away – it moves the wood under power and (usually) in a predictable, 'fixed', rotary direction. As the lathe does the work, we can spend all our time, concentration and effort on controlling the tool. However you can stop a plane or a chisel in mid-cut – it is not so easy to stop a modern, high-power lathe in mid-rotation. Because it is moving the wood fairly fast, everything happens much faster. The merest slip with a tool edge can cause a disaster in milliseconds. There are stages in turning where the edge of the wood is only a blur – you have to make some guesses and go in boldly. Lathes are 'decisive' and they require decisive operators.

The biggest consideration of all is the obvious one. Lathes move the wood, but can only do so in a circular motion – so we can (broadly speaking) only produce round (or oval) objects with the lathe. So, while we think of chisels and planes as travelling in feet per second, we normally convert the feet per second of the wood passing the lathe tool into revolutions per minute of the lathe. What governs the choice of the speed of rotation that is used is still, effectively, the speed of the wood passing the tool tip as measured in feet per second.

There are optimum speeds of traverse of cutting tools across wood; and there are similarly optimum lathe speeds. As a basis, the rougher or coarser the work, the slower the speed we use. The finer the work the higher the speed. Within this framework we try to keep the speed of the wood past the tool fairly constant. This means one thing above all others – that the bigger the diameter of the wood we are turning the slower the speed of rotation that we have to use if we are to keep the rim speed (the speed of the surface of the wood past the lathe tool) roughly constant.

If you read some of the published recommendation of master turners you will find considerable variation. First, and not surprisingly, you find that each gives a recommendation on basic lathe speed. Some provide tables relating the diameter, and the length of the piece to the speed. They also differentiate between face plate and 'between centres' work. However not only will you find major variations, but also several inconsistencies.

Most of the well-known turner/authors recommend rotational speeds which give somewhere between 20 and 30 feet (6 and 9 metres) per second for the actual wood surface to be passing the turning tool. One turner, however, has a table which gives a rim speed range of from 1ft 6in (45cm) per second to 65 feet (20 metres) per second.

In subsequent chapters we will look at tables of recommended speeds for different types of turning and different sizes of workpiece. These will show the theoretical speeds as well as the actual speeds that I use, because it is the nearest that I have available on my lathe.

You may find some of the speeds on the high side. Don't worry. Find a speed that you are comfortable with even if it is somewhat slower. If you feel that you could go a little higher, and are confident about the firmness of the mounting of the wood, then go higher. In broad terms the higher the speed, the easier it is to get a good finish. The limitations are questions of safety and the speed with which mistakes can occur (and the distance which a piece of wood will travel if it does break free from the lathe).

There is another point to watch. Turning at high speed does set up stress in the timber and if there are any hidden flaws the wood may fly apart. It happened to me recently when demonstrating with an 8in (20.5cm) diameter 4in (10cm) thick yew bowl blank; it very nearly had disastrous consequences.

In broad terms you can use the more desirable faster speeds when turning between centres because the wood is more securely held in place. You can use faster speeds for shorter workpieces because there is again a more secure mounting. You should do roughing at half the speed of finishing turning for a similar sized piece of timber because of the strain that roughing puts on timber, mountings and tools.

If we start with the base line of aiming for a standard cutting speed of 25 feet (7.5 metres) per second, the following table

would hold good for a 2in (5cm) thick bowl blank or a spindle of up to 6in (15cm) in length. Looking at a table like this causes many turners to realise that on smaller items – say 6in (15cm) diameter and down – they do not turn fast enough. It also shows up the inadequacy of many lathes which have clearances capable of accepting 12 to 14in (30 to 36cm) diameter blanks but the lowest speed that they offer is 800 r.p.m.

You may also have identified another problem. Let's say that you are turning an 18in (45.5cm) diameter bowl. You set the lathe to 400 r.p.m. which gives a rim speed of 31ft/sec. But what about that sweeping cut where you are trying to get a nice tear-free finish on the inside base? As you near the centre the effective cutting speed is continuously decreasing. At 2in (5cm) out from centre the wood is travelling at about 3½ ft/sec.; at an inch you are down to 1.7ft/sec – hardly the speed at which to make a clean shearing

Table 1   Lathe speeds for different diameters of work.

Diameter of workpiece in inches	Theoretical revs for 25ft/sec	Likely available revs	Actual speed ft/sec	Probable roughing revs
1/2	11,457	3,000	6.5	3,000
1	5,728	3,000	13	3,000
2	2,864	2,500	22	1,500
3	1,909	1,800	24	800
4	1,432	1,500	26	800
6	954	1,000	26	500
8	716	800	28	500
10	572	500	22	250
12	477	500	26	250
18	318	400	31	250
24	238	250	26	250
36	159	250	39	250

cut with a tool as crude as a wood-turning gouge!

Later we will consider some of the special problems of turning different woods, particularly burrs and knotty materials, and the requirements of turning natural edged or 'waney' pieces. In general I find that I prefer to work at half to three-quarters of the normal speed for a given diameter when I am working on 'scrubby', 'pippy', or rough woods.

There are some other basics to consider whilst talking about lathe speeds. Green wood cuts more readily than dry timber but it requires sharper tools to cut through the fibres and is more likely to tear when cutting across the grain. However, the sap does have some lubricating property.

Dense, tropical hardwoods blunt the tool very quickly and respond best to the use of smaller tools, lighter cuts and a higher speed of rotation. Some woods, such as Iroko, are particularly aggressive.

One thing is certain. When the wood first goes into the lathe – when it is not a perfect round, when it may be square or have warts, bumps or dents on it – then it must be turned slowly. Remember the chisel exercise. In roughing you are taking deep cuts in a series of jerks as each protrusion passes the tool. You are not concerned about the surface finish, you just want to remove wood! Deep cuts means slower cutting speed – or, on the lathe, slower revolving speed.

If the normal speed for the diameter that you are turning is 'x' then when roughing down, drop the speed to half 'x'. For instance the normal speed for shaping and finishing an 18in (46cm) diameter bowl is 400, but for roughing the outer rim it would be only 250 r.p.m. A 2in (5cm) spindle may be worked at 2,000 and even higher; but it should be roughed from a square to the round at about the 800 mark.

So to conclude this chapter, let's try that. If you have never used a lathe at all then it would be useful at this stage to read the first few pages of the later chapter on lathes just to become familiar with the names of the parts.

Any sort of timber will do. In fact for practice it is a good idea to use poor wood, not because you will be 'wasting' it anyway, but because the poorer the wood the more precise you have to be with your tool control if you are not to end up with torn surfaces.

It is useful to befriend a local builder and ask for any off-cuts – the ends of floor joists and rafters provide useful practice. If it is used wood watch out for the nails, and for early practice avoid the knotty pieces. A second source of good practice wood is a local window-frame maker. They often have pieces of Meranti and other low-grade hardwoods which are quite suitable for general practice and for the making of tool handles. Frame-makers will give you a bag full in return for the occasional handle.

For this exercise we want something about 2in (5cm) square and 9 to 12in (23 to 30cm) long. If the wood is not roughly square it is worthwhile squaring off on a saw table as this saves turning time.

We are going to turn this piece 'between centres' – that is, with the headstock drive in one end and the tail stock point supporting the wood at the other. This is also known as spindle turning as with chair legs, banister rails and so on. The closer you can get the centre axis of the wood to align with the axis of rotation of the lathe, then the less wood will be wasted and the larger will be the diameter of the spindle you are left to work on. So

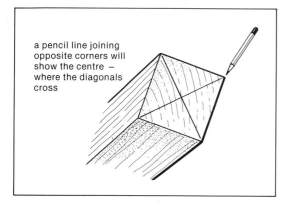

a pencil line joining opposite corners will show the centre – where the diagonals cross

Finding the centre of a square section.

Finding the centre of the squared timber by linking the diagonally opposite corners.

first find the centre of the ends of the piece of wood.

There are three ways of finding the centre of a squared piece of timber:

(a)   Guess.
(b)   Link diagonal corners.
(c)   Use a centring gauge.

Guessing is OK and some people are very good at it. For most it wastes wood! Linking diagonals is readily available, cheap and takes only a few seconds. Using a centring gauge is fast and reliable, once you have made a gauge! For now we will adopt the linking corners approach.

Using a steel ruler link the diagonally opposite corners and scribe a line with a sharp, hard grade pencil or an awl point. Repeat, linking the other two opposite corners. Where the two lines now intersect is the centre of the wood. You can use the same method for rectangular, square, or nearly squared wood. Next use a centre pop to indent the intersection point. A four or six inch nail makes a good 'pop' for this purpose. Repeat to find centre on the other end of the wood.

It is important that the drive spur is

Marking the point of intersection with a centre punch.

13

Indenting the drive spur to give a firm seating. Use a rubber hammer to avoid damage to the spur threads, or use an old spur. Never do this by hammering the wood on to a lathe-mounted spur.

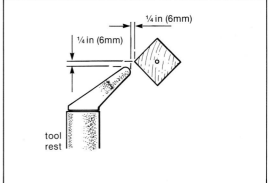

Tool rest position for roughing down.

firmly indented into the wood. Do not hammer the wood on to the spur whilst the latter is mounted on the lathe – this very quickly damages the lathe spindle bearings! It saves a lot of time if you have a spare spur for punching the drive end of the wood. Using a rubber hammer will avoid damaging the spur.

Offer up the timber to the spur on the lathe. Bring up the tailstock until the point sits in the centre popped mark on the outboard end of the wood. Clamp the tail stock, wind in the quill and lock it in position.

Set the tool rest so that it is parallel with the length of the wood and sufficiently far from it so that there is 1/8in (3mm) clearance between the rest and the corners. The height of the rest should be such that it is just below the centre axis of rotation of the lathe (to be precise, about 1/4in (6mm) below centre height). Rotate the wood by hand to check that all corners are clear. Always, after every adjustment of the tool rest, turn the work piece by hand to ensure that it clears the rest.

The tool that you want is the roughing gouge – that is the big, deep fluted one. You are going to start with the tool in a position where it could not cut anything. Rest the gouge with the flute vertically upwards, and with the underside of the blade bridging across and resting on both the tool rest and the top of the piece of timber. It should be near the right-hand end of the rest and towards the right-hand end of the timber. The tool should be at between 30 and 45 degrees to the axis of the lathe with the blade pointing to the left. The tool handle will be down at about 20 degrees from the horizontal.

Start the lathe, hold the gouge handle firmly in one hand and bring the tool down into the position just described. As each corner of the wood hits the underside of the blade it will bounce. To dampen out the bounce place the first two fingers of your free hand on top of the

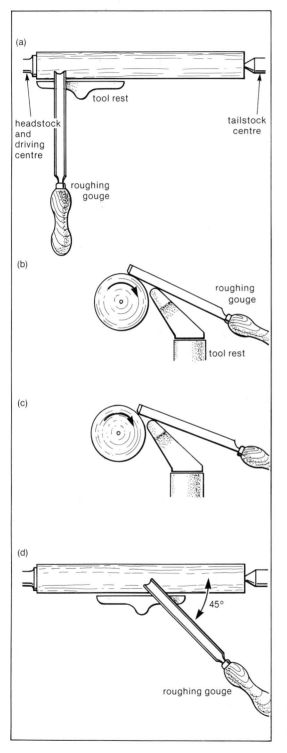

blade over the rest, and press the blade on to the rest.

At this stage as you look at the turning wood there will be two images. There will be a dark core and a fuzzy or blurred corona. The core marks the round diameter you will get down to, the hazy part is where you have the rapid interplay of the corners of the wood and the spaces between. This is the wood that you will have to remove.

Now, draw the blade back slowly. There will be a point at which the underside of the blade is no longer on the wood but now the bevel rubs. Again it will be bouncing on the corners of the rotating timber and it makes a sound like a world war one aeroplane engine. There are still no chippings coming off the wood. This is what is known as the 'bevel rubbing' position and, whatever the cut or the tool, this should be the starting position every time you take a tool to a piece of wood.

So, you always start with the tool firmly on the rest and the bevel rubbing. This is the control position and avoids the huge dig-ins you are likely to get by pushing the tool straight into the turning wood. Remember – over the top, and then draw back.

Once you have a feel for the chattering bevel rub, then draw back the handle of the tool a fraction further. Immediately, chippings will start to fly.

Left: Bringing wood to the round with the roughing gouge – 'roughing out'. (a) Tool rest is ⅛in(3mm) from the widest part of the wood (check by hand-spinning the wood). (b) Start with the back of the tool resting across the tool rest and rotating the wood. (c) Draw back the gouge until the bevel rubs on the wood, then draw it back a fraction further until cutting starts. (d) Angle of 45° at which normal roughing will later be done.

Roughing with a massive gouge. The blade is positioned to an angle of 45 degrees to the axis of the wood.

Keeping the tool firmly down on the rest move it slowly sideways. As the turnings fly, the hazy corona reduces in diameter. You are taking off the corners! Stop the lathe and have a look.

Start up again. Tool on the rest, bevel rubbing, and then draw back to start the cut. This time as you move the tool sideways roll it on its axis so that the flute is not vertically upwards but is just off the upright. Point the open flute in the direction of the cut. Continue the cut by moving the tool sideways on a line parallel with the lathes axis. As you reach the end of the timber (or that part of it within the compass of the tool rest) angle the tool the other way, again tilting the flute in the direction of cut and move sideways to make a cut in the opposite direction.

Repeat this, back and forward, until the corona just disappears and you can now

The cutting zone is at about 10 o'clock.

Roughing with a large bowl gouge.

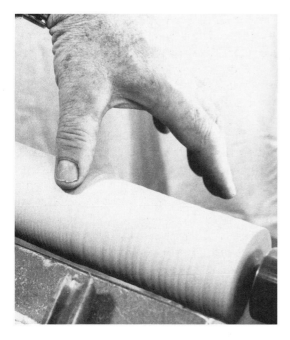

Testing for round. The tip of the thumb must point in the direction of rotation.

see a sharp outline of the turning timber.

You can check to see if you have completed the rounding out without stopping the lathe by resting the thumb lightly on the top of the rotating piece. Have the hand over the far side of the workpiece with the tip of the thumb pointing towards you. You will feel bumps if the corners have not quite gone.

Words of caution! A finger caught between the timber and the tool rest can be lost! Always have the tool rest close to the timber and make sure that the tip of the finger (or thumb) is pointing in the direction of rotation and never against it. Always keep it well clear from the rest, and make sure that your sleeves do not catch.

So we now have a cylinder. Stop the lathe and look at the finish. If you are using poor timber it is extremely unlikely that the finish will be good.

Try an experiment. Make sure that the tool is sharp and make a pass or two with the gouge at a different angle to the axis. You will find that there is an optimum. If too much towards the right-angle you get small chippings and a rough finish. Too fine an angle and you get fine ribbon shavings and burnished wood, but it takes a long time to get much off. Somewhere between, the cut is quite fast, the turnings are larger, and the finish is reasonable. The more that the alignment of the gouge is angled to the axis of the lathe the more the bevel rubs, and the more rubbing there is the better the finish.

Using the roughing gouge to round out a squared section equates broadly to the use of the chisel in our first exercises. The bevel is rubbing then we lift the handle slightly to get a cut. Some people use the roughing gouge more as a scraper, just chipping flakes off the corners. Why have a gouge in this case?

Perhaps, now we have a cylinder to work on, it is time that we looked at the other basic tools of woodturning.

2 Woodturning Tools

Chisels and planes cut wood. They peel off slices. According to the type of wood, the angle of approach to the grain, and the sharpness of the tool, you get either long, thin peelings or short, thick ones. If you use a rasp to shape wood, you tear off mini chips which look like sawdust.

In woodturning most of the tools that are used work in a planing fashion; they include chisels, skew chisels, gouges, and beading tools; we do, however, also approximate the rasp in that we also use tools called scrapers. There are some turners who only use scrapers, and others who regard scrapers as taboo! In fact each and every tool has its uses: and its problems!

CHISELS

The simplest chisel for the tool maker to make is, of course, a square-ended flat chisel with a single bevel. However, such a tool is useless for getting inside rounded corners and under the rims of bowls. So turning chisels are made into a variety of shapes to handle different types of jobs. Flat chisels have angled ends to work across the surface; these we call skew chisels. Corners are cut back and the whole blade is rounded into a semi-circular section to give what we call gouges. By having the sides of the chisel blade bent up to the gouge form, we can keep the corners out of the way when

cutting into concave recesses. Gouge bevels are ground at different angles to enable them to get deep inside rounded forms.

Scrapers, too, are profiled into various forms to get into round or square corners or under the lip of a recess. Sometimes we grind scrapers to special profiles to produce particular cuts or beadings.

Let's start a detailed examination of the different tools with the simple chisel. A conventional woodwork chisel has a square end and has the bevel on one side only. The woodturning equivalent normally has an angled end and has a bevel on both sides. The reason is simple.

If you took a square-ended chisel and went straight in at right-angles to the axis of rotation, the chisel would not cut while the bevel was rubbing. The moment that the edge caught, the wood would peel, the bevel would cease to rub and the pressure of the shaving on the top of the blade would force the blade deeper into the wood and in no time at all you would have a horrendous dig-in.

In order to keep the bevel rubbing we angle the blade to the axis of rotation (as we did with the roughing gouge). This way we also keep the corners clear by making sure that the cut is being taken somewhere near the centre of the edge. Obviously with a square-ended blade the whole tool would have to be held at a fine angle to the axis – it would almost be lying along rather than across the tool rest, and would be difficult to control. The

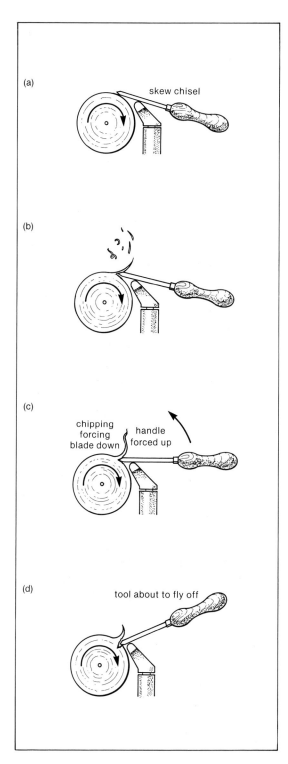

(a) skew chisel

(b)

(c) chipping forcing blade down — handle forced up

(d) tool about to fly off

tool handle (and our knuckles) might come close to the rotating wood, and the end of the handle would probably foul the tailstock. By grinding the edge at an angle we can maintain the correct angle at the cutting edge while having the tool at a more acute angle to the workpiece.

A 20 degree skew means that the edge can be presented to cut at 45 degrees to the axis of rotation while the tool handle is only 25 degrees from the right-angle.

The double-sided bevel means that the chisel can be worked from either end of the workpiece into both left- and right-handed corners (a substantial degree of ambidextrousness is invaluable to a woodturner).

The skew chisel is used in two basic ways. One is for planing down the outside of a cylinder working almost along the grain; the other is for cutting into corners, as on facing cuts, or making a round 'bead' where the cut is across the end grain.

The secret of planing with the skew chisel is to keep the cutting edge to about 45 degrees to the axis of rotation, to keep the actual cut somewhere near the centre of the edge thus keeping the corners clear, and, of course, to keep the bevel rubbing,

Left: How to get a dig-in! (a) Starting position, with the bevel rubbing on rotating wood – no cutting taking place. (b) Bevel still rubbing to support the blade, but the tool has been brought back until the tool edge just lifts fine shavings off the surface. The tool edge is now being pushed down into the wood by the shavings but the rubbing bevel and tool rest prevent dig-in. But – (c) The tool is drawn further back – no support from the bevel. Added pressure from shavings forces the blade down. It pivots on the tool rest and the handle is forced up. (d) The blade is pinched between the wood and the rest – it may wrench the wood off the mounting.

both to prevent the blade digging in and to burnish the surface of the cut wood.

Some instructors, when teaching a novice, put a little insulation tape over the long point corner of the chisel. This is a reminder of the 'danger zone' – if you catch the corner on the workpiece it digs in, skews across the surface and leaves a deep spiral groove.

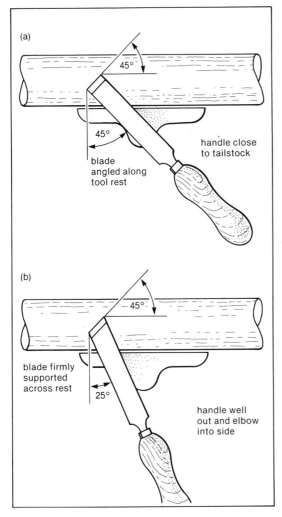

(a)

45°

45°

handle close to tailstock

blade angled along tool rest

(b)

45°

blade firmly supported across rest

25°

handle well out and elbow into side

Why skews are angle-ground. (a) Problems with square ended chisels. (b) The advantage of an angle-ground skew chisel.

How about trying it – not digging in (that will happen soon enough) – but planing with a skew. Until you are used to delicately handling a fine chisel you should work with a large broad one (the corners are further out of the way). Make sure that it is sharp. Work on the cylinder you previously roughed down. You can increase the speed of rotation now.

Position the tool rest higher. Ideally it should be half to ¾in (1.9cm) below the top of the workpiece for planing with a skew. Some lathes will not allow you to come this high as the tool rest posts are too short.

Again, for the first time start with the blade bridging the tool rest and the rotating timber. Present it so that the cutting edge is at 45 degrees to the axis of rotation. Draw the handle slowly back until the bevel rubs. Make sure that the contact between wood and blade is somewhere near the centre of the edge. Now draw the handle back a fraction more until the edge starts cutting. Do not draw back

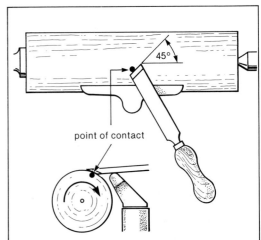

45°

point of contact

Planing with a skew chisel. The tool rest is raised to just below the top of the workpiece, with ⅛in(3mm) clearance from the wood.

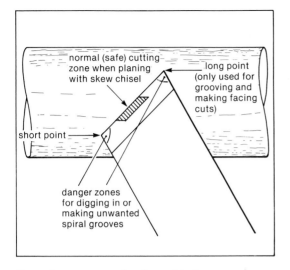

Go and no-go areas for skew chisels.

any further, but slowly move the tool sideways along the tool rest, keeping the cut in the centre of the edge. Just make one pass, stop the lathe and look at the finish. It should be smooth and burnished. Take two or three more cuts practising tool position, bevel rubbing, and sweeping, gentle cuts. If you centred your work properly, you stopped roughing as soon as you achieved a round cylinder, and your planing cuts were well-controlled you should now have a clean cylinder a fraction under 2in (5cm) diameter. The surface of the wood should have a polished appearance.

All other chisels and gouges work in exactly the same way as the skew. They are presented to cut at an angle, the bevel rubs and burnishes, but with gouges the corners are bent up so they cannot dig in.

The angle of grind on the skew bevel is not critical. The shallower the angle the keener will be the edge (and the quicker it will get blunt). The higher you get the tool rest, the shallower the angle of bevel you need. The thicker the chisel the steeper the angle of bevel you tend to get.

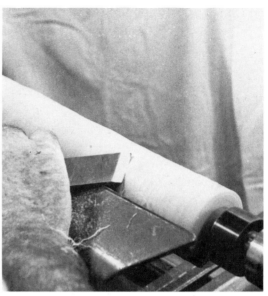

Planing with a skew chisel. The cutting edge of the blade is at 45 degrees to the axis of the wood, and the cutting zone is kept clearly in the middle of the blade.

The tool rest is set to just below the top of the wood for planing. In this example, the gap between the tool rest and the wood is too great.

I like broad skews made from high-quality steels of thin section with, as a basis, the edge set at an angle of between 10 and 20 degrees, and the bevel ground to about 18 degrees. Some turners curve the edge in a gentle arc – this helps to keep the corners out of the way, and a recent development has been the introduction of skews with the body made of an oval section instead of the usual flat bar. This helps when rolling the skew on to its side when turning beads.

One type of flat chisel that is set square is the beading tool used for turning small beads. It has a narrow section, and a thick blade.

Parting Tool

While considering square-ended chisels we have also to look at the parting tool. This, as its name implies, is used for parting off a finished workpiece or a section of the timber. The basic pattern is that of a flat chisel but the edge is ground vertically through the thickness of the blade rather than across its width. This means that the edge is on the end of a long, tapering point. It is used with the blade held in the vertical axis.

To use a parting tool, set the rest at the height of the rotation axis. The tool is held on the rest and at right-angles to the axis. Again, as always, start with the bevel rubbing. Draw back the handle until the edge starts to cut and grooves into the timber. Continue to draw the handle slowly back, lifting it slightly at the same time. The edge will cut deeper and deeper into the wood until it is cut right through.

There can be problems with a parting tool. They work very nicely taking what is a peeling cut into nice, clean, even-grained wood. They are not particularly

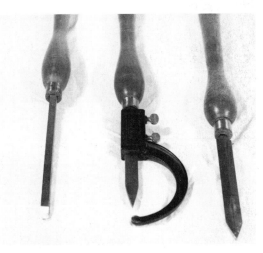

Parting tools. From right to left: diamond section parting tool – this section reduces wall friction and therefore heat build up; diamond tool fitted with a sizing gauge; beading and parting tool for broader groves and small bead cutting.

happy when used on knotty or burred wood. There are indeed times when the 'down and in' arc cutting has to be abandoned and the tool has to be pushed slowly in to the wood, pointing continuously at the axis of rotation. This way it scrapes its way through.

Equally, as they get deeper into the narrow groove the sides of the blade are rubbing on the wood, generating considerable friction. To reduce this problem some parting tools are made with diamond section blades and others have the cutting edge wider than the blade behind. You can manage without these refinements if you rock the blade from side to side fractionally on deeper cuts, thus making the groove slightly wider than the tool blade.

Let's try another exercise on our cylinder. Using the parting tool reduce the diameter of the cylinder at the tailstock end for the last eighth of an inch

Marking off a cylinder for grooving. A pencil point is held lightly against the rotating wood. Sometimes a steel rule is placed along the top of the tool rest to give dimensions.

Grooving with a parting tool. The tool rest is set on or just above centre height. The tool starts in the bevel rubbing position and is then drawn slowly back until a peeling cut starts. Thereafter the tip is arced down and in towards the centre of the wood.

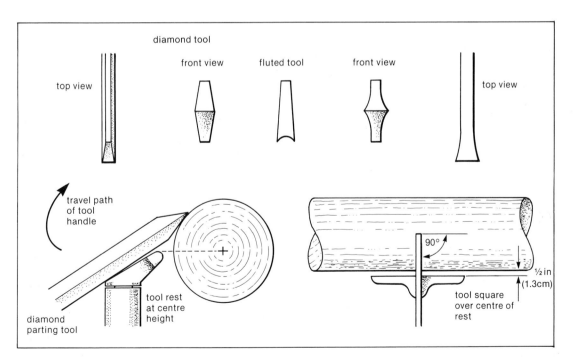

diamond tool

top view   front view   fluted tool   front view   top view

travel path of tool handle

diamond parting tool

tool rest at centre height

90°

tool square over centre of rest

½ in (1.3cm)

Parting tools.

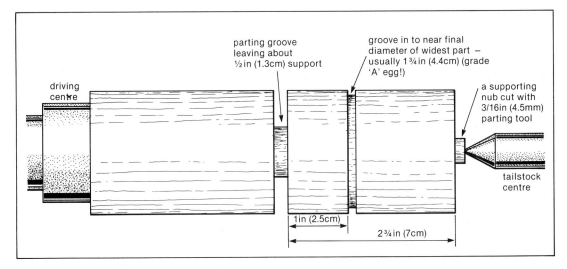

parting groove
leaving about
½in (1.3cm) support

groove in to near final
diameter of widest part –
usually 1¾in (4.4cm) (grade
'A' egg!)

driving
centre

a supporting
nub cut with
3/16in (4.5mm)
parting tool

tailstock
centre

1in (2.5cm)

2¾in (7cm)

Grooving the cylinder to give the working dimension for a turned egg.

to about half an inch. 2¾in (7cm) from the end face, cut into the timber as if parting off, but again leave the last half inch. You are going to start to make that 2¾in (7cm) piece into an egg.

Many turners use gouges to fashion eggs. That is the easy way! It is more satisfying, and good practice, to do your

egg-making with a skew chisel. Ultimately it is quicker and produces a better finish.

Have the point of the egg towards the tailstock end. The widest part of the egg will be 1in (2.5cm) in from the deep groove. If you hold the point of a pencil against the side of the cylinder at 1in

The marked and grooved cylinder for an egg. A nib has been left for the tailstock point. The parting groove is 2¾in (7cm) in from the end. One inch (2.5cm) back from the parting groove is a shallow groove which presets the finished maximum diameter of the egg.

Working down towards the point. Using a broad blade skew chisel reduces the chance of a dig-in.

(2.5cm) from the groove you will give yourself a working mark. This line is the area of maximum diameter.

You now have an option. You can shape the tapering pointed end with the skew held in your right or left hand. Left-handed people have no problem. The ambidextrous should also work this end left-handedly. If you are right handed and find left handed work too difficult then for this exercise angle the body and work with the chisel in the right hand, but mind your elbow and clothing on the rotating timber and chuck.

In future, practise right- and left-hand cutting with all tools, particularly the skew, until it becomes second nature.

Starting well to the right of the maximum diameter mark make a pass with the skew moving from left to right. This time as you move the tool sideways raise the

A long piece of timber is being used to produce several eggs one after the other. A long work steady can be seen — this prevents whip in the cylinder.

25

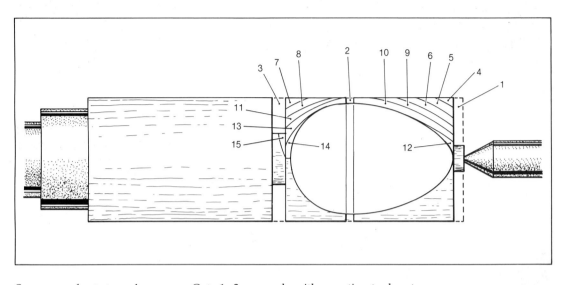

Sequence of cuts to make an egg. Cuts 1–3 are made with a parting tool; cuts 4–13 with a skew, long point up (planing); cuts 14–15 (and so on) with skew long point down (facing).

left hand (the handle of the tool) slightly so that the cut deepens and you start to chamfer and curve the pointed end of the egg. At all times watch the tip of the blade and ensure that the cut is being taken somewhere near the centre of the cutting edge. With each succeeding cut start a little closer to your working mark.

Now change hands to the right-hand hold so that you can round off the blunt end. To do this you will have to roll the skew on the tool rest; it will start flat and finish in the vertical axis. The handle of the tool will move to the right and rise quite considerably as you arc in. As you get deeper into the groove you may find that the rest is now too high. Set it down a quarter of an inch or so.

There are two things to watch for. First, you are working into the narrow space of the groove – if you do not like this, take another pass with the parting tool on the waste wood side of the parting groove to widen the gap. The second problem you may already have found out about – the dig-in! As you roll round the curve and into the deep groove you may lose sight of the lower corner of the skew and it could have caught. If it does, the tool will be forced out, it will bang on the tool rest, and there will be a spiral groove in the egg. You have had your first dig-in.

Novices go in fear and trepidation of dig-ins – until they have had a few! They rarely lead to anything more than a shock. Oh, and, of course, a smaller diameter egg as you have to take further cuts to hide the grooves!

It is worth practising this stage of egg making for some time until you can produce nice rounded blunt ends with a clean, polished cut; and you only dig in once in each dozen. I still calculate egg making on the basis of the 'Baker's Dozen' – one scrap for every twelve good eggs made!

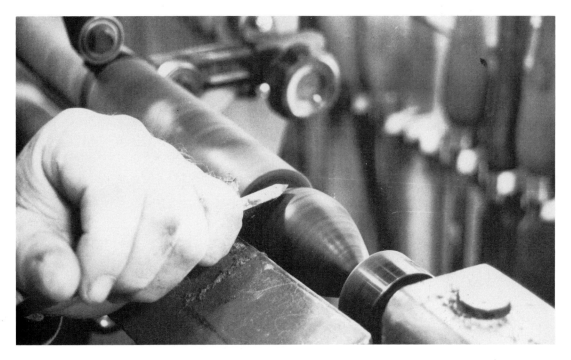

Turning the chisel on its axis to round off the blunt end of the egg.

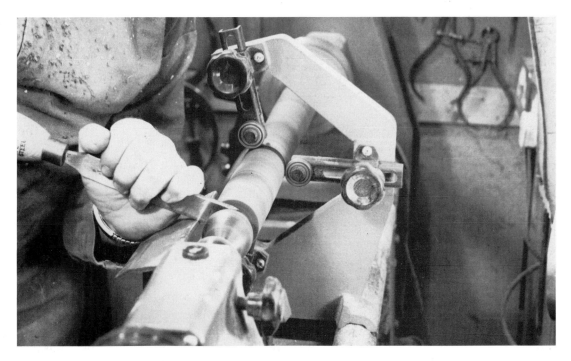

Parting through with alternating facing cuts on the headstock side and
rounding cuts on the base of the egg.

You could have done much of the shaping with a spindle gouge. There would have been less likelihood of a dig-in, but then you would not have produced such nice smooth curves, nor would you have got right round the blunt end. So where do the other tools fit in?

GOUGES

Spindle Gouge

The edge of the spindle gouge is curved, and for different purposes and to individual preference, the end profile may vary between a smooth, continuous arc to a more pointed finger-nail profile. The basic bevel is about 30 degrees, although I do have a couple with 20 degree 'skew' bevels. Some spindle gouges are made of a half-round bar with a shallow flute; others have a deeper hollow over a wider section and tend more to the 'flat chisel with bent up sides'.

Spindle gouges may be used for rounding beads, but their primary function is cutting covings and taking out rounded, concave areas.

Think of it this way. If you are rounding over (as with eggs) the shape of the work-piece is such that the corners of a skew chisel are going to be well clear. So we use a skew because they produce smooth surfaces free of ridges. If you are working in a confined space or producing concave curves the corners of a skew would too

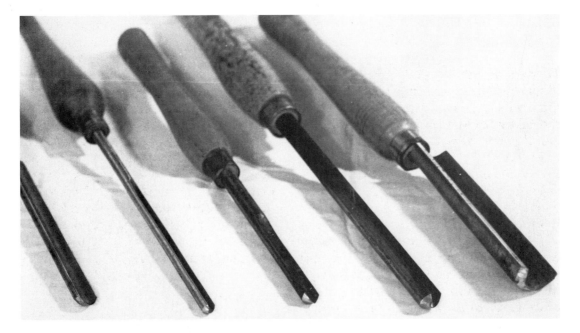

Gouges. From right to left: large roughing gouge with a square end; deep flute ½in (1.3cm) bowl gouge (known as a long and strong) in which the shoulders are ground back about ³/₁₆in (4.5mm); spindle gouge with pointed end; small bowl gouge with shoulders taken back a little; open gouge with slightly radiused end.

frequently catch, so we use the gouge in which the corners are bent up out of the way.

Roughing Gouge

The roughing gouge is a big, rugged gouge with the corners even more bent up. It is made so big and robust because in taking the corners off rough wood it takes a massive pounding. The bevel may be as fine as 30 degrees but can go up to 45 degrees with the heavier tools.

There are 2in (5cm)-wide roughing gouges available. However, many have small tangs and quickly bend under rough usage. I prefer tools of a much heavier section but possibly only an inch wide. Marples used to make a magnificent one – the blade was some 20in (51cm)-long and the tang a massive square section. This, in a 24in (61cm)-long handle, can cope with anything.

There is an advantage to big tools. The more solid the tool the more of the shocks it absorbs so that less are transmitted to the elbow of the arm holding the tool handle. If working on large, rough blanks or knotty or burred timber it is very easy to develop elbow trouble: usually what is known as 'golfers elbow'. A solid tool with a long handle held firmly against the thigh can help to minimise this problem.

Nice, shallow bevel angles give keener edges and cleaner cuts. Against this, the shallower the bevel the more frequently it needs sharpening. When working inside vessels, deep bowls, vases and the like, you cannot get the correct angle of attack through the mouth of the vessel and at depth it is impossible to maintain bevel contact with shallow-grind angles. So we have to increase the angle. We also want

to work with the tool approaching from many different angles. Furthermore, deep inside it would be even easier for the corners to catch. To overcome these problems we have the bowl gouge.

Bowl Gouge

These are usually made from round bar stock, the flute is deep and the bevel angle steeper, and the shoulders are ground back. No single tool is adequate. For a long time I worked with two, one ground to 42 degrees and one to 50. Then I found that going down the inside of a long curved taper, a pointed gouge with about 20 degrees was useful and that when trying to get a nice, flat inside bottom something nearer the 60 degrees-plus of a scraper was useful.

Hence I have a range of bowl gouges all ground to different bevel angles. All have the shoulders ground back a little. Every so often I experiment with the shoulders ground right back so that the tool can be used almost upside-down. Some of the experiments have been more useful than others – particularly a tool ground similar to one that the great American turner David Ellsworth uses. Liam O'Neill from Ireland offers specially ground bowl gouges that I find very useful for more advanced work. Both David and Liam's tools, however, have angles so compound that they cannot be described by a simple set of measurements.

Scraper

We are still trying to slice or cut rather than tear wood when we use the last of our basic types of turning tool – the scraper.

Used properly, the scraper is almost like

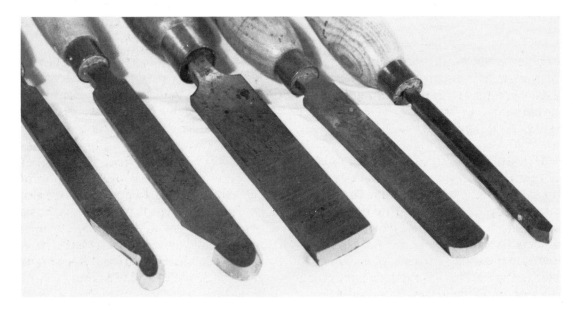

A range of scrapers. From right to left: small diamond point used for inside corners; large domed scraper for inside bowls; large square end for cleaning convex surfaces; medium rounded side scraper for inside concave surfaces; small rounded-side scraper for working under overhanging rims.

a gouge! If it is sharp enough, and it has been ground to give a burr on the leading edge, the burr peels off tiny shavings rather than tearing off splinters. The moment the burr has worn down the scraper really 'scrapes' and it is time to resharpen!

Broadly speaking, we profile scrapers to do the sort of job we require. Hence some have corners that are just under the right angle for getting into right-angle corners, others are rounded to get into curves. Some are designed to cut on the end, some on the side. Some have an incut rounded end for getting in under overhanging rims.

The action of scraping is a little like that of planing across the end grain. It requires more effort, it takes off only fine shavings, and it can easily tear the grains apart. The action tends to set up vibration in the tool blade and there is no bevel rubbing to prevent dig-ins. To overcome this we use

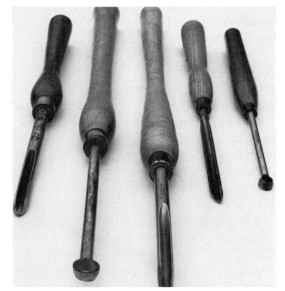

Special gouges. A medium and small ring gouge for end grain work, and three sizes of bowl gouge with the shoulders ground back to provide a cutting edge along the first inch and a half of the top of the flute. The centre gouge was profiled by Liam O'Neill.

heavier tools, support them on heavy-duty rests, position them to cut below the axis of rotation and tilt them slightly downwards so that if they vibrate they will get knocked outwards rather than dig in.

The normal bevel angle is about 60 to 70 degrees but can be as high as 80 for particularly heavy tools. Some turners do use shallower angles of grind on scrapers and Richard Raffen says he only ever uses 45 degrees.

If we take the principle of working below the centre axis when scraping the outside of a turning cylinder so that the edge cannot dig in, then when we start to scrape the inside of a hollow cylinder we must work above the axis of rotation for the same reason. The second difficulty when working inside is that of vibration. It is usually difficult to get the tool rest close to the cutting edge, and the greater the length of overhang from the rest to the edge, the greater the vibration level. Again this drives us towards using bigger and heavier tools as internal scrapers; but then the bigger they are the more difficult it is to find the space to keep them above the centre axis of the walls.

By keeping the edge really sharp, those turners who only ever use scrapers produce work with quite acceptable finishes.

Basic Tool Kit

There are those woodturners who only have a small range of tools – possibly two scrapers, two spindle gouges, a bowl gouge and a parting tool. Others seem to spend more time collecting tools than they do using them. I am afraid that I tend more to the school of having different tools for different jobs, and of trying

everything new that comes along. Therefore over the years, with purchases and gifts and manufacturers requests to try things, I have built up a considerable collection. (I daren't admit to over 60 – sorry that was last week. Over 70 now!)

It is difficult to recommend a basic set of tools; so much depends upon the sort of turning that you are doing and the type of lathe that you have. If we take as a basis an average hobbyist lathe to be used for spindle work and light bowls then the following starting-up kit would be suitable (HSS = High Speed Steel):

1in Roughing gouge
1in Skew chisel
½in Skew chisel
¼in Beading and parting tool
⅛in Parting tool – waisted or diamond
⅝in Spindle gouge – fingernail
¼in Spindle gouge – fingernail
½in Spindle gouge – square ended
¼in Bowl gouge – HSS deep-U
½in Bowl gouge – HSS 'Long and Strong'
1in Round nose scraper
1in Left hand corner scraper
½in Diamond point scraper

If working on fine items such as lace bobbins, then a finer skew chisel and an ⅛in square-ended scraper have to be considered. If working on large bowls then a bigger roughing gouge and a 2in dome scraper are essential.

I still prefer the older tools – they were usually bigger and heavier, and were often made of superb steel. Of today's tools I prefer High Speed Steel (HSS) as the tools do retain their edge longer and they can outlast by four or five times an equivalent tool in plain carbon steel. HSS also takes more punishment on the grinding wheel without loosing its temper. So far I have not tried chrome vanadium tools, but they should be good.

Some of the sets of tools on offer in DIY stores are a complete waste of money; the steel is very poor, they bend easily, do not hold an edge at all, and the handles are far too short for proper use.

One thing to avoid at all cost is home-made tools made from old files. This used to be a favourite cost-saving wheeze of schools. The temper of a file is unsuitable and one can shatter under shock, producing missiles far more deadly than an Exocet. You can of course retemper the steel if you know how, but the whole process of grinding and retempering requires considerable skill and takes so long that it is usually cheaper to buy the proper thing. Having said that, I have to acknowledge that some of the best minia-ture tools for detailed work are often made from masonry nails and similar.

It might be worth noting here that every year new tool shapes appear, as well as revamps of ideas from centuries ago. At various places in this book mention has been made of special tools used by some experts. Whilst it is always interesting to experiment and to try something new, do not look to fancy tools as a means of solving problems of technique. Some of the best old turners only ever used two or three types of tool. 'Two sizes of skew and three gouges is all you'll ever need, boy!' one turner of sixty-three years' continuous experience told me. He produced everything from four-poster bed legs to small goblets, and the finish was always perfect.

The time to experiment is when you have learned to make the proper use of all the basic tools and you now want to make some special shape which is physically beyond the capability of existing equip-ment.

3 Keeping an Edge

We all know that tools need to be sharp to be effective, but you meet very few people who keep them sharp enough. I know that I do not. The result is not only that extra energy and effort is required in using the tool; there is also the considerable amount of extra time that is required to put right the damage that blunt tools create. A quick lick on the grindstone to fine-up an edge can save five sheets of sandpaper and three-quarters of an hour of tedious buffing and grinding.

Unfortunately it is the lathe's motor that puts most of the effort into the turning process. You may therefore be unaware that a tool needs sharpening until you stop the lathe, thinking you have finished, only to see a mass of torn fibres where you have crossed the end grain.

I have already mentioned the angles at which the different types of tools should be ground; further reference has and will be made to this as each different type of turning work is considered in more detail. Tool sharpening and the angle of grind is the subject that causes most concern to beginners and generates the most heated argument amongst experts. There is a basic set of theories; these are tempered with personal preference, and then everything is modified according to the type of work that we want to do.

First, just think back over the theory. Chisels and gouges are frequently used working along the grain. You are trying to cut cleanly through the fibres producing thin shavings by lifting a little off the surface. You use the tool in such a way that the bevel rubs on the cut surface behind the cutting edge. This does two things. First it provides control and prevents the tool from cutting in too deep, and second it polishes or burnishes the cut face. All this means that we need a keen cutting edge and a shallow bevel angle.

Parting tools are vertical chisels and work in the same way; thin shavings with a bevel rubbing. Gouges are chisels with the corners bent. They are designed to work inside curves. Sometimes the curve that you wish to work is deep inside a confined space. You could not present the tool and keep the bevel rubbing if the bevel was ground to a normal chisel angle, so you must modify the bevel angle on gouges. For this reason the angle of grind on an average bowl gouge has to be steeper than that on a skew chisel.

But that is the average. To get in under the lip of a narrow mouthed bowl or vase you may need a gouge ground to a much shallower angle than that of a standard chisel. To get deep down to the bottom of a deep vessel the gouge will have a much steeper bevel – at times approaching that of the scraper.

The scraper, on the other hand, is used in such a way that you do not have the bevel rubbing. In fact you should deliberately go the other way. The cut is now made by a little feather burr raised on the tip of the cutting edge, and the tool is

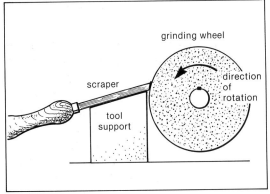

Grinding a scraper on a rotary grindstone.

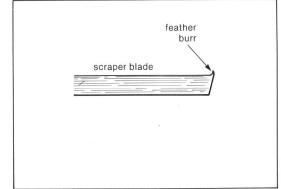

The feather burr, produced on a rotary grindstone, should not be removed. It helps to give clean scraping.

used both for cutting across end grain and for working along or with the grain.

At one time the greatest controversy amongst turners revolved around the manner of sharpening tools rather than the specific angle of bevel. A few still insist on doing all sharpening on flat stones. Some roughly sharpen on power grindstones and then finish on flat stones with a final strop on leather. The increasing majority sharpen on a grind wheel only, and use the tool 'straight off the wheel'. I must admit to being one of this school. It not only saves time, but with the single exception of the skew chisel it produces a better cutting edge. Indeed it is almost the only way to get a good edge and burr on a scraper.

It is undoubtedly true that finishing on a flat stone (and maybe then stropping on a leather) does give a skew the keenest finish and produces an edge that lasts a trifle longer in use. However, sharpening this way takes so long that many who follow the practice do not sharpen their tools as frequently – they let them get that little bit blunter before stopping to sharpen.

Tools properly sharpened on a suitable grind wheel are very keen, the edge lasts nearly as long, and they can be constantly resharpened, virtually without interrupting the work flow, as it takes only a second and a half to give them a quick touch-up on a handy grind wheel.

One of the great problems with powered grinding wheels is that of overheating the blade and destroying the temper. High-speed steels are much less susceptible to this problem than are even the best carbon steel tools; but even these need care. If the sharpening requires two or more passes across the wheel, it is advisable to quench the edge in cold water between passes even when using the high speed steels; indeed many turners always dip the tool into water before putting it on to the grind wheel.

In flat stone sharpening of hand tools (wood chisels and plane blades), we use a coarse-grade grit for shaping and then a much finer one for honing an edge. Water or oil is used not so much as a coolant but to carry away the particles of stone and steel created, and thus prevent the pores of the stone clogging.

Sharpening of lathe tools on a powered grind wheel is done dry and to avoid the clogging problem we use a very coarse grade of grit. Many experts use high-speed wheels of 60 grit, a few tend towards the 100. I compromise and do everything with 80 grit. A few turners also finish off on fine grit or slow-speed wheels.

Sharpening on a rotating wheel does mean that the bevel is going to be ground concave. This does not matter as long as it is not overdone. With a scraper a quite pronounced concave to the bevel is no problem, but on a skew it can be. Wheels of less than 6in (15cm) in diameter are not really satisfactory; 8 to 10in (20.5 to 25.5cm) are better and the massive old hand-turned farm grind wheels are still ideal though not very practical for a quick sharpen.

Typically, a coarse grit powered wheel will be driven at 1,000 to 1,250 r.p.m. and the bevel is always ground against the direction of rotation.

There is one problem which we all encounter, and that is of getting and keeping the grind angle correct and even across the face. Most powered grind wheels have a small table which can be preset to the required angle. The angled table is difficult to set accurately, a little tricky to use to produce an even face, and has to be slackened, moved, reset, and retightened for each different type of tool. Fortunately there is a better alternative.

In my early days of turning I went on a course with a superb teacher, Cliff Willets of Melton Mowbray. Cliff had developed many teaching aids and some useful tools of his own. His grind wheel was a supreme piece of ingenuity. The power unit was a 1,250 r.p.m. washing machine motor (obtained cheaply from the local scrap yard). The shaft had a coupling which connected it straight through to a Picador arbour. On the arbour was an 8in (20.5cm)-diameter by 1in (2.5cm)-wide grind wheel. The whole was held in a wooden box structure which cradled the motor and clamped it in position to prevent the motor body rotating. Around the grind wheel was a platform the height of which corresponded with the height of the centre of the arbour shaft. Rigidly mounted into one side of the platform was a vertical rod. On this pivoted a stack of 'leaves'. The lowest couple of leaves were of aluminium – one of about $\frac{1}{16}$in (1.5mm) thick and the other about $\frac{1}{8}$in (3mm). The higher leaves were of wood of different thicknesses. The leaves could be swung in and out to provide platforms in front of the grinding rim of the wheel.

Using the aluminium (packing pieces) and the first, the lowest wooden leaf, you

The 'Cliff Willets' tool grinder (with spark guard removed). Each leaf provides a flat platform for a different angle of grind.

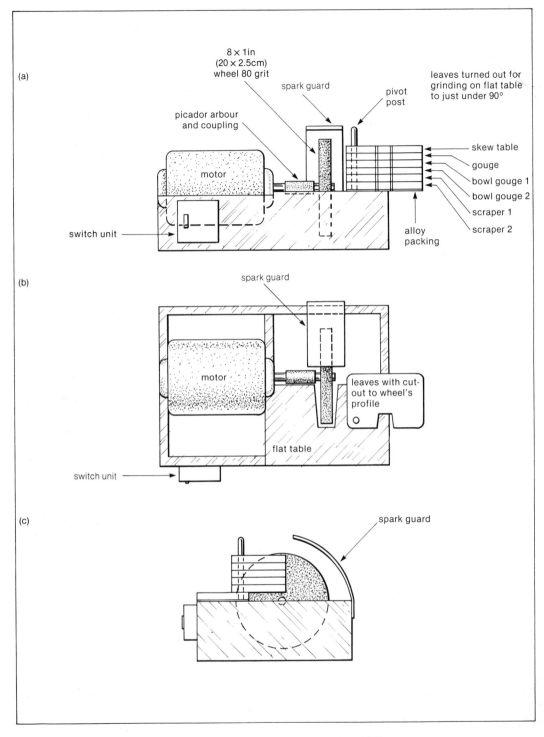

The 'Cliff Willets' tool grinder, with leaves to give pre-set angles. (a) Front view showing motor cradled in frame. (b) Plan view showing leaves rotated outward. (c) Side view with 70° leaf and alloy packers turned in.

had a flat platform on to which you could lie a scraper. When held flat on the platform and fed on to the wheel this leaf automatically gave a 70 degree bevel on the scraper. Swing in one more leaf and you got 60 degrees. Succeeding leaves gave a series of gouge grinding angles of gradually reducing bevel angle until the top leaf gave an 18 degree bevel for a skew.

The beauty of the machine was that each leaf allowed you to grind to the correct angle by holding the tool flat. The angles were preset by the thickness of the leaves and the height of the stack. If you wanted a round edge as with the domed scraper, then the tool was still held flat

and merely pivoted around. With deep bowl gouges you pivoted slightly but rotated the handle of the tool to cut back the shoulders. Whatever rotating or pivoting you did you still retained the pre-set grind angle of the platform height.

As the wheel wore – and they all do – the correct bevel angle was maintained by removing the aluminium packing leaves. I came straight back and made myself a couple based on this design, and now, daily, say a prayer of thanks to Cliff.

I did change mine slightly. I have a few more leaves, giving a wider range of bevel angles, and I painted the faces of each leaf a different colour. Then I put the appropriate colour dot on the butt of the chisel

Table 3 gives about 37 degrees for a bowl gouge.

37

Table 6 allows a 60 degree grind on a scraper. The box platform, table 7, gives an angle of 72 degrees.

handle. Mistakes are now very difficult. An 18 degree bevel skew has a green dot and uses the top, green-painted leaf. The 55 degree bowl gouge is red to red, 80 degree scraper blue to blue, and so on.

The rim of a grind wheel used for a lot of gouge grinding does itself become grooved. It will need dressing at regular intervals with either a dressing wheel or a Devil stone (a block of very coarse grindstone which is held against the rim of the wheel for a few seconds). When dressing it is advisable to move the grinder close to a dust extractor inlet as grindstone dust has been connected with pneumoconiosis.

There are some very specialised tools which have to be sharpened in different ways. American turner Ed Moulthrop, who makes five foot high, two foot diameter bowls, uses two forms of tool of his own design – both he forges himself

from massive used high-speed drill bits or old machine taps. One tool is tapered off to a spear-like point. This he calls a 'lance', the other is made by first tapering the end of the tap to a ribbon and then forging the ribbon round to form a hook. The top edge of the hook is the cutting edge. There is a ring turning tool available in Britain which is like a closed-up version of Ed's hook. Both the ring and the hook have to be sharpened from the inside and this requires a long but small-diameter rotary grinding point which is usually powered by a hand drill. The outside face of the ring may or may not have a bevel, but if the tool is made with an outside bevel the edge is still sharpened from inside the ring.

Ed, incidentally, uses the lance and the hook by levering them off pins set into the tool rest. This coupled with the fact that

Using a dressing wheel to flatten off the rim of a grind wheel. The unit is placed close to the dust extractor inlet for this task.

some have handles over 5 ft (1.5m) long, means that he can exert considerable leverage and work very quickly through huge tree trunk-sized blanks. His approach is very much one of brute force – but certainly not of ignorance!

David Ellsworth, already mentioned for his specially ground gouges, is also known for his hollowed spheres. He can work through an aperture of 1½in (3.8cm) diameter into an 18in (45.5cm) diameter sphere. He can not see the tool point so he is working blind, yet he will get the wall of the sphere to an even one-eighth of an inch thickness all round. The tool he uses for this type of work is made up of a long rod, into the end of which are clamped small point 'scraper' bits similar to the tools used on metal work lathes. The bits may be high-speed steel or are sometimes made of tungsten carbide (TC). To sharpen TC bits you still use a grind wheel but this time a much finer grade, soft green grit stone wheel.

To summarise on tools and the angles of grind, have a look at the table over. Beyond these, many turners have their own modified tools. Some are bowl gouges where the shoulders are ground back over the length of an inch or more. These are used for overhand or backward cutting inside vessels. The nose of such gouges is sharpened in the normal way. The tool is then pivoted and is rotated on its axis as the tip is pushed up the grinding wheel while grinding the shoulders.

Most of us have scrapers with a particular profile for making odd shapes or getting in under difficult corners, but these are all ground normally, merely pivoting the tool on the appropriate height of leaf.

39

Tool type	Size range	End shape	Bevel angle	Normal uses
CHISELS				
Straight	¼ to 1¼ flat section	square	18 to 25	planing, roughing
Skew	¼ to 1½ thin blade	skew angled at 10 to 20	18 to 25	planing cylinders, cutting beads, cleaning vertical faces, shearing off, decorative grooving, dovetails
Skew	½ to 1¼ thick blade	skew 10 to 20	20 to 25	roughing, beading, heavy rounding
Beading and Parting	⅜ to ⅝ square section	straight	20 to 25	beading, grooving, flat shoulders in confined spaces, parting
PARTING				
Straight	⅛ to ¼ flat section	straight	50	parting off, grooving, cleaning into corners, very fine beads
Fluted	⅛ to ¼ fluted end	straight	45 to 50	parting off into deep recesses
Fluted	³⁄₁₆ bottom flute	straight	45	parting fibrous woods
Diamond	⅛ to ³⁄₁₆ diamond section	straight	45 to 50	parting off into deep recesses
GOUGES				
Roughing	¾ to 1½ deep U	straight	35 to 45	roughing to round
Bowl	¼ to ½ round section deep U flute	straight with shoulders cut back	30 to 45 (normal) 25 to 70	inside bowls, tight coves, special purposes, steep walls, deep vessels
Spindle	⅜ to 1 shallow	straight	30	covings

Tool type	Size range	End shape	Bevel angle	Normal uses
Spindle round	⅜ to ¾ shallow U	rounded	30	hollowing out, coves, beads
Spindle finger	⅜ to ½ half-round	rounded	30 to 40	hollowing out
SCRAPERS				
Square	¼ to 2 flat	straight	35 to 70	outside of bowls, inside boxes
Skew	¼ to 1½	angled 60 to 70	35 to 60	inside corners
Corner	½ to 1½	off-square	70 to 80 on end 60 to 75 along sides	deep corners
Round nose	¼ to 2	round	35 to 55	inside bowls, goblets
Round side	¾	semicircle	35 to 45	inside hollow wares, under returns
Diamond side	¾	off-square	35 to 45 85 corner	inside small boxes
Diamond point	¼ to 1¼	diamond	35 to 70 point	roughing burrs, angled grooves, dovetails
RING				
Ring	⅜ and ½	ring	80	hollowing out

Table 2   Turning speeds for bowls.

There are, also, various patent tools of varying degrees of utility. A cranked parting tool is supposed to allow the removal of rings from inside bowls. It is more likely to remove fingers and tool rests. In America there are even more extreme ideas. Dennis Stewart of Oregon has produced an interesting tool kit with handle, scrapers, hooks, chatter tools and various cutting bits. With a massive handle and an elbow cup they are capable of tackling very rough jobs.

Old hook tools in a Norwegian folk museum.

Most tools can be ground on the same type of wheel.

As was mentioned earlier, it is very easy to build up a large collection of tools. If now, to the various profiles and sizes, you are going to add a number ground to different bevels, the workshop walls will soon be covered. It may be because I specialise in bowls many of which have complex internal profiles that I do have a number of gouges and scrapers with different angles. It is also why the table above includes a range of bevel angles that goes beyond the recommendations of many turners. Indeed Richard Raffan says that he tends to stick within the range of 30 to 45 degrees for all tools. I suggest that you experiment to find what suits you best.

4 Holding the Wood

In order to demonstrate the roughing gouge and the skew chisel, I clamped the wood between the centres – the headstock drive spur and the tailstock centre. This is only one of the many ways of holding wood.

Basically there are two systems of turning. One is the between centres method already used, and the other what is broadly classed as 'face plate' turning – however, within these two there are many variations.

Let's start with the 'centres' systems. So far you have used a drive spur, probably the one supplied with the lathe as a standard fitting. Most of these have a centre point in the middle of a cross-head of chisel edges or 'prongs'. Some are made as a single piece, whereas in others the centre point is separate, and is clamped in by a grub screw. This can be adjusted to give varying levels of penetration. The normal position is to have the point about ⅛in (3mm) proud of the prongs. The crudest form of drive centre is the two-prong. This is ground out of one piece into a single chisel with a small point notched out at the centre.

The tailstock invariably has a single point. On the cheaper, and some older, lathes the point in the tailstock is fixed. This means that the turning wood rotates around the centre point, setting up friction. Grease or oil (even soft soap) can be used to lubricate the point, but the problem with any fixed centre is that they quickly wear a hole in the end of the wood and the tight grip soon slackens, necessitating constant adjustment of the tailstock.

Drive and tail spurs. Left to right: simple two prong, ground from a solid piece; fixed tail stock spur, number 2 morse taper fit; live tail stock spur with ball race, number 3 morse taper fit; four-prong drive spur, number 2 morse taper fit; lace bobbin chuck on 2 morse taper; centre punch for indenting.

Three face plates. The largest is an 18in (45.5cm) diameter for a Wadkin RS. The smallest, already screwed on to a blank, is for a Multico.

The alternative is the live centre, where the point is mounted in a bearing and rotates with the wood. These are infinitely preferable.

There is one drive centre that should be listed with the 'between centres' methods. This is the lace bobbin chuck. It is used at the drive or headstock end and is a form of what I call 'cup chuck'. It has a square recess into which the end of a half-inch square length of timber can be wedged, half an inch (1.3cm) being the typical size of blank for the turning of lace bobbins. When using a bobbin chuck, always support the outboard end of the wood with the tail stock as this helps to keep the timber firmly held in the chuck – hence it is used as a between-centres driver.

The basic concept of all so-called face plate methods of mounting is that the wood can be held without the need for a tailstock. In practice, however, we do still add the additional support of the tailstock when rough-turning some items.

Face Plate

The first device in the face plate category must be the face plate itself. This is a disc with a centre boss, which screws on to the lathe spindle. The diameter of the plate can be anything from 3 or 4in (7.5 or 10cm) to as many feet. There will be holes or slots through the plate through which screws are driven into the piece of timber to be turned. It is not unusual for a turner to have more than one face plate. The smaller the plate the easier it is to get at the back of the timber when turning. The bigger they are the more securely they will hold big pieces of off-round wood when roughing out. So one small diameter plate for fine work with a second much bigger for heavier duty is a reasonable starting point. I have a 4in (10cm), a 12in (30cm) and, hidden in some dark corner of the workshop and never used in anger, a 20in (51cm) diameter inboard and a monster 26in (66cm) diameter outboard, plate.

Screw Chuck

Probably the simplest holding device is the screw chuck. This consists of a woodscrew, mounted in some form of holder with a boss for the lathe spindle. Most screw chucks have a small backing face plate. Some manufacturers produce tiny screw chucks where the screw is welded into the mount. These are not very good, as you have to replace the whole thing if you break the screw or damage the threads – something I seem to do every third month! The better chucks have a screw which can be replaced and which is held in by a grub screw. Where there is a small face plate incorporated it can provide additional support for the timber and will usually offer the option of driving in a few extra screws to hold particularly tricky bits.

There are limitations to the screw chuck. First on the run-of-the-mill chucks the screw is likely to be a number 10 or 12 woodscrew – sometimes as big as a ¼in (6mm) coach bolt. The smaller ones are

Screw chucks. The pair are for a Multico. The screws are welded in and are therefore not replaceable, and are so small as to be useless. Above is a combination chuck in the screw mode. The large ply disc is a home-made chuck using a coach screw (it is mounted on a small face plate).

not very strong and can break off under the shocks of roughing out. Secondly they are usually only ¾ to 1in (1.9 to 2.5cm) long. This is not a great deal if you are trying to support a long piece of timber – hence the need to supplement with support from the tailstock. Also, the shortish length of even a 12 gauge screw may be fine in firm, medium grained, dry wood. If used on soft or green wood they are very likely to tear out and spin round inside a disconcertingly static workpiece.

Where the screw chuck does come into its own is for the quick mounting of small bowl blanks of up to about 8in (20.5cm) diameter.

You can easily make your own screw chucks and these are often better than bought proprietary items. Unfortunately, home-made screw chucks do tie up a face plate, but it may be worthwhile purchasing a spare plate for this purpose.

To make a screw chuck, fix a disc of hard wood – beech is very good – on to the spare small diameter face plate. Between the disc and the plant insert a thin disc of ply or aluminium. Mount the face plate on to the lathe and turn up the outside rim of the disc using the bowl gouge as a roughing gouge. Make the edges smooth and round off the corners. You will need to use a file to clean up any part of the aluminium disc that protrudes, as the edge can inflict nasty cuts.

Now bring the tool rest to lie across the front of the disc and set it ¹⁄₁₆in (1.5cm) below the centre height. With the point of a pencil, mark the exact centre of the rotating disc, then confirm the mark with the point of an awl or the dividers.

With a ⅛in (3mm) drill bit held in a hand drill and the bit resting on the top of the tool rest, push the drill into the centre and make a hole about three-quarters of

the way through the disc. Take the whole off the lathe and mark the discs relative to their position on the small face plate. (Holes on face plates are not always perfectly symmetrically placed.)

Dismantle, put the aluminium disc to one side, and then complete the ⅛in (3mm) hole through the beech disc by drilling through with a ¼in (6mm) drill. With a wood chisel cut a recess in the rear of the disc to precisely take the head of a ¼in coach screw. Fit a ¼ by 1¾in coach screw and reassemble. The disc of aluminium now acts to hold the coach screw firmly in place in the recess and the square shoulders of the recess should stop the screw turning. If you ever need to do a really heavy job you could use a longer coach screw, or even use a heavier disc to take a ⅜in screw. In extreme cases additional screws may be driven through

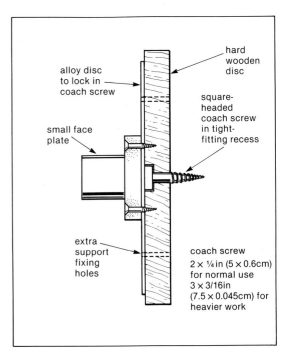

alloy disc to lock in coach screw

hard wooden disc

small face plate

square-headed coach screw in tight-fitting recess

extra support fixing holes

coach screw 2 × ¼in (5 × 0.6cm) for normal use 3 × 3/16in (7.5 × 0.045cm) for heavier work

Home-made screw chuck.

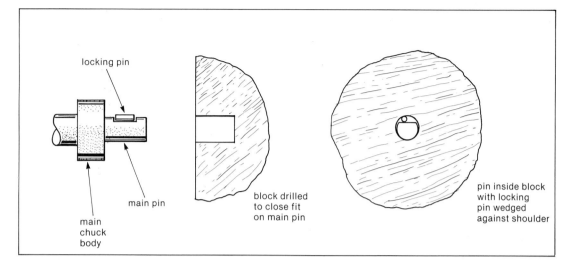

Pin chuck for mounting rough blank.

the discs and into the base of the timber blank.

I use the screw chuck extensively on bowl blanks up to 10in (25.5cm) diameter and for 4 by 12in (10 by 30cm) long candle lamp blanks. The latter are supported with the tail stock while roughing and shaping the outside and the support is removed only when drilling the hole for the candle mechanism.

Neither screw chucks, nor the screw-held face plates should be fixed into end grain. They grip poorly and quickly work loose so that the work piece soon begins to wobble. It may be only an imperceptible degree of movement but it can be enough to cause a major dig-in which will wrench the timber from its mounting, and you will have to duck pretty quickly!

Pin Chuck

To overcome the problem of the fragility of the small screws in screw chucks, there is another alternative – the pin chuck. This has as a centre piece a rod of any-

Cup chucks including two wooden chucks for holding eggs for finishing.

47

thing from ⅝ to 1¾in (1.6 to 4.4cm) diameter. There is a small flat on one side of the rod, and a small diameter pin sits loose on the flat. A hole of exactly the right diameter is drilled into the timber that is to be mounted. This hole is pushed over the rod and pin and is rotated until the pin locks on the shoulder of the flat. To demount you simply rotate the timber in the opposite direction.

The pin chuck is good for holding larger pieces of timber but is really only effective on denser and dry woods. When used on green timber the small pin tends to become embedded in the wood, no longer holds against the shoulder of the flat and the wood soon spins freely on the rod.

CUP CHUCK

Another simple device is the cup chuck. This provides a hollowed cylinder into which a spigot on the end of the timber can be driven. The chucks have a small taper which tightens up on the wood as it is driven home. Again they are fine for relatively short lengths of wood but can only take the side-thrust of a turning tool when working close to the chuck itself. The other disadvantage of the cup chuck is that you lose the length of wood in the chuck and this can be as much as 2in (5cm), which, with some very expensive exotic timbers, can be quite an important consideration.

Although the usual form for a cup chuck is that of a hollow cylinder, there are variations such as the lace bobbin drives mentioned earlier. Later we will make our own cup chucks for holding wooden eggs while finishing the ends – these are 'egg cup chucks'!

We frequently find that there is a need

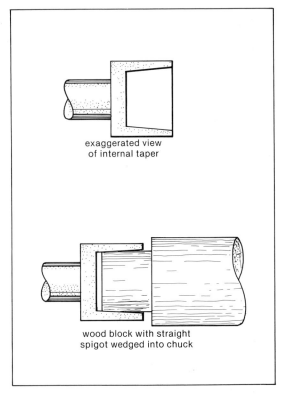

exaggerated view
of internal taper

wood block with straight
spigot wedged into chuck

The cup chuck

to mount a piece of work on a spigot. This is called a mandril, and it is often mounted off a screw or jaw chuck. Here the work to be mounted is already hollow, and we need to hold the piece from the inside. We also make frequent use of a mandril at the outboard end, to form a stabilising centre.

For instance, we have made a candle stick and drilled the candle hole. Now we wish to finish off the lamp column. A wooden mandril to fit the candle hole will, together with the tailstock point, hold the work steady.

When making totally hollow cylinders – as with serviette rings – we use home-made wooden mandrils at both drive and tailstock end.

When talking of the prong and the spigot chuck the phrase 'driven on to or into' has been used. We use a rubber hammer to get the prong drive to bite into the end of the timber and we use a rubber hammer to drive the wood spigot into the cup chuck. In both cases we do this on the work bench and not direct on to the lathe. Hammering wood into a chuck that is mounted on the lathe will damage the spindle bearings.

JAW CHUCK

Unfortunately one of the most useful holding devices is also one of the most expensive. This is the traditional jaw chuck. Two patterns are in normal use,

Three- and four-jaw chucks.

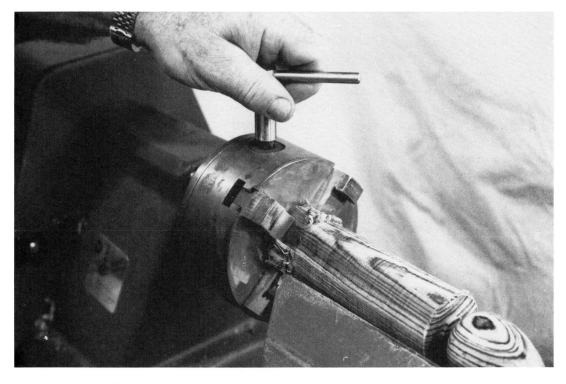

Four-jaw chuck holding a cylinder for egg making.

one with three jaws which is very useful for holding uneven or oddly shaped pieces of timber, and the other with four jaws which is ideal for round or squared stock. The jaws can grip a quite small spigot (as little as ¼in/6mm) and will hold very firmly against all sorts of abuse. The better chucks have two sets of jaws – one for clamping down on to a spigot, and the other for expanding outwards into a hollow cylinder (or small bowl). Some of the cheaper jaw chucks on the market do not self-centre and are not really very effective. Buy one and you will soon wish to replace it with a better one.

Beside the price there are other problems with jaw chucks. They are heavy and add considerably to the starting torque of the lathe; but the real danger is that the jaws stick out from the body, and with the least moment of inattention you can get a very severe rap over the knuckles (you can, in fact, smash them). A guard, although inconvenient, is a very wise precaution.

A good jaw chuck will hold almost any type of wood, could well accept 5 to 6in (12.5 to 15cm)-diameter pieces, and will satisfactorily hold timber up to 18in (45.5cm) long without the support of a tailstock.

GLUE CHUCK

Not everybody wants to waste a spiggot, nor do they want a screw hole in the bottom of the piece. One way round this is the use of a glue chuck. Here a piece of scrap timber is glued to the base of the timber to be turned and the screw chuck is then driven into the scrap timber. Alternatively the scrap can be turned to a round and this spigot is then held in either a cup or a jaw chuck.

Hot melt glues from a glue gun, or any of the PVA synthetic wood glues are suitable for mounting the scrap block. However, in later removing the block you will sometimes pull away fibres from the main timber. This problem can be overcome by gluing a piece of paper between the timber and the scrap. Now when you part the scrap away, the joint should separate along the line of the paper gasket. This method is generally known as the 'glue sandwich chuck'.

COMBINATION CHUCKS

There can now be very few of the 20,000-plus woodturners in Britain who do not own one or other of the modern combination chucks. These units offer a number of different facilities. Usually there is one or more diameter of cup, a screw, split ring and dovetail, spigot, expanding dovetail, collar, pin, and various adjustable collets. All who own one swear by it and could never do without it; each make has its own devotees. I normally use the Craft Supplies precision combination chuck which is both robust and versatile. The only damage I seem to be able to do to it is that I have torn the threads off the stainless steel screw, and do break a fair number of the largest size of cast collets (only the 3¾in size, however).

One very useful facility with the combination chuck is the range of face plate rings. These provide a screw on dovetail, and they are designed so that the expanding collet will clamp into them. They can be screwed to the bottom of a timber blank with quite small screws and hold very firmly. The great advantage is that they can be mounted on the chuck in a matter

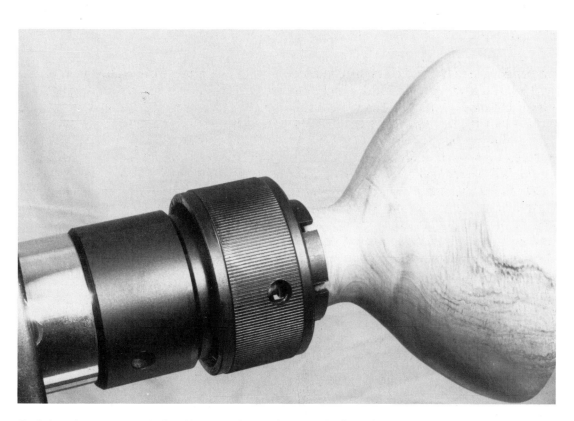

Craft Supplies Precision Collet Chuck can be used to grip the foot of smaller items while allowing free access to the outside of the vessel.

of seconds and, if you have a few of them, can be left on a partially-worked piece for later remounting and finishing. They are particularly useful when rough-turning unseasoned wood. If you part-turn green wood and cut a dovetail into the wood itself, then the chances are that the dovetail hole will become oval in drying and the piece cannot be remounted. Re-fixing a face plate ring overcomes this.

There is another thing. Cutting a dovetail into the wood does leave an unsightly hole in the base of the finished object. I know that few people ever see the base, but it is so much nicer if that dovetail is not there. If a ring has been used it is only a matter of seconds to fill the four small screw holes or to hide them under a cork or baize ring.

Craft Supplies' combination chuck used in expanding collet mode.

JACOBS CHUCK

While talking of work-holding devices we have to include the Jacobs chuck which is sometimes used as a driving end stock for holding very small-diameter work as in lace bobbins.

The Jacobs chuck is more normally used by mounting it from the tailstock to hold drill bits to hollow out work. This means having the work piece mounted on the drive stock on a screw chuck or in jaws or similar and locking the drill bit into a Jacobs chuck mounted on the tailstock. We will talk more about this when we start to consider the turning process of hollowing out.

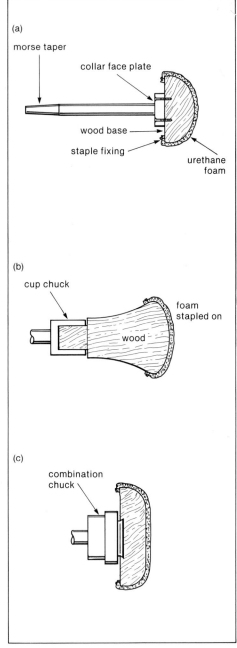

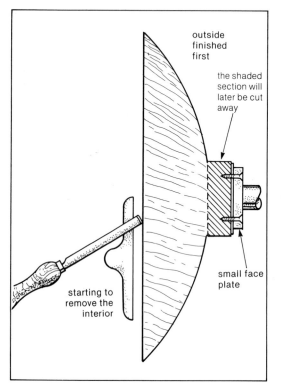

Reverse chucking, first stage. The bowl is being turned for reverse chucking; the shaded section will later be cut away.

Chucks for reverse chucking. (a) Made-up chuck for deeper vessels. (b) A variety of sizes can be made to fit a cup chuck. (c) Several sizes for use with shallower bowls to fit a collet chuck.

To finish this chapter let's go down the road a step. You are showing your finished bowl to the club expert. He looks at it, strokes the inside and makes 'Mmm!' noises of approval. He looks at the profile and says: 'Yes! Good! I like it.' Then he turns it over, his face clouds, and he hands your masterpiece back with a non-committal, unenthusiastic 'Yes, coming on.' What went wrong? Why did his attitude change? It was because he looked at the bottom – there was the tell-tale dovetail recess of the expanding collet chuck. To make matters worse, the edges of the recess were still rough.

It may seem unnecessary, but the finish underneath should be just as good as it is on top and inside. It should also obscure the question of how it was chucked. One answer is reverse chucking.

REVERSE CHUCK

Once the piece has been sanded and finished, it has to be remounted so that with a small gouge you can carefully clean up the base and remove all traces of the chucking method used.

In its simplest form, a reverse chuck is a contoured wooden block mounted on the headstock. On the face of the block is fixed a little padding. An ideal material is the dense polyurethane foam used in car upholstery. This can be lightly stapled in place so that it can be replaced when worn.

The bowl (or whatever) is mounted over this block and is held in place by the tail-stock point bearing lightly on the centre of the base. Always check that the piece is centred by spinning by hand before the

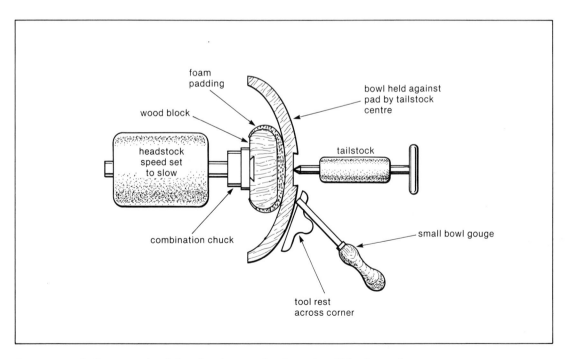

Arrangement of reverse chuck for cleaning up chuck marks off the base of a bowl.

lathe is started. Adjust the tailstock centre until right.

Now use a slow lathe speed (800 r.p.m. maximum) and a fine bowl gouge to remove the shoulder of the spigot recess and possibly to incise a little design.

You will need various sizes of block and some means of dealing with deeper vessels. As a basis start with a 3 to 4in wide by 2in (7.5 to 10cm by 5cm) thick block and recess this for expanding collet chuck mounting. For deeper vessels, a block on a small face plate which itself is mounted on a morse taper shaft is a useful permanent accessory.

The pressure of the padded block is sufficient to grip and spin the workpiece at slow lathe speeds and the tailstock point needs only minimal pressure to hold it all together.

When you have cut away all that you require to hide the chucking marks, take the piece off the lathe and clean up with a rotary sanding pad. Finally, rub in a little oil, polish, or whatever finish you have used, on the outside.

I love it when at craft fairs another turner picks up a piece, looks at the base and then asks, 'How did you mount it on the lathe?' If they have been making approving smiles, I will tell them!

5 Working between Centres

Even if your interest lies mainly in platters or bowls, it is probably best to start on spindles or 'between centres' work. Most training courses start here, and they do so for a good reason. The tool control needed for fine spindle work is more precise, and spindle making also involves the use of a greater variety of tools. If things do go wrong when turning spindles, you are less likely to do any damage; flying pieces of broken spindle are usually much less lethal than are pieces of disintegrated bowl.

We have already looked at the preparatory stages of roughing to a round and using the skew chisel to plane the round down to a smooth finish. So let's now move forward from that point.

The skew chisel is used whenever possible because it is the best tool for planing a flat surface to a very smooth finish. It is used with the tool rest above the centre axis line so that when the bevel rests on the rotating wood, the tool is near-horizontal. It can, of course, cut into shallow concave areas, but it is more frequently (and safely) used for flat areas or convex curves, as in the egg shape you partially completed earlier.

The other common use for the skew is for slicing in to wood to produce vertical faces. When used for this purpose we are usually cutting across end grain, and a keen edged skew can, in doing this, produce a very smooth, burnished cut face. It is very similar to the face produced when in the early exercises we used a sharp bevel chisel to cut the end walls of a mortise.

It is workshop time; and the exercise piece that you are going to make is a tool handle. It is a matter of pride with many turners that they have made the handles for all of their own turning tools. It is also a comment upon the poor handle design of some commercial tools!

Handles are usually made from hardwoods. Box, hornbeam, and yew (if clean-grained and check-free) are all ideal but are not always readily available, and it is better for us to make our first handle or two of something a little softer. Beech is good, as is window-frame off-cut mahogany (Meranti or similar). Look for a piece 2in square and a couple of inches longer than the length of handle required, and use wood with a straight grain.

There are one or two points to bear in mind in making handles. First, in broad terms, the denser the wood the stronger the handle. Tools which take a pounding, such as roughing gouges, need touch handles and are very likely to split at an angle if the grain is not straight down the length. A tool has to balance in the hands and be of such a shape that it can be held easily. So not any shape will do. Finally, the longer the handle the more firmly it can be held. Oh! but make sure you have the room to swing a long handle without catching the lathe bed, the wall, or whatever. Probably an optimum timber size to start with would be with a 14 to 16in (35.5 to 40cm) long by 2in (5cm) square piece.

Centre the wood, tap in the prongs of the drive spur to give a good firm grip, and mount it on to the lathe. Incidentally, when driving in the spur, although you need to ensure that the prongs bite well into the timber, don't overdo it. In driving a spur into a piece of lignum vitae I hit it too hard and split the timber! If using a hard wood the prong location can be facilitated by marking the two diagonal pencil lines with shallow cuts from a tenon saw. Set the lathe speed to about 900 r.p.m. (Note: This is a little slower than you will later use, but it will allow you to get the feel of things.)

Rough down to a round with the roughing gouge. Remember – tool rest at axis height; tool on to rest with blade back on top of the rotating timber; tool offset to about 45 degrees off the right-angle. Flute upwards but inclined slightly towards the direction of travel; draw back the handle until the bevel rubs (the noise is quite distinctive); tool handle back a little more until cutting begins; and then move the tool sideways along the rest. It is good practice to take only the smallest chippings off in the first pass or two until you have removed the worst of the corners. When you reach one end of the rest (watch that you do not fall off the end), angle the tool the other way and make a pass in the opposite direction.

To get the length of handle required, the length of timber you need is likely to considerably exceed that of the standard tool rest. You will probably have to move the rest twice at least to get from end to end. When working the ends of the timber always work from the middle of the wood towards and off the end. Never try to come in from the end.

Check with a backward-pointing thumb on the top of the rotating workpiece. If you feel any bumps at all the wood is not yet round.

Once the touch is smooth, raise the tool rest to a little above the axis line. On later handles when you are more used to working with the tools you can increase the lathe speed to about 2,000 r.p.m. once you have completed the roughing.

Now take the 1in skew chisel. The skew has a long point and it is normally used with this point up and the cutting edge diagonally across the line of axis at an angle of about 45 degrees. It is even more important with a skew chisel that you do not go straight in – you must start with the bevel rubbing and then carefully draw back and raise the handle until the middle of the blade just picks up a cut. When the long cylinder is planed smooth, drop the rest to axis height.

The next step is to mark off dimensions. This is done with the wood still rotating. Lay a straight edge along the tool rest; hold a pencil on the rest with the point against the wood. Mark off the full length of the finished handle – we have allowed an inch spare at each end. Next mark off the length of the collar – I prefer this to be at the tailstock end. Back from the collar, about 3in (7.5cm), is another mark – this is the point of greatest diameter on the finished handle. Finally, roughly half way down the handle, make another mark – this is where the smallest diameter will occur.

The parting tool and a pair of external callipers are our next requirement, as is a ferrule for the collar. Proprietary ferrules are available, but lengths of copper water pipe are wholly satisfactory. They are sold in metric diameter size. 15mm is fine for small tools, 22mm for the average size, and 28mm for the larger. Really massive roughing gouges or scrapers may require

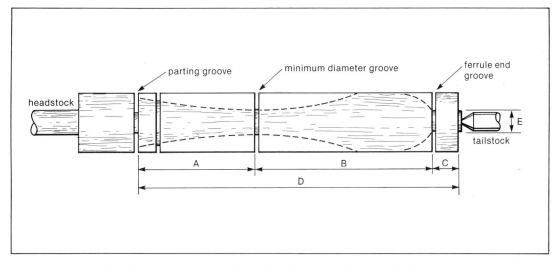

Grooving to establish dimensions for a tool handle. Dimension B is usually 1½ to 2 times A – this is down to personal preference. Dimension C is 1 to 1¼in(2.5 to 3.2cm). Dimension D is to suit tool and personal preference (for a ½in(1.3cm) bowl scraper, about 18in(45.5cm). Dimension E is to suit the ferrule (probably a 22 and 28mm water pipe).

35mm. The length of ferrule required is about 1in (2.5cm).

The parting tool is used to make grooves at the various marked points. The grooves are made to almost finished diameter. Start at the collar end and set the callipers to a fraction over the inside diameter of the ferrule.

Start the lathe, and position the parting tool to cut at the end of the handle at the collar end. Hold the tool to bridge from the rest to the top of the wood and then draw back until it starts to cut. Raise the handle and continue to draw back slightly as the point cuts down into the wood. To hold the tool firm a useful grip for the steadying hand is with the thumb hooked over the blade and the forefinger under the rest – a pinching stop grip.

There are two methods of checking the depth of the groove. One is to stop the lathe and test with the callipers. This is slow and tedious and can involve several stop-starts. There is also a strong possibility that you will go too far!

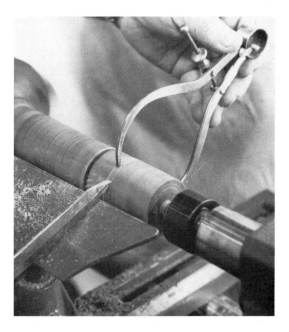

Grooving to a required diameter using external callipers. The parting tool is held firmly in one hand while the callipers are held in the groove until they just drop across the diameter. It is advisable to use callipers with rounded rather than chisel point ends.

A sizing tool or depth gauge is set to the required diameter. This is a little less frightening for the beginner but usually requires a slightly wider (more wasteful) groove.

The second method looks a little scary the first time you see it. While the piece is turning and you are continuing the parting cut holding the tool in the one hand, you offer up the callipers from the far side and hold them firmly in the groove until they drop across the finished diameter. Stop the cut immediately the calliper drops over, and you have a very accurate diameter.

Now you have made the first cut, use exactly the same procedure to groove at the back end of the collar. Remove the wood between the two grooves using the beading and parting tool (it is a bit quicker than using the narrow parting tool). Continue to cut away the wood from the end of the collar right up to the tailstock, giving the very end a slight taper such that it is clearly of lesser diameter than the main collar zone. This provides a lead for the ferrule.

The handle cylinder marked off. The inboard groove marks the butt of the handle; the middle groove the point of the narrowest finished diameter; and the right groove the ferrule end. A shallower groove just inboard of the ferrule end sets the diameter for the fattest part of the handle.

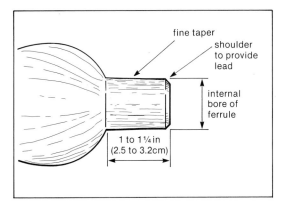

Ferrule end of a tool handle. Average tools use 22mm copper water pipe. Larger tools use 28mm pipe.

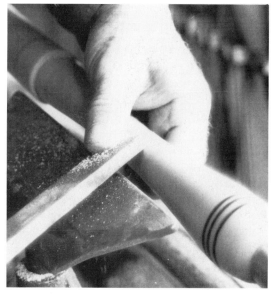

Planing down the concave area with a small skew chisel.

Ignore the maximum diameter mark and make the next groove on the minimum diameter mark. Cut in here to almost what you want the finished diameter to be (probably about 1¼in (3.2cm) for an average tool). Again use the callipers to establish an accurate depth.

Finally groove in to about an inch diameter in the parting zone to mark the end of the handle by the drive stock.

If you want to show off, you can now do all the rest with a skew chisel (readjust the tool rest height); however, it is quicker if you first use the roughing or other large gouge to shape the handle from the point of maximum diameter to the minimum point and back out again to the end of the handle. The diameter of the end is usually halfway between those of the maximum and minimum diameters but the end should be long and heavy enough to balance the weight of the blade. Depending upon your hand size, and the nature of the work that you intend to do, you may wish to leave the maximum diameter at the full 2in (5cm). It is advisable to avoid having tool handles that are too small in diameter as these are very tiring to hold for any length of time.

Once roughed to shape use the skew to plane down the concave part of the body of the handle and bring it to a fine finish. Always cut from the high points down into the hollows. This means starting one cut at the point of maximum diameter and sweeping down to the minimum diameter area, and then starting another at the butt of the handle – the other end – and also bringing this down into the middle.

If you have a very gradual concave curve you may find that you can make a continuous cut from one end to the other, but the chances are that as you start to cut uphill you will pick up the grain and cause some roughness. It might be worth trying just to see what happens!

Now, remember the egg exercise. You are going to round the shoulder of the handle from the maximum diameter point down to the collar. Start the cut half-way between the maximum mark and the collar end. Long point up. Steadying fingers pushing down on the top of the skew blade. You cannot hold the rest as the tool is going to travel sideways. As you start the cut move the skew sideways but at the same time raise the handle, moving it away from the body in an upwards diagonal. This will cause the cut to go in deeper as you near the end. You will find that there is some resistance as the wood tries to push the chisel backwards. You are cutting deep and across end grain. Obviously the blade is having to roll on the rest as the rounding develops. The blade starts flat in the near horizontal position, but ends near-vertical with the handle considerably higher than the cutting edge.

Keep an eye on the edge to ensure that the point of cutting is in the middle and that the corners are kept well clear. If the long point catches you will dig in and tear off large splinters. If the short end catches the tool will be forced back up the developing shoulder and leave a spiral groove.

With each succeeding cut start a little closer to the maximum diameter mark and rotate the blade further to round off the shoulders.

Most turners like to cut a few ring grooves on the handle; usually some around the maximum diameter part and others towards the tail end of the handle. These serve to provide a better grip, but they can also be used as identification marks – 2 rings = skew, 3 rings = spindle gouge, 4 a bowl gouge, etc. These can be useful for rapid location of the correct tool when, late in a session, the blades are covered in shavings.

You can use the skew chisel to make grooves. For this the tool rest is set just above the axis line. The skew is positioned vertically on the rest with the long point down and with the underside of the blade touching the rotating wood.

Cutting grooves with the skew. The blade is held vertically and at an absolute right-angle to the surface of the wood. If off the right-angle, the blade will be skewed sideways on contact with the wood.

Take a firm overhand grasp with the steadying hand. Draw the handle back until the point just bites into the wood and then raise the tool handle so that the point arcs downwards in towards the centre axis. This is the simple 'grooving cut'. Make the required number of grooves.

When satisfied, stop the lathe, slacken off the tailstock and feed the ferrule on to the taper. Try to run it on to the collar. If it will not run right up, bring up the tailstock, start up, and take a little off the collar with the beading and parting tool. The ferrule ring should, however, be a tight fit and require knocking home with light hammer blows.

Once the ferrule is in place give the whole handle a light sanding. Move the

The ferrule (a length of copper water pipe) is in place and a pilot hole for the blade is being drilled with an ordinary twist bit held in a Jacobs chuck mounted in the tailstock quill.

tool rest out of the way so that you do not trap any fingers. Start with sandpaper of about 100 grit to take off the roughness. Hold it against the rotating piece with a sorbo rubber pad or in a thick gloved hand. Next a rub with 240 grit and finally a polish off with 400 grit. Finish with lacquer or oil according to preference. We will discuss the alternatives later under 'Finishes' (page 123). I now use Danish Oil for most things and this is certainly suitable for handles.

Now to a tricky bit. Back with the tool rest and set it the merest shade below axis height. With the parting tool, cut the groove at the butt end of the handle down to about ½in (1.3cm) diameter. Now use the skew to make a facing cut to round off the end of the handle. The tool is held with the blade vertical as in grooving.

The critical thing is to ensure that the bevel of the skew is always rubbing on the wood at the end of the handle. This means working at about two to three degrees off the vertical with the skew's handle just leading towards the tailstock. The long point should be pushed firmly into the wood about $\frac{1}{32}$ in (1mm) from the end. This will take off the corner. From here we continue with the chisel in this position but instead of cutting with the actual point the cut is on the edge, an eighth of an inch above the point – this is what is known as the 'shearing cut' and is widely used in cutting grooves and beads with the skew as well as for trimming up vertical end faces. Continue making shearing cuts until the corner is well rounded. With each cut go further in towards the centre until it goes in as far as the bottom of the parting tool groove.

Now see if you can part off the end of the handle at the headstock end using the skew. Working from first the handle side, then the drive side, and then back again, cut a groove into the remaining wood. As the groove deepens and is nearly through take the steadying hand from the skew blade and loosely hold the turning piece from the rear. Continue to cut in with the skew until you part right through and the handle is free in your hand. Take the handle out of the lathe and finish off the end with a little sandpaper and oil, and finally saw away any wood that protrudes beyond the ferrule. Mount the handle in a wooden jawed vice and drill a pilot hole (usually tapering) for the tang of the blade you are going to fix in to the handle.

There is an alternative method of making the decorative grooves, and this is to use a cheese wire and burn the groove in by friction. This can give an attractive dark coloured groove on lighter-coloured woods.

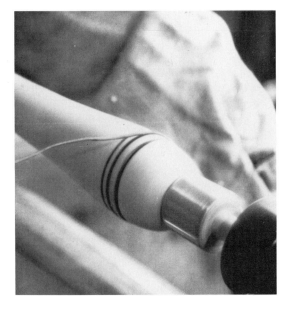

Burning decorative grooves into the handle
by friction, using a piece of steel wire.

Parting off the completed handle with a
parting tool. The wood is held lightly with
the left hand to catch it as it parts through.

Before we leave the skew there are a few
points to underline in connection with
fine control of the tool. With any of the
shearing cuts it is essential to ensure that
the bevel is rubbing on the shoulder of the
work before cutting begins. If you are
trimming a vertical face and you want it
flat, this presents difficulties as the flatter
the face the greater the tendency for a
corner to catch. As the face becomes more
rounded the problem decreases.

First the blade has to be so angled that
the bevel rubs. This means that if the tool
bevel is ground to 20 degrees then the
blade has to be first offered to the work at
18 to 19 degrees. Secondly in order to
keep the upper corner clear then the blade
needs to be inclined over on its side by a
couple of degrees.

The third is a general principle, and like
all general principles we may bend it from
time to time; you may indeed already
have tried. With the skew you should
always cut downhill. This is why in

making the handle you started the final
planing cuts at the ends and worked
down into the hollow in the middle of the
handle. If you did try a continuous cut
and started to go uphill, you probably
picked up some of the grain. What the
edge of the tool was in fact doing was to
get under the end of a fibre and lift it up.
As there were no overlying fibres to
support it, it may have torn away rather
than have been cut through. Going
downhill you shear through the ends of
the fibres because the main body of the
fibre is supported by those underneath.

The keener the edge and the higher the
speed, the more likely you are to get away
with it; and there may be times when
cutting uphill is the only way to get into
an awkward corner.

It is worthwhile remembering these and
similar problems when you are designing
objects. Always try to keep the design
such that you can use the best tooling
practices.

When you are cutting grooves or round-

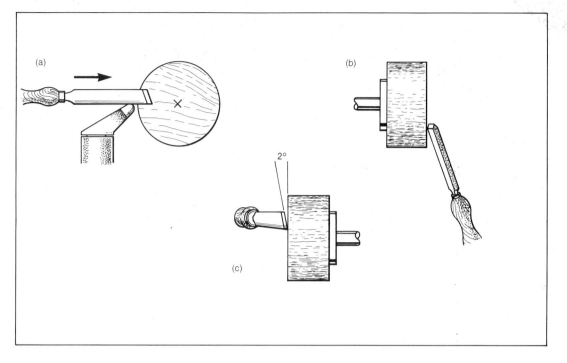

Facing cut with skew chisel. (a) View from tailstock, rest at centre height, long point down. (b) View from above, the bevel rubbing on the bottom edge, the skew slightly tilted (2° from the vertical). (c) View from the 'far' side. The bevel is not seen – the blade is inclined over at 2°.

ing off the end of an item you really appreciate two things. First, and yet again, the importance of keeping the edge very sharp; and secondly of having shallow angled bevels on skew chisels. Big fat skews with steep bevels are very difficult to get into small spaces!

In grooving down to a particular diameter we used the parting tool and a pair of callipers. This is normal practice and once you have the knack of it, it is quick and simple. It does become a little more difficult when working on knotty or burred wood. On really rough timber you will find it particularly hard to keep the bevel of the parting tool rubbing, and to get an even cut. Dig-ins are not uncommon and the splitting off of chunks is not unknown. It can be particularly trying if what splits away is the base of a goblet!

If the wood is such that it gives parting tool trouble it is also likely to catch on the ends of the callipers. The callipers that I use for sizing have therefore had the ends rounded – some are supplied with an almost chisel-like point and these are positively dangerous. A quick touch with a file is all that is needed.

There is, of course, the sizing tool. This has a semicircular arm which is clamped to the end of a parting tool. The idea is that you set the distance between the tip of the blade and the end of the arm to the precise dimension you are trying to create. The end of the arm now sits in the groove on the far side from the tip of the tool and the tip arcs downwards into the wood, virtually pivoting off the end of the arm.

Sizing tools are excellent for repetitive

Sizing tool used to make a fixed dimension spiggot on a repetition job.

work where you wish to make several grooves or objects to the same diameter. They do, however, work better on ⅜ or ¼in/or 6mm beading and parting tools, and hence make wider grooves. Also by their very nature they position the tool blade such that it is a scraping rather than a bevel rubbing cut. On the plus side they reduce the tendency to dig-ins on rougher woods.

With extremely rough woods and with timbers that are soft and fibrous, it can be useful first to mark the limits of the groove with a couple of grooving cuts from a vertical skew – this will give you a clean edge to work to, and will produce much cleaner corners.

There are times when parting becomes more and more difficult the deeper the groove gets. Here I resort to another 'dangerous' practice. With the lathe rotating at its slowest speed a very firmly-held

tenon saw may be used to almost part through. If the timber is fibrous you have to take the saw out frequently to clear the teeth and to ensure that the blade is not heating up at all (to protect the temper). The final parting is also made with the saw, but now with the lathe stopped!

To finish off, how about remounting the part-turned egg. If the main body has a reasonable finish, sand it off smooth; otherwise first give it another couple of light planing cuts with the skew. Now, still using the skew, work the blunt end of the egg until you have practically cut through. Try to get a smooth, even curve using shearing cuts. If you do get a ridge it probably means that in your caution you had a little too much bevel rubbing. To remove the ring start outside it with light bevel rubbing, and then slowly swing the handle until the cut begins, and make a nice sweeping shearing cut in towards the centre. Do not try to take too much off at a time. If you do you will find it requires enormous effort, generates a lot of friction, and usually leaves a burn mark on the end of the egg.

Don't go right through yet. Go back to the pointed end and bring this in finer, again without finally shearing off. You should get to the stage where the tailstock supports through only the merest nub. Finally part off at the blunt end. You can cut the nub off the pointed end with a pad saw or sharp knife.

Put the egg on one side – you will smooth off the ends later when we have made an egg cup chuck to hold it.

Perhaps this would be a good point at which to consider the various ways in which we hold tools. Let's consider two separate elements. First there is the hand holding the handle of the tool. We will call this the 'tool hand'; and with right-handed people this would automatically be the right hand. Secondly there is the hand which holds the tool on the rest. It usually bears on the tool blade and sometimes also on the rest. This we call the 'steadying hand'.

The tool hand normally takes a firm grip around the handle of the tool – fingers round one side and the thumb wrapped around the other.

For roughing and rugged work with long-handled tools you will find it best to hold the handle well down towards the outer end. This means that the holding hand is well behind the body, and often the butt of the handle is locked against the thigh. In this way the shocks are taken by the whole body and not just the elbow.

The 'average' position is to hold the tool handle somewhere just behind the widest part. When rolling beads and incising detail the hand moves forward slightly with the fingers wrapped round the full width zone, and the rolling motion is made by a rotation of the wrist.

For fine control, particularly when planing with a narrow skew, or cutting fine beads with a parting tool I find that I like to hold the handle just behind the ferrule with the index finger pointing up along the blade. I don't know why – it just feels right!

Reference has already been made to the usefulness of being ambidextrous. In fact it is more than useful; it is essential. Unless you can get round to work on both sides of the lathe you just cannot get into every corner with a single, right-hand grip.

How you hold the tool affects both the quality of the work, and to a lesser extent safety.

The right-handed person will find it easy to skew plane from right to left, but if you do not change hands to go from left to right then you are going to have to angle your body awkwardly and bring your left elbow and sleeve very close to the rotating chuck. It is also so awkward that getting a smooth finish is difficult.

In fact if you do try this difficult position, your basic stance will be completely wrong. Smooth cuts require the elbow into the side with the forearm parallel to the floor. You should sway from one foot to the other (without actually moving them) and with a little bending at the waist as the tool moves across the front of the body. If you try to make a right-handed, right pass you are in fact pushing the tool away from the body, the elbow moves away from the side and firm tool control is lost.

So we cut across the body, and this means away from the holding hand. The handle of the tool is held in the right hand

65

while making a leftwards cut and the left hand for a rightwards pass. The elbow occasionally moves from the side and although we sway from the waist the shoulders move only slightly. This is not always the case and a notable exception arises when rolling beads (or rounding into a corner with a skew). Now the shoulder starts low and rises as the tool rolls down into the vertical. During the process the elbow may have come well away from the body.

The word ambidextrous could be misleading – all we are talking about is alternating the tool hand. The steadying hand has just as much work to do and requires just as much control.

There are many positions and grips adopted by the steadying hand. We can start by differentiating between grips that allow the blade to move sideways and those that lock it into a fixed position. In the former the steadying hand only holds or rests on the tool blade; in the latter it will in some way hold both blade and rest, 'clamping' the two together.

In planing cuts the steadying hand guides the blade along the rest in a nice, even-flowing straight line. In making entry or grooving cuts it locks the blade in position at a fixed point on the rest so that the blade cannot skew sideways.

In turning beads or hollowing out covings, a stop grip with the steadying hand not only limits the sideways travel, but working in unison with the tool hand it rolls the blade on to its side.

There are then a number of quite different steadying hand grips. The first and most basic is the overhand grip. The hand is over the top of the blade with the fingers wrapped round and the thumb wrapped under. This is one of the strongest grips and is used for roughing and

The overhand grip. The blade is held firmly and pushed down on to the tool rest. The steadying hand is clear of the rest and sideways movement is free.

The underhand grip used here with a bowl gouge. The tool is pulled down on to the rest. The side of the hand against the rest limits the depth of cut on sideways sweeps, and there is a clear view of the cutting edge.

major timber-removing cuts with a bowl gouge. One advantage it gives is the facility for deflecting the stream of shavings away from the face with the side of the hand.

A much lighter grip is merely resting the fingers on the top of the blade. This is useful in light planing where it merely guides the blade along the rest.

In slightly heavier planing (rougher wood or broader skews) we use the underhand grip where the blade is pinched between the thumb and fingers from underneath so that the blade can be pulled down on to the rest but no part of the hand obscures the view of the cutting edge.

When we get on to cutting coves in spindles and making grooves with a vertical skew chisel another grip is used. This is a stop grip. Here the thumb is hooked over the top of the blade and the side of the forefinger grips the underside

The pinch grip. The blade is pinched between the thumb and forefingers and the index finger is hooked under the rest, pinching the tool to the rest. This prevents any side movement. Here it is used with the beading tool.

The overhand grip in the semi-stop position. The fleshy part of the side of the hand is pressed firmly on to the rest to prevent side kicks.

of the tool rest. The thumb and finger 'pinch' together and clamp the tool very firmly to a fixed point on the rest.

Another form of stop grip used in hollowing out is the overhand grip with fingers wrapped round but with the fleshy part of the side of the hand pressed firmly on to the rest. Now the side of the hand acts as a pivot point.

Later, when we start to look at thin wall work, we will have to consider how the grips need to be modified in order to provide support for the walls.

6 Ornamental Spindles

You have jumped in at the deep end! Well done! Some turners never use skews other than as scrapers, other turners fear them to the extent that they do not even have one in their kit. Certainly it is the most difficult tool to handle, but once mastered it is one of the most useful. If you managed the egg, then you can also produce beads with a skew. The skew is worth the effort because with it you can produce finer detail and a better finish than you can ever get with a spindle gouge.

One of the secrets of good skew work is lathe speed, so let's take a closer look at speeds. Earlier I laid down some ground rules which directly coupled speed of rotation with the diameter of the turned work. We also saw that the higher the speed the better the finish. There was then a problem of differential speeds across the face when turning discs. When turning long spindles we have additional problems.

The first is whip. A long spindle unsupported in the middle will whip considerably and the higher the speed the greater the whip. Also, the thinner the spindle the greater the whip. There comes a point, when making items like standard lamp columns, where they are almost impossible to turn without a centre steady unless you leave them so thick and massive that they are ugly. It is therefore important to get the speed right.

The table below covers the optimum rotation speeds when working with properly centred fully rounded workpieces. The speed should be halved in all cases for roughing down. The table shows where centre steadys are likely to become necessary. Steadys are shown against all the longer, larger diameter pieces not so much because of whip, but more to provide overall stability and safety.

We do have one thing going for us in spindle turning. It is likely that the surface speed is roughly constant across all the worked areas on a spindle as all faces are much the same distance from the centre axis.

The spindle gouge is the next tool to consider. Start with the square ended pattern. It is useful to think of this as a skew chisel with the corners bent up out of the way so that they are less likely to catch. It is used in a similar way to all the tools that we have considered so far, particularly the skew. The bevel rubs behind the cutting edge and this means presenting the edge at an angle to the line of axis. Worked with the edge at between 15 to 45 degrees to the axis and tilted at about 15 degrees towards the direction of travel the edge will cut cleanly, and the wood will polish. Just as with the skew, the tool rest is above the centre axis height, the tool handle 10 to 15 degrees below the rest. The gouge is normally used for working into concave areas such as covings and this means that the tool has to be rotated around its own centre axis to hollow out, just as you 'rolled' the skew to round off the ends of the egg.

Diameter	Lengths					
	6in	12in	18in	24in	36in	48in
1in	3,000	2,500	1,500*	1,000**	800**	800**
2in	2,500	1,800	1,500*	1,000**	800**	800**
3in	1,800	1,500	1,250	1,000*	800**	800**
4in	1,500	1,000	1,000	800*	800**	500**
6in	1,000	1,000	800*	800	500*	500**

* steady desirable   ** steady essential

Table 3 Optimum rotation speeds when working with centred fully rounded workpieces. All speeds are shown in revolutions per minute; one star indicates that a steady speed is desirable, two stars that a steady or centre bearing is essential.

Remember in the very first exercise, planing across the end grain and breaking out the unsupported corner? There can be a similar problem with the gouge if you try to work the whole of a cove all from one side and angle. Everything is fine while going down the one face into the cove, but the moment you start to cut up the other wall the grain is unsupported and the shoulder will break away. So you cut down one side with the edge at something between 15 degrees and 45 degrees to the axis, edge leading, and the tool well on its side for the vertical part of the cut. To make a clean entry on the near-vertical lip of the cove the tool blade may be presented 'over square' to the lathe axis with the blade axis vertical in order to get an initial bevel rub. Then roll the tool on its axis as you move down into the middle of the cove. Finish with the blade tilted over at about 10 degrees. Try to keep the actual cut somewhere near the centre of the edge of the tool at all times.

Having completed the cut down one side, change direction (ideally change hands) and approach the other wall from the other side. Again start at right-angles to the lathe axis, edge leading, tool on side, down the wall and roll the tool into the base, gradually decreasing the angle to the axis. The tool handle is sweeping in a scooping arc.

You may find that the best grip for the steadying hand is with the hand on top and the fingers wrapped lightly round the blade – the overhand grip that we used in roughing. For smaller coves the underhand, stop grip is better.

One problem that you will encounter initially, whether you change hands or not, is that when cutting coves it is difficult to get the two sides of the coving symmetrical. The only answer is practice!

By now you will probably have noticed something in your own turning. Your eye is constantly moving. First you watch the cutting edge, checking the angles, noting that the corners are well clear, and seeing that the depth of cut is about right. Then the eyes flick up to look at the top of the workpiece and see that the profile that is developing is what you require. You can not see the profile in the cutting zone as it is obscured by the tool edge, so you have to look at the top where it appears in silhouette. If you find that you do not do this naturally and you gaze fixedly at the cutting edge, start now to develop the habit of checking the top. Later you will find that you can make quite intricate cuts without looking at the edge at all. It is like playing the piano – the novice looks at his fingers, the master does not need to – they know where their fingers are.

On many occasions when working on the exteriors of larger bowls I find that I am looking at the top profile very much more than at the point where cutting is occurring. You can feel the condition of the cut through the tool handle. You should soon be able to tell where the edge is and the blade angle from the finished cut on the far side of the item – but you do have to actually look to tell what profile is emerging.

CUTTING COVING

Before we go any further it might be useful to get the feel of cutting some covings and at the same time checking upon your eye contact.

For this exercise rough down and plane smooth with the skew a piece of cleanish scrap wood. Another piece of about 2in (5cm) square by 18in (45.5cm) long will do. Once round, mark it off at 2in (5cm) intervals (use a pencil point against the spinning work piece).

For this cove cutting exercise you are going to work to a complex set of instructions and you will find that frequent reference to the drawings will help. To give you a little assistance in making entry

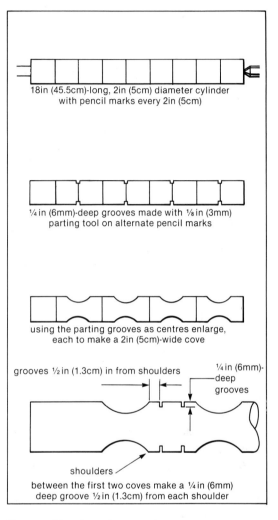

18in (45.5cm)-long, 2in (5cm) diameter cylinder with pencil marks every 2in (5cm)

¼in (6mm)-deep grooves made with ⅛in (3mm) parting tool on alternate pencil marks

using the parting grooves as centres enlarge, each to make a 2in (5cm)-wide cove

grooves ½in (1.3cm) in from shoulders

¼in (6mm)-deep grooves

shoulders

between the first two coves make a ¼in (6mm) deep groove ½in (1.3cm) from each shoulder

Cove and bead cutting exercise.

cuts, you will be using the parting tool to make some entry grooves to work to.

Working from the headstock end, at the second of the 2in (5cm) marks, make a parting groove about ¼in (6mm) deep. Do the same with each alternate mark from then on.

Now make a 2in (5cm) wide cove using each parting mark as a centre (where the deepest part of the cove will come). The tool to use is the shallow flute, square

71

Making an entry to cut a cove. The tool used here is a broad, shallow gouge with a near-square end. It is held dead vertical with the cutting point on the centre axis. A very firm pinching stop grip is used to prevent side skewing.

An entry has been made and the blade is starting to roll in a scooping action.

ended gouge. To start the cove, present the gouge rolled right on to its side with the edge into the groove and with the bevel rubbing on the side wall of the groove. The tool will almost be at right-angles to the axis line. Now start the cut by first slightly decreasing the angle to the axis. Once you pick up the cut, roll the tool and then decrease the angle to the axis making a scooping action. Aim to cut the shoulder off the groove first. With each succeeding cut take the shoulder further towards the adjacent pencil mark indicating the end of the coving. Each cut should stop once the bottom of the cove is reached; do not try to work uphill yet.

Take two or three cuts on one side then work the opposite face for two or three cuts; then back to the original side. With

each cut, roll the blade until there is very little tilt by the time it reaches the base of the cove. Try to get each cove to the same depth and profile; working to a 2in (5cm) width they should be quite shallow and have nice, even sweeping curves. Leave the timber in the lathe for the moment.

Although you started cutting coves using a square ended gouge you will find that this is not too easy when working inside smaller coves; it became easier as the cove opened out. For fine work it is normally the round ended or finger nail gouges that are brought into service.

CUTTING BEADS

For the remainder of this chapter we will consider the various ways of cutting beads.

In effect you were cutting half-beads

Subsequent cuts start with the bevel rubbing on the side wall. Each cut only goes down the side to the deepest point. It does not continue up the far wall.

The tool is reversed to cut the other wall of the cove.

when first rounding off the blunt end of the egg. There you also started by cutting into a groove that had been made with the parting tool.

Normally when cutting beads or coves on a spindle we do not start with parting tool grooves; we work directly on the smooth cylinder. For the moment you can again give yourselves a little initial help with some parting grooves. Working to the right of the first cove and ½in (1.3cm) from its top edge make another ¼in (6mm) deep parting groove, and a second groove a quarter of an inch to the left of the next cove. Do the same on the smooth part of the cylinder between coves three and four.

Using a medium to small skew (with the long point up) start to work the area between the first pair of grooves and cut this into a bead. Remember that you will

need the tool rest a little higher. First work one side then change tool hands and work the other. As you make these cuts be careful to cut only within the safe zone of the skew. If the short point catches it will dig in, be forced back up the bead, and leave a spiral groove. Should it happen, then recut the bead deeper until the groove has been worked out.

To cut the beads properly the greatest care has to be exercised when the edge is deep in the recess; this is when the point is most likely to catch. Keep a firm grip at all times.

Next, mark off the workpiece with pencil rings on the uncoved bits ½in (1.3cm) from each cove end. This will give a series of flat collars which will have an inch wide centre area marked off. Working on a couple of these sections, make a groove on each of the two pencil marks using the long point of a skew chisel.

Cutting beads with a narrow-blade skew chisel.

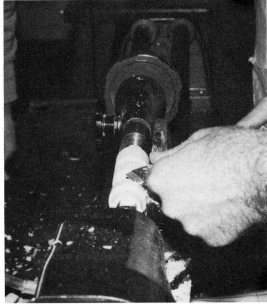

Using a medium skew for larger beads.

Remember you did this in making decorative rings on the handle you turned earlier. For this exercise use either a ½in (1.3cm) or ¾in (1.9cm)-wide skew. Set the tool rest at centre height, chisel on its edge, long point down, blade firmly held on the rest with steady hand pinching together both blade and rest, tool at exactly 90 degrees to the lathe axis. Push the tool forward firmly to give the depth of groove required. You will find that you cannot go in too far and that further pushing only creates friction.

Now reset the tool rest to just above centre height and about an eighth away from the cylinder. This time use the skew the other way up – still on its side, long point uppermost, but tilted over at about 45 degrees and now at about 25 to 30 degrees to the lathe axis. The first cut is the tricky one. It takes off the corner of the groove, it is made with the corner of the

Beads can also be cut with a shallow gouge or a spindle gouge.

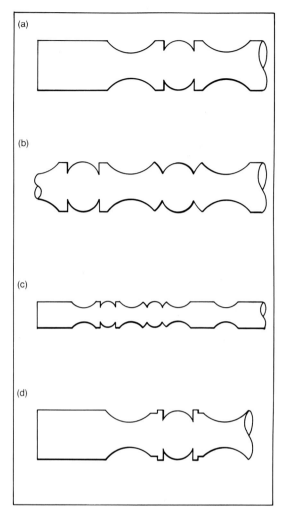

(a)

(b)

(c)

(d)

Cove and bead cutting exercise. (a) Cut the bead with the skew, keeping the long point up. Repeat to put bead between coves 2 and 3. (b) Round off the shoulders facing bead number 2. (c) The workpiece so far. (d) Put a step into the shoulders either side of the first bead, using a parting tool.

short point and there is really very little for the bevel to rub on. It therefore requires a firm grip with both hands. The steady hand must hold the blade down on the rest but must also be so firmly positioned on the rest that it will prevent the chisel's tendency to kick sideways (the pinching stop grip).

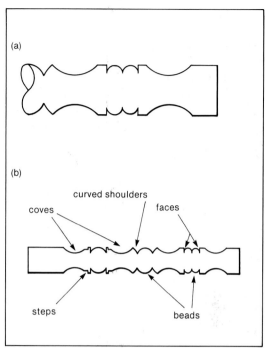

(a)

(b)

curved shoulders

coves

faces

steps

beads

(a) Two small beads cut into the cylinder between coves 3 and 4. (b) The finished workpiece.

Once the first cut is made things get easier. Now there is a shoulder for the bevel to rub on and you can start to cut using the skew's safe cutting zone.

As you are rounding over a bead, the blade will start flat and will be rolled to the near-vertical. A good position for the steady hand is the index finger over grip. Here the index finger is wrapped round the blade, the remaining fingers lightly clenched, and the side of the hand pushed firmly down on to the tool rest.

Finish the rounding-off with cuts into the corners. When that is complete have a go at the second marked off bead. You now have two beads cut into two of the flat sections. There should be half an inch (1.3cm) of flat cylinder between the ends of the bead and the adjacent cove.

Clean the faces on both sides of the first bead using the skew in the facing cut

75

position (tool rest at centre height, skew long point down, blade tilted only about 2 degrees over from the vertical). Get the bevel rubbing very clearly before any attempt is made to cut, then swing the handle very slightly until cutting begins. Take off a very fine disc. The swarf may hang up in the corner between the bead and the vertical face. Clean this up by coming in from the bead side – don't forget the shoulder rubbing. Work from both sides until you are satisfied with the finish. Sharp tools are essential at all times – doubly so when making vertical cuts across the end grain.

You still have the second bead between two untrimmed vertical faces. Round these off with half-beads again using the skew long point up.

You may now be asking 'Why, if I can make beads with a skew chisel, do I have a thing called a Beading and Parting Tool?' Good question! Actually if you think of a beading tool as being a very narrow but thicker skew chisel you have some of the answers. The beading tool is useful for making smaller or sharper curved beads. It is also much more likely that the corners will catch and the extra thickness gives the tool sufficient strength to withstand the occasional major dig-in. The tool can also be used as a parting tool to produce wider grooves or to reduce the diameter to make a shoulder. Try it.

Work on the shoulder between the first cove and the first bead, and using a beading tool put a step in it to the full width of the beading tool.

Next, working on one of the remaining flat sections between coves 3 and 4, scribe 2 marks ½in (1.3cm) either side of the original 2in (5cm) pencil mark. You should now have five rings at ½in spacings. The centre three pencil rings will mark the grooves for two small beads. Make these with the beading and parting tool in exactly the same way that you made the larger beads with the skew chisel. You will have to exercise a little more caution to ensure that you do not catch the corner of the beading tool, and because it is square ended this will mean that it has to be used at a much narrower angle to the lathe axis. The cutting edge will be near 45 degrees to the axis. At this angle there will be a greater tendency for the tool to be pushed sideways so the initial cuts again require a very firm grip (again try the index finger wrapped round grip).

You will probably make some mistakes in the early days, but if you accidentally take the top off a bead, make the bead again but of a smaller diameter. Somewhere between starting and parting right through the timber you should end up with at least one good one!

Problem solving theory suggests that whenever you do something wrong you should stop and analyse what caused it. Unfortunately in spindle turning everything happens so fast that it is difficult to see what happened or to think back to what was going on a millisecond earlier.

In fact the possible causes are very few and can generally be assumed from the effects. Most problems result in a spiral groove. Other, less frequent occurrences are great splinters being wrenched out. Most spiral grooves are caused by the lower point catching and the tool being forced back up the surface of the wood by the rotation of the work piece. Chips and splinters are mostly caused by an unsupported bevel edge or the upper corner digging in, and being forced down under the grain and into the wood by the power of the rotation.

Finally, there is the possibility of making beads as we made covings – with the gouge. The safest tool of all is the round ended (fingernail) gouge. It is almost impossible to get a dig-in unless you present the blade flat at right-angles to the axis, and go in straight without the bevel rubbing! It is, however, very easy to make spiral grooves when making the initial entry grooving cut with a gouge.

To avoid this problem it is best to start with the rest at half the tool's width below centre height. The blade must be absolutely vertical and at a perfect right-angle to the face of the wood. If on entry the gouge does kick sideways then if it kicks in the direction it is facing it was tilted slightly over the vertical. If it kicks away from the direction it was facing then it was not quite up to the vertical.

On the remaining flat sections at each end of your practice piece make a couple of beads using a gouge. Now with a roughing gouge plane smooth all your good work, plane up the cylinder with a skew, and start all over again. And again. And again. And yet again!

It is a good idea to go through this exercise several times (and to keep repeat-

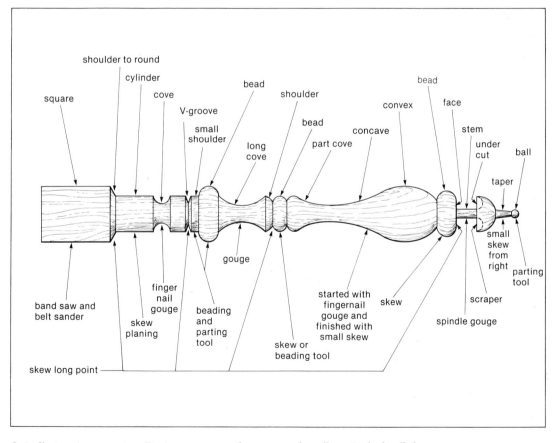

Spindle turning exercise. Design your own beer pump handle – include all the cuts shown here. First draw out your idea, then mark the wood off carefully.

ing it every so often in the future). Practice with the skew is important, as is working to a given (complex) set of instructions. It is also useful to repeat the exercise to get practice in making pieces that actually look alike – it takes skill to get all four legs of a stool to match!

From here on it is up to you. This time you might like to try a slightly longer piece of wood, of about 20in (51cm). Design yourself a handle which incorporates each and every one of the cuts we have so far identified. What you will finish up with may have no utility, it might not even be a thing of great beauty – but at least it will be interesting. First look at the diagram which shows all the cuts and identifies which is the proper tool to use for each. Then sketch out your own handle. It is good practice to draw the shapes of objects before you try to make them; it does not matter that you do not have particular drawing skills. Plane your piece of wood down to a cylinder and mark off the main features. You may care to establish a few reference grooves with a parting tool, but make sure that you incorporate into the exercise the making of entries with a skew and with a gouge.

7 Getting Inside

Turning between centres will produce columns, handles, part-finished eggs, lace bobbins, table legs and similar. Few turners would be satisfied with that alone. Before long you will want to start putting holes into things and to hollow out; so let's take a look at 'getting inside'.

The first issue to address is that you can no longer use the tailstock centre to keep the work piece pushed against the drive prongs. Without this the prongs will not bite, so you now need to adopt another method of transferring the drive to the work piece.

In Chapter 4 we talked about spigot, cup chucks, jaw chucks and the screw chuck. Using spigot, cup or jaw usually means allowing an extra length of wood that will ultimately be parted off and may be wasted. Provided you can accommodate the screw hole in the base of the finished piece, using the screw chuck means that the whole length of the timber can be utilised. This is very useful in that with the screw chuck we can make small items from off-cuts of wood that might otherwise have been wasted. Ring-stands and light-pulls spring readily to mind.

There are other reasons for focusing first upon the screw chuck. It is a standard component with most lathes and therefore every turner is likely to have one. Not everyone will have a jaw chuck – certainly not to start with. The screw chuck is also more forgiving than is the cup. With the latter the fit has to be perfect, and even then the workpiece will work loose if you use too much side pressure on the outside surfaces.

Having said that all the wood can be used with a screw chuck, on our next assignment we are going to waste a little wood because we do not want a hole in the base of the finished object. We are going to make a box, but will use the screw chuck for convenience.

MAKING A BOX

This is one thing over which there can be no short cuts. There can be no 'Well, it looks dry! I'll try it and hope I get away with it'. For the making of boxes you have to have dry wood – not even air dried or part-dried, but fully kiln dried and then allowed to stabilise down to normal room moisture levels. The reason is simple. When a thick piece of wood is turned and hollowed out, any moisture in the walls will quickly dry off. In drying, as the moisture leaves the pores in the wood they contract. Those near the centre of the tree contract less than those nearer the outside. However you cut the wood, part of it will have come from nearer the centre of the tree; and across your finished object, however small, there will be parts that will contract more than others. You may well start by hollowing out a perfect cylinder – the vessel you make may start by being round, but in the weeks, even the hours, that follow it will become slightly oval. If the wood was reasonably

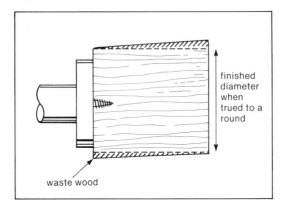

Wasteful effect of mounting blocks off square with sloping end.

6in (15cm)-long block of 3in (7.5cm)-square wood would be ideal (5in/12cm of 2×2in/5×5cm would still be OK). Again to make things easier, a nice clean piece of even-grained wood is preferred – beech, steamed pear, meranti or similar are amongst the more dimensionally stable.

First ensure that the end of the block that is to be mounted on the screw chuck is at right-angles to the axis of the wood – sloping ends are very wasteful when it comes to reducing the outboard end to a cylinder. A bench sander or sanding table can be used for this purpose. Mark off the centres on both ends of the block, and drill a small pilot hole in the centre of what will be the base. Screw the squared end on to the screw chuck and take the block up tight. Now bring up the tailstock to the outboard end. It is not essential to use the tailstock support but it is a useful safeguard for the roughing-to-a-round stage.

Rough out and then plane the cylinder

dry to start with, the degree of ovality may be small; it may not even be visible. But if you have made a box with a nice, snug-fitting lid you will know! Either the lid will not come off at all, or it will rattle around. So you *must* start dry!

To give yourself plenty to play with, a

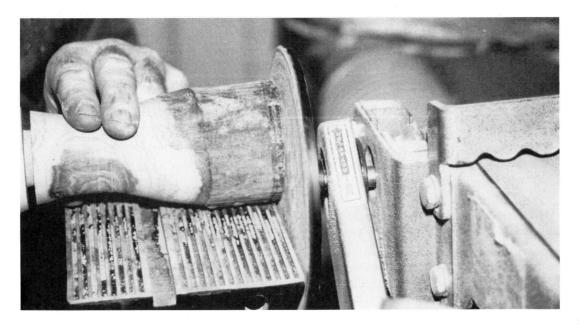

Sanding off the base to get it square on a part-worked piece.

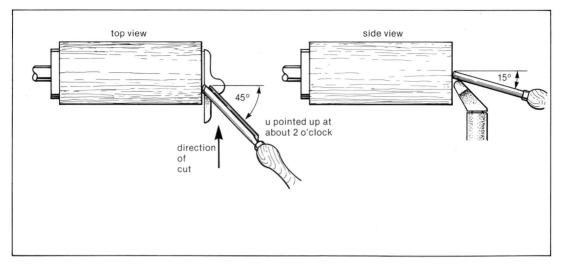

Truing the face with a bowl gouge forward cut.

with the skew. Aim for a good, polished finish as this will provide the outside of the box without further working. Tool rest close to the workpiece, parallel to the sides, an eighth of an inch below the centre line for the roughing stage and then just below the top of the workpiece for skew planing.

Remove the tailstock and reposition the tool rest so that it lies across the outboard end of the block. As usual it should be about an eighth of an inch away from the face and be a little (¼in/6mm) below the centre axis height.

The first task is to true up the face. Previously, in between centres turning, you did this by working from the side and making shearing cuts with the long point of a skew. This time use the small bowl gouge.

You have three options in terms of methods of attack. Which you choose will depend upon how close to square the end face is to start with.

If it is rough and way off square then it is best to work from the outside in towards the centre, using the bowl gouge. The angle at which the tool is presented will be about 45 degrees to the end face of the wood. The handle should be down about 15 degrees off the horizontal, and the flute of the gouge pointing in the general direction of travel but upwards at something like two o'clock. Use a firm overhand or stop grip with the steady hand.

The more off square the end, the greater will be the blur that you are working into. You will be starting the sweep of your cut outside the diameter of the cylinder so in this case the bevel will not be rubbing. Aim into the tip of the blur and move the gouge in until cutting starts. Continue to sweep in towards the centre. If you try to take too much at a time you will probably wrench the wood off the chuck. So care is the key word until you have located the corners.

While the face is out of true, each rotation will give an arc of cutting and an arc of space. You will feel this through the chisel handle as a series of gradually lessening bumps. However, the bumps seem to disappear before the face is finally true. The truing can be finished by continuing with a number of succeeding

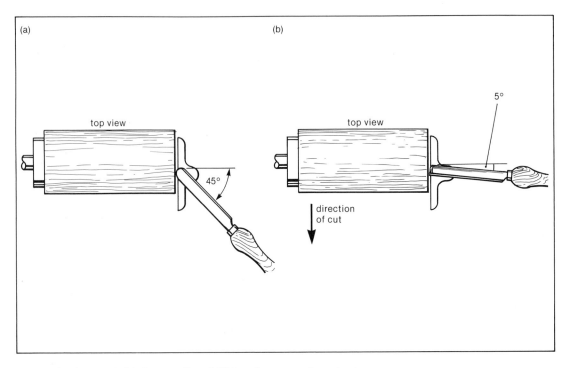

Truing the face with (a) fingernail and (b) bowl gouges, draw back cut.

cuts in exactly the same way, but I prefer to use a second cut when I think the job is almost done.

The second cut accentuates the feeling of bumping whilst there is any unevenness left. This cut is a draw back cut which starts from the centre of the face and works out to the rim. It is made with the cut being taken by the shoulder of the lower side of the U of the gouge and it is more of a scraping than a true shearing cut. The gouge is held at a more acute angle to the end face of the wood than were the first shearing cuts. The handle is raised to just below the horizontal. The blade is rolled over so that the flute is pointing wholly in the direction of travel (at nine o'clock). Two or three passes with this cut, and any bumping will have gone. You now have a clean end face.

Of course the face may not be square. You may have made it slightly concave or convex. Try to judge by eye. Line up an eye with the rim of the face and look across towards the centre. Move the head a fraction from side to side. Does the face look square? If not, take another scraping cut or two. When you think it is right, stop the lathe and try with a set square. With a little practice you will find that you can dispense with the set square in the checking process. As it happens for this exercise, it does not matter if the end is not perfectly square because we are going to do further work on it.

The third method of truing up the end with a bowl gouge is very similar to the first except that you use shearing cuts working from the centre out to the edge. This means working across the bed with

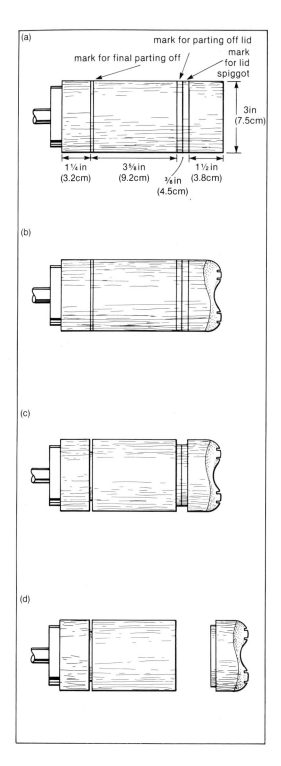

(a)

mark for parting off lid

mark for final parting off

mark for lid spiggot

3in (7.5cm)

1¼in (3.2cm)   3⅝in (9.2cm)   ⅜in (4.5cm)   1½in (3.8cm)

(b)

(c)

(d)

the gouge handle away from you. The flute now points towards you, aiming at your chest. Blade angle is determined by the bevel rub and the tool handle is dropped to about 15 degrees below the horizontal.

Once the end is true you can begin to mark it off and to work it. Start by rounding off the corners of the top of the lid. Here we meet a fundamental principle of turning. On face work, unless you are working into end grain, you should always cut from the smaller diameter to the larger. This means that while working on the outside of the object you start at the centre of the outboard end and work towards the greater diameter which will usually be at the drive or headstock end.

There is a reason for this principle. If working uphill, from smaller to larger diameter on the outside surface, the segment of the grain of the wood that you are cutting at any one time will be supported from behind by adjacent grains. It will be more likely to cut cleanly and less likely to be merely pushed up and tear away from the adjacent grain. Uphill cuts are less likely to leave a rough, torn finish than are downhill cuts.

In making boxes it is usual to have the grain running down the box. Hence you are working on end-grain when shaping the lid. So in this instance you work from its outside in towards the centre.

To round off corners, therefore, begin on the end face and work inwards from

Left: Marking the outside of a lidded pot. (a) Dimensions for marking off. (b) The top of the lid finished, with two decorative grooves. (c) A parting tool is used to take out ⅜in(1cm) – wide recess at lid joint, to a depth of ³/₁₆(4.5mm). (d) Lid parted away from base.

the cylinder wall. Start with the bevel rubbing. The first cut or two should be very fine as the corner grain is initially unsupported. As the corner becomes rounded you should reposition the tool rest to lie diagonally across the curve.

As you know, you could have produced the rounded corners another way. In fact you could have done it two other ways. When planing off the surface of the cylinder with the skew, you could have continued to roll the skew over the corner. Alternatively you can round off with a spindle gouge again, working from the long wall of the cylinder and on over the edge on to the face.

Go on to shape the top of the lid, but for this first box keep it fairly simple. Try a shallow depression in the centre – two or three gentle cuts in with the bowl gouge,

To round off the ends, position the tool rest across the corner. Start cutting at the centre with the tool handle across the lathe bed and slowly bring the butt towards you. Always cut 'uphill' from smaller to larger diameter.

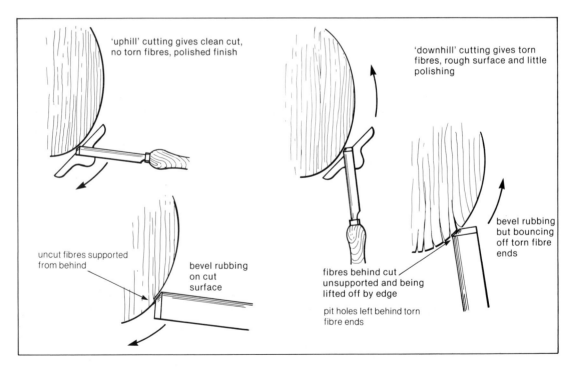

'uphill' cutting gives clean cut, no torn fibres, polished finish

'downhill' cutting gives torn fibres, rough surface and little polishing

uncut fibres supported from behind

bevel rubbing on cut surface

fibres behind cut unsupported and being lifted off by edge

pit holes left behind torn fibre ends

bevel rubbing but bouncing off torn fibre ends

Up- and downhill cutting.

and then possibly incise a couple of decorative groove rings with the long point of a skew just as you did on the tool handle. Remember to lift the tool rest to the centre axis for the grooving cut; skew at right handles to the work face – in other words, dead in line with the lathe axis; long point down and tool handle horizontal. A firm stop grip is needed.

Once you are satisfied with the shape of the lid it can be finished off. Indeed, when making lidded objects it is advisable to sand off the lid and the side walls practically to the final finish before the lid is parted off.

The lid of the box that you are making is going to have a spigot on the bottom of it that will fit into the box.

Bring the tool rest to the face of the cylinder, ⅛in (3mm) away and just on the centre height. With a pencil, mark off a ring about 1½in (3.8cm) in from the top of the lid. Working on the tailstock side of this mark and using the parting tool, incise a groove about $\frac{3}{16}$ to ¼in (4.5 to 6 mm) deep (err towards being deeper rather than too shallow at this stage). If you are using the narrow eighth-thick parting tool widen the groove until it is ⅜in (1cm) wide.

Now, working in the drive stock side of this groove, part off the lid with the parting tool. There will be some roughness on the parted face of the lid, so rub this smooth on a belt sander or on a piece of sandpaper placed flat on the top of the workbench. Put the finished lid to one side for the moment.

To give dimensions to work to, partially part off the base of the box. Draw a pencil ring well clear of the point of the screw of the chuck – allow at least ¼in (6mm) beyond the length of the screw. Using the parting tool, cut a groove on the outboard

Sand the lid of the box to a near-finished state before parting off. This reduces the chance of spinning the lid in the box later.

side of the pencil mark. Do not part right through; leave at least one-third of the overall diameter. This groove will eventually be used to part off and to form the external base of the finished box, but if you go in too far at this stage you will make the body unstable for clean hollowing.

So to hollowing out. There are three options: gouge, scraper, or drill. We are going to use a combination of the first two. The drill will be discussed later.

First you need to mark out the working dimensions – depth and inside diameter. You will be working to produce a wall thickness of about $\frac{3}{16}$in (4.5mm). The base thickness should be roughly the same as that of the wall. Measure the height of the wall from the base parting

85

groove to the rim. Take the small diameter spindle gouge and with a wrap of masking tape around the blade mark off the depth of the inside of the box. This will be the outside wall height, less the $^3/_{16}$in (4.5mm) base thickness, less another $^1/_{16}$in (1.5mm) 'cleaning up' margin.

Position the tool rest across the end face and fairly accurately to the radius of the spindle gouge below the centre. Start the lathe, offer up the point of the spindle gouge to the centre of the work piece – handle dead horizontal and lying straight along the lathe axis. Now push the gouge into the wood. It should go in cleanly and without oscillation. Once you have penetrated about an inch (2.5cm) draw the tool out and clear any swarf from the flute. Re-enter and push the gouge in until the masking tape mark shows that the full depth has been reached. If very deep, withdraw the gouge from time to time to clear the flute.

You can do this job with a drill bit mounted in the tailstock, but the spindle gouge is quicker for small work. For really big work many turners have the lathe stationary and drill the depth mark with a brace and wood auger (again using a wrap of masking tape on the bit to mark the required depth).

The next task is to mark off the inside diameter with a pair of dividers.

A robust pair of dividers is an essential piece of equipment to the turner, and I do mean robust. They are used for scribing against turning end grain and, unless strong, the points bend or burn away. I find the old, solid, 'antique' ones to be ideal.

Set the dividers to the diameter of the spigot on the base of the lid (again you might initially like to go a fraction undersize to give yourself a working margin).

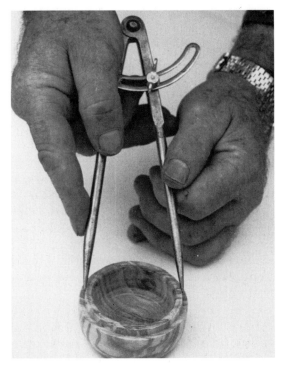

Setting the dividers to the size of the lid spigot. To hollow out the lid in the picture, it was wrapped with a couple of turns of masking tape and was lightly held in a four-jaw chuck.

The tool rest is still across the end face so raise it until it is exactly on the axis height. Start the lathe. Rest the dividers on the tool rest. You will be scribing a mark with the point nearest to you and ensuring that the further point does not actually touch the rotating wood. Try to judge that the scribing point and the free point are the same distance from the outside of the cylinder. Now make a mark into the rotating wood with the scribing point. If you have it right the free point will be exactly in line with the groove on the far side. If the free point is outside the groove you will need to reposition the scribing point a fraction outside the first

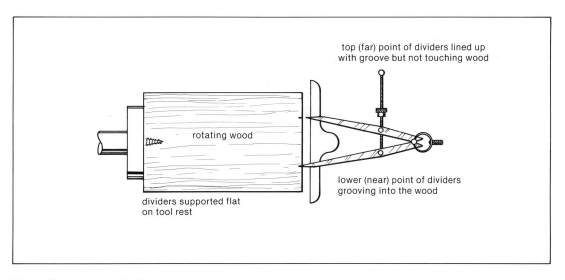

Using dividers to mark dimensions.

groove. Free point inside the groove will mean the scribing point is too far out. With practice you will develop an eye, and your first entry will often be spot on. You will later use this method of marking off diameters to make the spigots and dovetails in the bases of items to be mounted on spigot and combination chucks.

Now drop the rest a fraction − for the diameter of wood we are working, about ¼in (6mm) below axis is suitable. The small bowl gouge is used for the hollowing-out of boxes 3in (7.5cm) diameter or less.

The first cut starts near the centre and goes in to the depth gauge hole made by the spindle gouge. Start with the bevel rubbing, the tip out at about one-third of the diameter and above the axis height (about 11 o'clock). The tool handle will therefore be well below the tool rest and the flute of the U-pointing at about half past two. The cut is made by raising the handle towards you in an arc. This causes

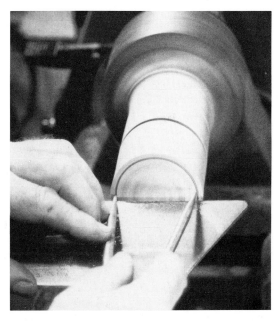

To mark off the wall thickness with the dividers set them to the lid spigot dimensions. The tool rest is set exactly on axis height. The nearside pointer is pushed into the rotating timber to score the wood while the far point is lined up with the groove but is kept just clear.

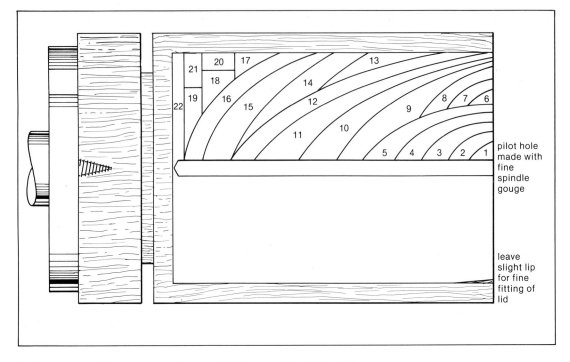

pilot hole made with fine spindle gouge

leave slight lip for fine fitting of lid

Hollowing out. The sequence of cuts to hollow out the body of the pot: cuts 1–16 with a bowl gouge; cuts 17–22 with a modified side-cutting square-ended scraper.

the cutting edge to arc downwards and inwards towards the centre axis.

Succeeding cuts go deeper and the

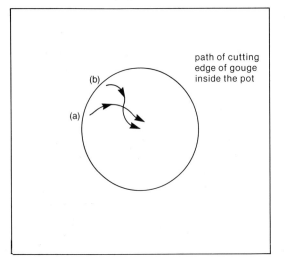

path of cutting edge of gouge inside the pot

(b)

(a)

The sweep of the bowl gouge. (a) Early cuts. (b) Later cuts.

swing of the handle now becomes a complex arc. The end of the handle starts away from you, low right and sweeps diagonally upwards (across your chest) to the left. Take several cuts from the same starting point so that you increase the depth of the hollow before enlarging the diameter.

Next move outwards a little and start another series of deepening cuts.

As you get deeper, and the inside walls of the hollow become more vertical, you will find a number of things are happening. First, in order to start the cut, you have to begin with the tool handle pointing away from you across the lathe bed. You will find that the cut starts at about nine o'clock, sweeps up towards eleven o'clock and then sweeps back down to the centre axis. The third thing you may find is that the deeper you get, the more diffi-

88

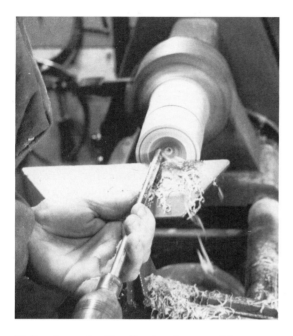

Hollowing out with a fine bowl gouge. The tool rest is just below centre height.

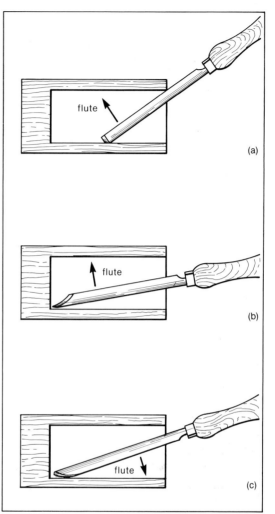

Gouges for deep vessels. (a) Limit of depth capability of a conventional bowl gouge. (b) Gouge with a long, pointed nose. (c) Ground-back gouges can be used inverted to shear-scrape into deep corners.

cult it becomes to keep the bevel rubbing on the vertical section. In fact if you have a steeper bevel angle on your gouge you may not even be able to maintain cut. This is where I change to a gouge with a shallower 20 degree bevel angle.

A similar thing occurs at the bottom of the cut. If you have an area deep inside which is flat (parallel to the base of the box), a conventionally angled bevel gouge will be scraping rather than shearing, and maintaining bevel contact is impossible. That is where my acute 65 degree angle bevel gouges come into play – they may be near scraping but at least you can maintain bevel contact and reduce the risk of vibration and dig-ins.

Continue to work downwards and outwards with the gouge until you reach the two dimension marks. In the base this will be the moment that you reach the bottom of the hole made with the spindle gouge or drill, and at the top, just inside the divider scribed marks. When working

close to the diameter marks, use a firm stop grip to start the cuts so that the gouge is not skewed out across the rim.

One thing that you cannot do with a gouge is to make a clean right-angled corner inside a box. This is where you have to turn to scrapers.

Scraper technique is fundamentally different from that used with chisels or gouges. First the tools are always used

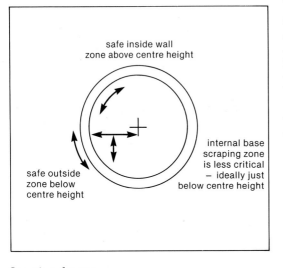

safe inside wall
zone above centre height

internal base
scraping zone
is less critical
– ideally just
below centre height

safe outside
zone below
centre height

Scraping the pot.

with the blade angled slightly down-wards – and, of course, there is no bevel rubbing.

Here we meet another principle. Think back to the principle of always cutting uphill with a gouge so that the grains being cut are supported by those behind. This is even more important with a scraper which has a greater tendency to tear grains apart rather than to cut through fibres. This means that we have to be very careful about the height at which the edge of the scraper is operating.

When cleaning a vertical face across the lathe axis, particularly if it is end grain, there is no problem. You can in theory work above, on, or below the axis height. If, however, you are working on side-walls of a cylinder the height is critical. At all times you must have the grain sup-ported from behind. When cutting on the outside of the cylinder wall the cutting edge of a scraper must be below the centre axis (and the tool edge be angled slightly downwards). If you try cutting an inside

wall of a cylinder and you work below the axis height, you will be tearing the ends off unsupported grain, and will certainly produce a rough, torn finish. You will probably also get pinched into a major dig-in.

When working inside on the side walls, therefore, you have to raise the tool rest so that with the edge of the tool angled slightly downwards it is still cutting well above the centre axis.

With a deep, vertically walled vessel, to cut down to the inside corners and still have the cutting edge above the axis may well mean that the tool rest has to be an inch or two above the axis height. On some lathes the tool post is not long enough to allow this.

There is another problem. The deeper you go into a vessel while still keeping the tool rest across the open face, the greater the overhang of blade that there is between the cutting edge and the support of the tool rest. This means that the blade is more likely to flex and vibrate slightly – this in turn could lead to a dig-in. When the edge digs in, and it is some distance out from the supporting rest, the shock and leverage are such that the blade dips down, the handle jerks upwards and control is lost. It is very aggravating when you are putting the finishing touches to a deep, incised corner if the tool catches and is jerked up so hard that it splits the rim of the work piece – and it usually does!

There are ways of minimising the problem. First, as already emphasised, ensure that the cutting edge is above the axis line. Second, use the biggest and thickest scrapers possible – they vibrate and flex less and are less prone to dig in. (Unfortunately, they also block the line of vision, may not be handled with sufficient

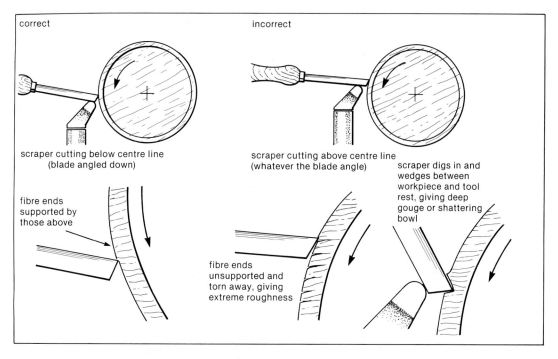

External scraping.

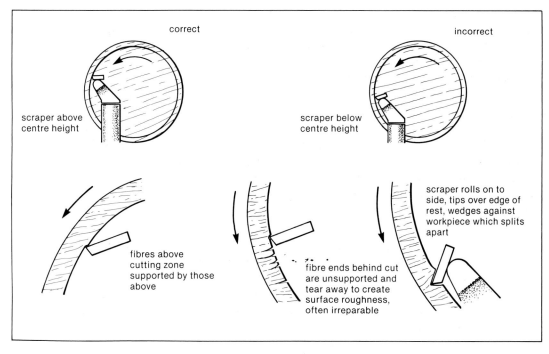

Internal scraping.

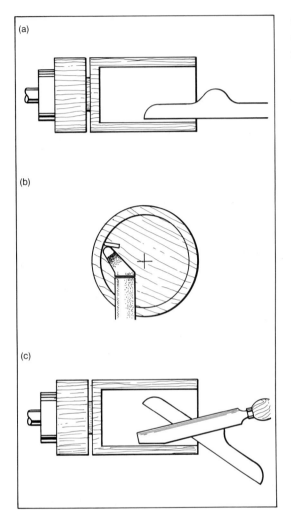

Tool rest problems inside the pot. (a) You want a tool rest that will support the scraper close to the wall, right down the pot. (b) But most rests slope and the scraper rocks on the edge. (c) The normal compromise is to angle the tool rest (and use the flat top rest if possible). This then provides a square across the blade support for the scraper.

delicacy or accuracy, and if they do dig in they will split the work piece right apart.)

A better solution is to have a tool rest that can be positioned inside the work piece, will support the tool close to the edge and right down to the bottom corners, be solid enough so that the rest itself does not flex, and still be sufficiently small to allow clear vision and access. No such ideal implement exists, but some useful compromise curved bowl rests do.

This still leaves one problem. If the rest is narrow and is positioned inside to lie parallel with the axis of rotation then a tool fed in from the open end of the vessel will be lying along the top of the rest and there will be a tendency for the pressure of the cutting action on the edge to cause the tool to rotate in your hand and to tip over the front edge of the rest. Again a dig-in, an almighty jam up, and a split side wall. Narrow tool rests positioned inside are best angled so that they are close to the vessel walls at the rim but are angled to the far side of the bottom.

So, where are we with the box? Fortunately it should be sufficiently shallow that you are not going to be faced with long overhangs of unsupported tool blade. It may be that on your lathe you can position the rest inside the hollow. Get it as close as you can to the face to be cut and ensure that it will hold the cutting edge above the centre axis.

The tool to use is the modified square nose scraper or the diamond side scraper. Work from the centre of the bottom, gradually cutting outwards towards the corner. Do not take too deep a cut with each pass but proceed in a series of gentle skims. (Remember you only have $3/16$ in (4.5mm) left.) While working the bottom in this way the rest can be a little lower, as you are cutting a vertical face across the axis and the cutting edge should be working just below centre height. However, as you are also impinging on to the side wall, a compromise at centre height would be in order.

With the bottom near-finished the rest needs to come up a little as we clean off the inside side walls. Start the cut at the rim. Keep a firm grip on the handle to prevent any rotation of the tool. The tool will have a tendency to chatter against the side wall although it shouldn't do if the edge is sharp and you are working on a small diameter vessel with walls $^3/_{16}$ in (4.5mm) thick. To prevent this happening, steady the tool on the rest with the thumb and press the fingers against the outside wall of the vessel to support the wall against the pressure of the cut. This is a variety of the support grip. Incidentally, the tendency to chatter will be increased if you parted in too far at the base and the work piece is not sufficiently well supported to cope with the vibration set up as the tool edge jumps from cutting one fibre to cutting the next.

You have worked the rim out almost to the scribing mark. Try the lid. It should nearly go in. I say nearly because you have yet to sand out the inside of the box. If it is clearly well off, then take another fine cut. If it does already fit then too bad, you will have a loose lid – this time!

Rough sand the interior until you can just get the lid in. Once you have achieved a tight fit, push the lid home and then complete the sanding off of the outside of the box and the lid as one. If you are going to finish with a friction lacquer or wax, do this now.

Next remove the lid and complete the interior sanding and finishing. Finally, part off at the base and smooth off on the belt sander, or reverse chuck the box and trim off with facing cuts. Don't forget to apply a little finish to the base – probably a rub of oil to seal it.

A well-made box with a correctly fitting lid is one where the lid is sufficiently close

that it is held in against removal by vacuum. There should be a 'plop' of in-rushing air as the lid is drawn out, and the box should stay that way if you really did start with dry timber!

Earlier in this chapter we said there are three methods of hollowing out. We have looked at two of them together. Obviously you can hollow out, leaving a rounded inside base using only the bowl gouge. Equally, you can hollow out using only scrapers – a diamond point to make the initial insertion and then a series of widening and deepening cuts with the modified square nose.

This leaves the third method; that of drilling. Using a drill to hollow out means that you need drill bits with a diameter of the required finished internal size. They need also to be of a pattern that will produce clean side walls and a flat bottom. Obviously you would have to make the spigot on the lid base the right diameter to fit into the drill hole. Here you would use the external calliper and parting tool method to cut lid spigot grooves to drill bit diameter.

The type of drill bit that meets all our criteria is the saw tooth or forstener bit. These have saw teeth around the outside rim to produce clean sided walls and two chisel edges on the face to cut a clean bottom. They are, however, quite expensive.

Most saw tooth bits have a ½in shank and have to be mounted in the Jacobs chuck fixed on to or into the tailstock quill. They are designed for slow speed cutting and the lathe has to be set at its slowest rate. They should not be used in hand-held drills.

The quill is wound right back and the tail stock unit is moved up until the bit is just touching the face of the workpiece.

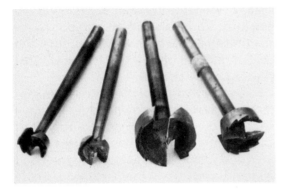

Forstner bits. The saw teeth round the rim cut clean-walled vertical holes while the chisels across the base cut the depth.

temperature build-up. According to the depth required it is sometimes necessary to wind in the quill and reposition the whole tailstock until the bit again contacts the bottom of the hole.

Drilling is a sure way of testing the moisture content of the wood. The heat generated internally will push any moisture to the outside surface and there will be a volume of steam. Obviously such an amount of heat can quickly split sensitive woods. The secret is dry wood, very slow lathe speeds, frequent tool withdrawal, and long cooling, rest periods.

The tail stock body is firmly clamped and the lathe started. Using the tailstock wheel, the quill is slowly extended and the drill cuts into the rotating wood.

It is advisable to draw the drill bit out after each additional inch of depth drilled. This allows for the clearance of swarf which in turn reduces the frictional

To drill smaller holes, as in the centre of lamp pulls, ordinary twist drills are quite adequate. A shallow hole with a ¼in (6mm) bit will accommodate the knot in the draw string, and an eighth diameter hole will allow the main string to pass through the body.

Longer holes, as in standard lamp stems, are drilled with special long-

Forstener bit held in the Jacobs chuck ready to drill the centre out of the outer of two Yew bud vases.

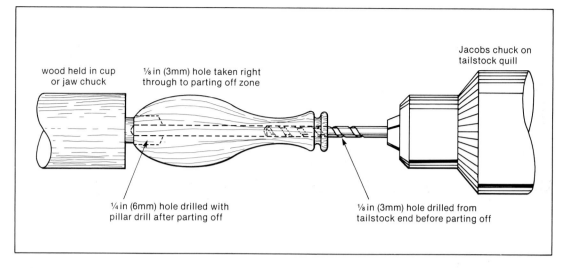

Drilling cord holes in a lamp pull.

handled augers. Most lathes have hollow tail stock quills which are designed to allow the auger to be fed through from the outboard end. Not all lathes have the same diameter hole; therefore you often have to have the lathe manufacturer's own long hole auger.

Long spindles cannot be adequately held by a screw or even a jaw chuck alone. It is essential when doing long hole-boring that work pieces be supported near the outboard end in a long work or centre steady.

COMPLETING AN EGG

Earlier, you part-completed an egg. You turned the overall shape, nicely rounded off the pointed end, and sanded the body smooth. It was parted off at the blunt end using a skew chisel, but unless you have become a master overnight it is unlikely that the parted face will be perfectly round and unblemished.

What is now needed is an egg cup chuck in which the egg can be held while finishing the rounding-off and the sanding of the

blunt end. You will need a piece of pine off-cut $2\frac{1}{2} \times 2\frac{1}{2} \times 5$in ($6.5 \times 6.5 \times 12.5$cm).

If you plan to make several eggs, it is likely that you will get some size and shape variation. You may therefore need three or four egg chucks where the inside

A long hole borer being fed in through the tailstock for a standard lamp column. The lathe is set to the slowest speed of rotation.

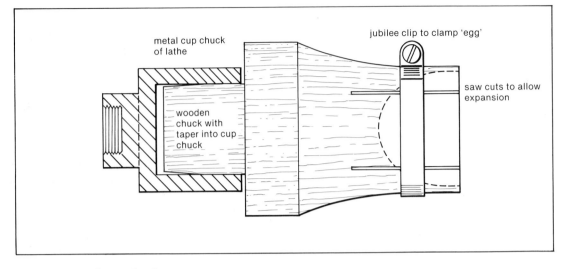

metal cup chuck of lathe

jubilee clip to clamp 'egg'

wooden chuck with taper into cup chuck

saw cuts to allow expansion

A 'sophisticated' egg chuck.

diameter differs in increments of about $\frac{1}{16}$in (1.5mm). These may all be made so that they can be mounted on either your basic cup chuck or a screw chuck. Here we will look at the cup chuck pattern.

To make the chuck, first mount the timber between centres and rough down to the round. Reduce the outboard end of the cylinder to a diameter where it will form a spigot that will sit firmly into your cup chuck, either by trial and error or by the parting tool and calliper approach. When done stop the lathe and remove the cylinder.

Mount the cup chuck on the lathe with the wooden egg chuck cylinder pushed firmly home; it should hold tight without any movement. Position the tool rest across the face about $\frac{1}{8}$in (3mm) away and $\frac{1}{4}$in (6mm) below centre height. True up the outside face.

With the dividers scribe on the end face a ring which is just a fraction smaller in diameter than your egg. My standard eggs are 1¾in (4.4cm) in diameter; some people make them smaller, and your first one or two could well end up on the small side. (Rest at centre height for scribing.)

Reposition the tool rest across the end face about $\frac{1}{8}$in (3mm) away and $\frac{1}{4}$in (6mm) below centre height, and using the small bowl gouge hollow out the chuck until your part-finished egg sits firmly in it with the rim of the chuck just short of the widest diameter of the egg. If you make the chuck carefully it will still hold the egg firmly whichever way round the egg is placed. Hence the hollow will have to be deep enough to accept the pointed end of an egg, whilst the internal diameter at the rim and inside profile is such that it will grip the egg rather than allowing the egg to drop right in loosely. Aim for a fairly rough finish on the inside of the egg chuck as this will give a friction fit that will hold the egg firmly when you sand off the ends.

Once you have the fit right you can finish off the outside of the chuck. The wall of the chuck should be thin near the rim to allow full access to the egg. It can then taper outwards to provide a little more body outside the spigot that is held in the cup chuck.

A more sophisticated, multi-sized egg chuck can be made as a single unit. The hollowed out cylinder is made large enough to accept a large egg and is then slotted with saw cuts into the open end. After the end has been tapered down a radiator hose clip is mounted around the outside to clamp on to different diameters of egg. Once the chuck is made, push in your egg and finish off the ends, sand smooth, and apply oil or lacquer. (*See* Chapter 9, Finishing and Finishes.)

To make an egg cup to display the egg in (or a cup for the real breakfast-table egg), you start in exactly the same way. Again you have the option of roughing to a cylinder between centres or simply mounting the timber directly on a screw chuck. If you use the latter you may decide to do everything off this single mounting and to leave the screw hole in the base of the egg cup. Rough down to the round as usual.

In hollowing out, use the small bowl gouge with the rest an eighth away from the face and about an eighth below the centre axis.

Eggs are funny things; they are all such varied shapes. If you try to make an egg cup that fits snugly to one egg you will find that some will sit awkwardly on top while others will just rattle around. Whenever I am making egg cups I have two or three different sizes of real eggs to hand and hollow out until I get a satisfactory fit for a range of eggs. What results is a cup that grips large eggs with its rim, and grips smaller eggs somewhere down its taper. There isn't a better method than that of trial and error!

In the making of egg cups (or small goblets) where the stem is going to be taken down to quite a fine diameter, the hollowing out and the finishing of the inside is completed before starting to work on the outside. The stem is worked

Supporting the fine stem of an egg cup from underneath with the middle phalanx of the index finger. The thumb rests on the top of the skew blade to steady it. Finger and thumb are pinched together to reduce vibration.

last. In this way you avoid putting too much twisting torque on to a thin stem.

Having hollowed out the inside, start to work from the outboard end of the item and shape the outside, working the bowl down to the stem. You are now back to near-spindle work; it is not true spindle work in that we have only one end supported. Again use the skew and/or the spindle gouge according to the shape required.

It is generally considered to be poor design if the profile inside the vessel is substantially different from the external profile. This is an idea that may be challenged later! Some turners take this to

Richard Raffan at a Buxton seminar demonstrates the support grip on a fine spindle.

finished diameter, clean down the outside of the bowl and sand it smooth. Again avoid putting any twisting torque on the thinner stem area.

When working a fine stem, the tool to use is a small skew chisel and the extra support grip with the steadying hand. The fingers wrap round the stem to support it with the middle phalanx of the index finger round the far side. The thumb bridges across the top of the stem, pointing towards the turner. The base of the thumb lies across the top of the rest and then the thumb tip rests on top of the tool blade. The tool rest is maintained almost level with the top of the stem and the skew is held horizontally. At these settings the skew takes off only the merest whisper of a cut.

It could be that you want a long, slender stem with a larger diameter bead at half height, so the beading and parting tool may also be brought into play. On goblets, ornamentation on the stem – beads, for instance – looks better on the top half rather than the lower section.

The making of goblets, egg cups and chalices involves the use of simple basic spindle gouge and skew chisel techniques. On all of these items, balance and design are factors of the greatest importance and are often more a question of personal preference and feel rather than following any set of design principles. We will return to the question of design after a closer look at bowl making.

mean that the walls should be a continuous, even thickness from top to bottom. While this does indicate a high level of skill it does not necessarily produce a sufficiently strong structure or one that will withstand the knocks and rigours of normal use.

On goblets and egg cups, a slight and gradual thickening from the rim down towards the stem provides a piece that is much more robust.

As the bowl of the cup is finished, and before you take the lower stem down to its

8 Bowls

My wife has christened me Drake. 'You always want to finish playing bowls before you come in and we do battle over the dishes!'

I love bowls, massive bowls with thick walls that will last hundreds of years. Bowls in English hardwoods that show off the swirling grain patterns and the burr figure. Bowls that are no longer mere utilitarian items but which demand their own space and often have to be integrated into, or even be designed as being a part of, a structured decor.

It is a fixation with big bowls that made me install a lathe weighing 17cwts. It means that I have to buy whole trees to get the sizes of blank I require. That in turn often necessitates the use of a chain saw and a hand-held power plane to part-round off the blanks because they are outside the capacity of any reasonable sized band saw. It has also led to constant experimentation into means of cutting in inaccessible places in difficult timbers.

Large bowl making is not without its problems! Each week there are at least three huge sacks of turnings to dispose of. There is an unfortunate level of wastage as some part-turned blanks that have been left to dry then split and are lost. There is golfer's elbow, and a frequently banged and bruised left hand. Fortunately my wife tolerates the houseful of rejects that I don't actually have the heart to throw away. There is also the need to use a van rather than a car to take half a dozen samples to a gallery.

Despite all the problems, I love it, and there is the immense satisfaction of knowing that some of my pieces are now cherished in homes in various corners of the world.

I have a particular point of style which is mainly concerned with the finish – it is also something of a hobby-horse! Here I am not only talking about what is applied to the surface, but what is done to the wood prior to the final finish. I like wood to look like wood. Its character should shout out at you. Some turners make objects where every corner is rounded and every coving perfect. Knot holes and checks are filled and camouflaged. They then fill the pores with sanding sealer and sand down until not only have all blemishes gone but so has all vestige of grain. Then the whole object is given several coats of varnish. Some are burnished and left high gloss; others are cut back with wire wool to an even matt, yet all look like plastic!

Perhaps we are jumping ahead a little. Let's first make the bowl before starting to worry about how it is going to be finished. So I will begin with the basic techniques of bowl making.

MAKING A BOWL

Start with blanks that have been made as round as possible. In most cases this will mean that a block or slab has been cut from the log or plank. The block is then cut to a round on a band saw. Regular bowl making can only be contemplated if you start in this way, as the cost of buying any quantity of ready-prepared blanks is prohibitive. For this reason alone a good-sized band saw quickly becomes an essential item to the bowl maker.

The implications are self-evident and immediate. Even with band sawn round blanks, we frequently start the bowl making process with pieces of timber that are not a true round and are out of balance. These have to be fixed very firmly on to the lathe.

There are four basic approaches to the mounting of blanks for bowl turning. In one you start by smoothing off one face of the blank; this will ultimately be the base of the object. A face plate is screwed direct on to this face and you then work the whole bowl of this one mounting. The base of the finished bowl has to be thick enough to accommodate the length of the fixing screws. When the bowl is finished it is removed from the face plate, the screw holes are filled and the base is sanded to a smooth finish. Alternatively, it is left near-smooth and some covering such as a cork or beige cloth ring or disc is applied.

The second method is very similar, but here, after working much of the outside and completely finishing the interior, the bowl is removed from the face plate, is reverse chucked, and the outside is finished by removing the base timber where the face plate screw holes were.

The third method involves first mounting the blank with the face plate screwed to what will ultimately be the top of the finished object. The outside of the bowl is then turned, finished off, the base is smoothed, and a dovetail or spigot is cut for remounting. The face plate is taken off the lathe and unscrewed from the wood. The dovetail, spigot or combination chuck is mounted, the blank fixed to that and the inside is hollowed out.

The fourth approach, that of triple mounting starting on the ultimate base, then mounting from the top, and then from the base again, is used on natural edged work. We will consider it later.

As a ground rule you do not mount face plates on to end grain – particularly with green timber. In end grain the screws quickly work loose and the blank flies off the lathe. If the job requires end grain work you have to start by mounting off the top (the third approach above) and use very long wood screws driven into that part of the wood, which will eventually be lost in the hollowing out process.

There are minor variations within the three basic themes outlined above, and one or two wrinkles which can help with all methods. But before considering these, let's look at the actual shaping techniques and the tools used.

It is normal to start by turning the outside of the bowl. Obviously the whole process is greatly simplified if the double mounting approach is used, and the blank is first mounted on to the plate with the bowl base to the outboard. This gives clear access to the lower outside walls.

Shaping the outside is now quite straightforward and uses exactly the same methods as those used in shaping the lid of the box. First, the face is trued, then the corners are rounded off, and finally the profile is worked, cutting uphill from smaller to larger diameter. The only difference to the box-making exercise is that for bigger bowls we tend to use bigger tools.

There are one or two points worthy of note. Nice blanks with the top and bottom

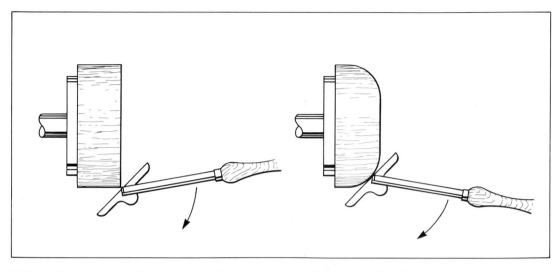

Taking off the corners. The rest is kept close to the apex of the corner (hand check the free swing before starting the lathe). The flute is toward you at 10 o'clock.

faces parallel, the outside rim a good circle (the sort you buy in the crafts store) and all properly centred on the face plate are fine. They present few problems. But once it becomes known that you are a turner, people start offering you wood – sometimes whole trees. This can give nightmares, rather than simply problems.

For the moment, forget all such questions as that of drying, and start by considering one of the worst scenarios. You have a huge rough block. It is too large to go on the band saw. It probably has two chain sawn faces (top and bottom) which are not really parallel. It has been cut to a square slab and then the corners have been taken off with the chain saw to produce a rough octagon. (It could, to make matters worse, have only one sawn face as we intend to make a natural edged piece – we will look at this additional problem in a few moments.)

First, you have to select which side of the blank is to form the top of the bowl. Usually this will be the face with no checks or splits near the edge. If this face is not sufficiently level or is angled in

some way, you may need to true it up with a power planer (I do find this a useful tool to have in the workshop). When reasonably flat, place the face plate on the surface and position it so that it is as central as possible. Use the largest face plate available and drive long wood screws through the outermost holes. On a 9in (23 cm) diameter face plate I use at least four 1½in (3.8cm) by 12s wood screws.

Ed Moulthrop, in making his massive tree trunk bowls, does not use big face plates – some are only 6in (15cm) in diameter; but they are fixed with 8 or so 2–3in (5–7.5cm) coach bolts, and are spun slowly.

The smaller the diameter of the face plate, or the larger the diameter of the wood block, the bigger the screws used as the loading while roughing down is enormous and will quickly tear the screws out of soft and green timbers. As already emphasised, the problem is even greater with end grain work.

Mount the block and plate on the lathe, and spin it by hand. If the whole is con-

101

Rounding off the corners, cutting uphill.

Levelling off the base with a backhand cut.

Scribing a mark for a dovetail collet.

Starting to hollow out (another lathe and another time!).

Getting down towards the base.

Cleaning up the rim with a large square-end scraper.

siderably off balance, or there are corners which stick out much further than others, I again use the power planer to take off the worst.

Any blank that does not start off as a perfect round, or that is not truly centred on the face plate, will cause considerable vibration when you start the lathe. This is where heavy-bodied lathes, bolted to the floor, come into their own. It is also where very slow speeds are required in the early stages of roughing. I make frequent use of the 200 r.p.m. setting.

Some timbers can still present a problem even when you do start with a properly centred, true round. I had a 4in (10cm) thick 14in (35.5cm) diameter blank of ash. One part, to about a third of the way across, was olive ash. The lathe I had at the time had a bottom speed of 800 r.p.m. I pressed the start button and

jumped back at the noise. Before I could get near enough to switch it off again the vibration had wrenched the lathe off its bed (it had been G-cramped down) and the whole thing was cavorting towards the door. I did not know then that the olive wood is almost three times the density of the normal white ash wood!

For these reasons a simple table of recommended lathe speeds is not really satisfactory. In the table on page 105 four speeds are given. The first is the theoretical speed which would give a peripheral speed of 25ft/sec for the wood at the rim of the blank passing the cutting tool. The second is the normal turning speed used, taking what is available on a typical lathe, and relating this to the diameter for a piece of clean wood that has already been roughed to the general

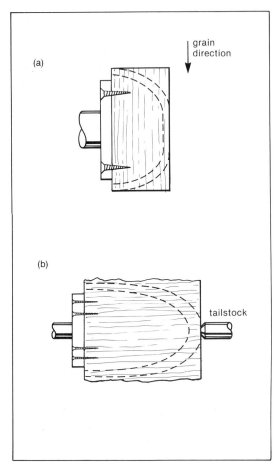

that is distinctly off balance. The speeds shown for 24in (61cm) blanks assume that the slowest speed available on most lathes is 200 to 250. If slower speeds, such as 150 r.p.m. are available then coarse roughing the outer faces should be done at the slowest speed. If your lathe does not have a particular speed shown on the table then go to the nearest slower speed. You may safely increase the finishing speed slightly, but the roughing speeds shown are already erring towards the maximum for general safety.

From the table over it can be seen that I usually turn bowls at faster than the 25ft/sec peripheral speed recommended

Face plate mounting of large blanks. (a) Long screws can be used as they are within wood that will later be removed. The blank is mounted on what will be the top of the bowl for truing the base and shaping the outside. (b) Very long screws (as many as is possible) are essential when screwing into the end grain. The tailstock is used to provide extra support while roughing and shaping. Note – this piece will also require a substantial spigot for base mounting.

shape required. The third is the roughing speed which you would use on a fairly clean rounded blank, and the fourth (in brackets) is the roughing speed for a chain saw prepared block or a piece of timber

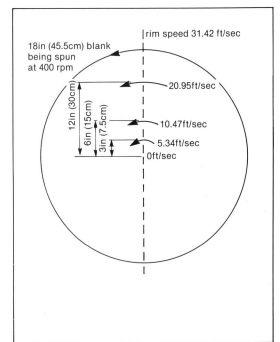

The surface speed problem. The closer a tool sweeps to the centre the lower the effective surface speeds. A higher speed is required to maintain a clean cut, but this would put the rim speed to a dangerously high level.

Thickness			2in	4in	6in plus
Speeds		Theoretical	Normal	Roughing	Coarse Roughing
Diameter					
6in		954	1500–800	1000–800	800–500 (500)
8in		716	1000–700	1000–700	1000–500 (500)
10in		572	1000–700	900–700	500 (250)
12in		477	1000–700	900–700	500–250 (250)
18in		318	700–250	400–200	400–200 (200)
24in		238	250–200	250–200	250–200

Table 4   Turning speed.

by some turners although this often causes me belt slip problems on the old Wadkin.

As we identified right at the beginning, there is a problem in turning the interior of larger diameter pieces where we work not only out at the fast turning rim, but also near the slow-moving centre.

The diagram shows the relative speed of the wood at varying distances from the centre on an 18in blank turned at 400 r.p.m. Based upon this a case could be made for actually rotating the blank at a slower speed while working out at the rim then increasing the speed to make a few sweeping cuts across the middle.

The blank is now on the lathe and we have either rounded it on the band saw or taken off the worst corners with mallet and chisel, planer, chainsaw or whatever;

now comes the roughing down stage. It is essential that you start by taking off the corners working from the open face – just as you did in rounding off the corners of the lid of the box. Should you try working into the corners from the wall of the bowl you will get massive banging and shock loading on the tool rest.

Tool rest position is important and in the early stages frequent adjustments have to be made. It is set diagonally across the corner, at about the centre axis height, with the post of the tool rest beside the apex of the outboard corner and ⅛in (3mm) clear of the most protruding part of the wood. *Always hand spin the wood all the way round to make sure it clears the rest before actually starting the lathe.* Incidentally, having the tool rest post on the apex ensures that the initial shocks are taken on the post and not on an unsupported end of the rest. Use the heaviest roughing gouge and go into the blur cautiously. The worst corners are cut back very quickly, so there are many stops to readjust the tool rest closer to the wood.

In your early days of turning you should stop the lathe to make each adjustment of the tool rest. It is very easy to catch the edge of the rest on a rotating projection, and if this happens it will be snatched from the fingers and slammed down into the tool post. Damage and injury are very likely. Later, as your eye develops you may adjust the rest while the lathe is still turning (although you will still probably get the occasional bang!).

Starting to rough a blank to a true round with the tool rest at the side and parallel with the lathe axis is dangerous with large, rough blanks. The tool can bounce off one projection, dip in behind it and catch the next projection full square. It digs in hard and can wrench the blank off the face plate. You are standing in line with one of the only two ways that the blank can fly!

So even with the roughest blanks the rule is the same as with perfect rounds. Right from the beginning you shape the outside of bowls working from the smaller to the large diameter (usually the base to the rim). This means working from the centre outwards. With bowls it is 'OOII' – Outsides Outwards, Insides Inwards!

Roughing completed, start working with the bowl gouge. I find the ½in gouge satisfactory for most sizes of bowl, from the big to the quite small; and for both convex and concave curves, insides and outsides.

Stance is important. For between centres turning, you only have to sway from side to side to move the tool along the length of the spindle. In bowl turning, particularly with larger bowls, you start working across the lathe on the outboard end of the workpiece with the tool handle pointed at the far wall, and finish working along the lathe as you get towards the headstock and the rim of the bowl. The upper trunk of the body describes a definite arc and this should be achieved without moving the feet!

Changing foot position in the middle of a cut is invariably reflected in the profile of the bowl; the result is usually a definite angle, a ridge or a groove.

Later, and finishing, cuts should be made continuous from the centre right out to the rim – this may necessitate long or curved tool rests – it certainly requires that the feet are correctly placed to start with. Ideally the right foot points at right-angles to the lathe axis and is almost under the lathe bed, and the left foot will be turned out pointing along the axis, at some distance to the side of the right foot and a little out from the lathe. With feet in this position and a little bending at the waist, the trunk, forearm and tool can move round as one in a continuous, graceful arc. The result is a beautiful, smooth, ridge-free continuous cut. If the tool is kept sharp it is possible to produce a cut that requires little or no finishing sanding.

It is possible! Most of us, however, are not that good. We are usually left with a few bumps and grooves that we then have to clean up with a scraper.

Remember to reposition the rest below centre height, and to clean the outside take the biggest, heaviest square ended scraper you have. Back of the blade on the tool rest, handle slightly higher than the blade tip, a light fingers over steadying grip, and with the gentlest of cuts take off only whisper swarf. This should iron out any tool marks left by the gouge.

We still have the base to attend to. Some like to work this first, others leave it until the rest of the outside is finished. Whatever, it first has to be trued with forward shearing, and backhanded scraping cuts using the gouge. You may wish to have a small plinth at the base of the bowl and may have to cut this in with a square ended scraper during the shaping of the walls.

You will also have considered how you are going to remount the piece in order to turn the inside and you now need to make the necessary provision. One possible remounting system is to rescrew the face plate to the base. This time you can use much smaller screws and they can be nearer the centre. Alternatively, but similarly, you may have decided to use a face plate ring with a dovetail collet chuck. In either case set your dividers to the outside diameter of the plate or ring and scribe a circle on the base – this is your mounting mark for centring the plate. It is extremely difficult to accurately remount on a face plate that is larger than the base diameter of the workpiece so this is best avoided. Even with a smaller plate you may find that the remounted bowl is not quite centred. You now have to decide whether to accept this or to rework the outside walls!

Cutting a dovetail for a collet chuck also starts with the dividers. A circle is scribed to the dimensions of the outside edge of the closed down collet. The rest, which was at centre height for the scribing, is dropped about $^3/_{16}$ in (4.5mm) so that you can take out the dovetail. The easiest way of doing this is first to cut just inside the scribed mark with a diamond point

scraper. A small bowl gouge will then take out the centre of the recess – working from the outside in towards the centre. Next, working outwards from the centre with the diamond point, clean up the bottom of the dovetail socket. Finally, using the long point of an old skew chisel as a scraper, undercut the dovetail to the scribed mark.

The principles are the same whether you are working on huge, knobbly out-of-round blocks, or neat little precut ash-tray blanks. The only difference is the size of tool used.

In all cases it is much easier to mount from the top first and to shape the outside on the outboard end. With round blanks of up to 10in (25.5cm) in diameter you may not even need a face plate – a good sized screw chuck will be quite adequate.

Obviously if you start by mounting from the base and completing the whole job from there, then there are problems of working the outside of the bowl down near the faceplate. You will sometimes be forced by the proximity of the headstock to cut into the faceplate working from the larger towards the smaller diameter.

With natural edge pieces we often need to treble mount. Here the block is first mounted on a face plate on what will ultimately be the base. This needs to be a particularly firm mounting as it is going to have to withstand considerable shock loadings, so first make the mounting face as flat as possible. The natural face of the wood starts at the outboard end.

The first stage is to prepare the natural face so that you can remount on to it. This may mean working a flat area of sufficient diameter to be able to screw on a face plate or accept the shoulders of the chuck body behind a screw or pin chuck.

Let me say immediately that as a

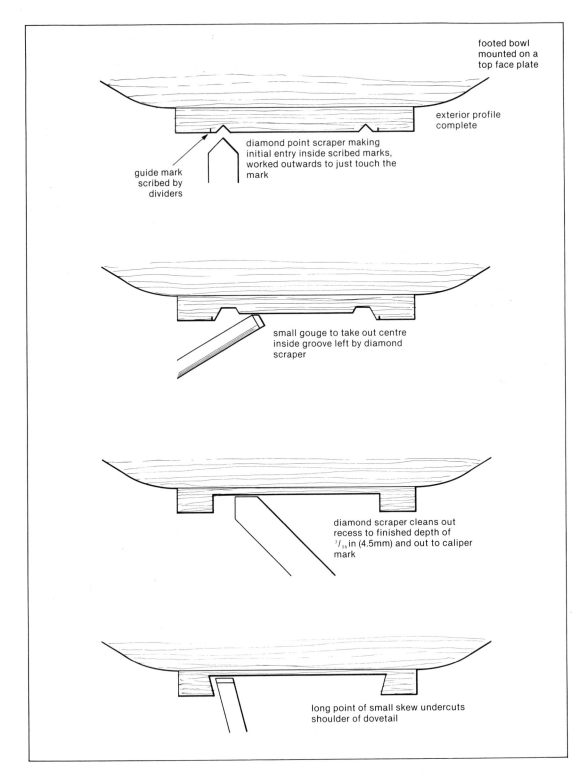

footed bowl mounted on a top face plate

exterior profile complete

diamond point scraper making initial entry inside scribed marks, worked outwards to just touch the mark

guide mark scribed by dividers

small gouge to take out centre inside groove left by diamond scraper

diamond scraper cleans out recess to finished depth of $^3/_{16}$ in (4.5mm) and out to caliper mark

long point of small skew undercuts shoulder of dovetail

Cutting a dovetail for a collet chuck.

Small pieces of natural edge wood can be held in a jaw chuck while the recess is cut into the natural top for a small screw chuck.

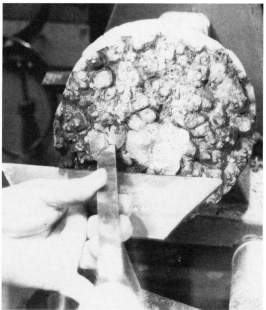

Starting to cut a face plate recess into the top of a medium sized natural edged piece. The base is firmly screwed on to a plate. A heavy diamond point scraper is used for taking very fine cuts until the worst projections have been removed.

personal preference I prefer the face plate approach as I have never found pin chucks really satisfactory, probably because I am rarely using them on dry, even-grained, firm timber. I know that some turners like them, but they are not for me.

Working into the top of a piece of natural edged timber is not easy, particularly if the face is something like a saw-tooth alpine mountain range as is often the case with a good burr.

Once rotating, all you can see is a blur; you are, to an extent, going to have to work blind. It is also very easy to catch a finger or the side of the steadying hand on the edge, and that can be nasty; above all, there is no way that you can avoid some tool shocks.

I alternate between two methods of taking the top off natural edge work. The first uses a heavy duty diamond point scraper or a massive ¾in (1.9cm) square section diamond side cutter. The second approach is to use a long and strong bowl gouge.

To use either of the scrapers, position the tool rest across the face so that the cutting tip of the tool will be just below centre height. Have the post of the rest half-way between the centre axis and the nearside edge of the timber. Swing the timber a couple of full rotations to ensure that it clears the rest.

Make the first cut by carefully trying to find the centre of the blur. Go in very slowly, make contact, and take a cut about ⅛in (3mm) deep. Now draw the scraper towards you very carefully for about ¼in (6mm). Next, draw the point out and move it ⅛in (3mm) closer towards you.

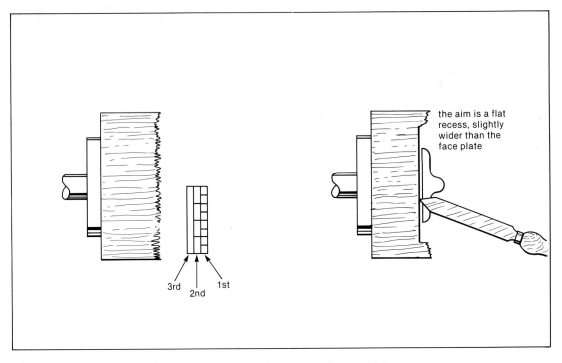

the aim is a flat recess, slightly wider than the face plate

3rd   2nd   1st

Preparing the top of a waney edged blank. A – first series of cuts with heavy-pointed scraper in about ⅛in (3mm). Move sideways ½in (1.3cm), pause, move another half inch, and so on. B – second series of cuts still ⅛in (3mm) deep, but move sideways up to 1in (2.5cm) at a time. C – third cut, ⅛in (3mm) deep. Move sideways through full distance. Slow and gentle movements avoid suddenly catching big projections.

Again advance the point in slowly. This time once contact is made, continue to feed the tool point into the wood until the new cut meets the ring of the first one. Do not now cut sideways. Continue to work slowly outwards in one-eighth steps in a series of shallow cuts, making each cut at right-angles to the face by bringing the tool in parallel with the axis of the lathe. If you try to sweep the tool sideways you are very likely to catch the side of a large projection and will almost certainly rip the block off its mountings.

Continue cutting until you have reached the diameter required. Now you can go back to the centre to make a second series of cuts to deepen the recess. This time you again start at the centre but now you can sweep the point of the tool side-ways (towards you) provided you keep the cut shallow (usually only about an eighth deep). Continue to make shallow cuts until you have a surface which will provide a firm base for a face plate.

Although the essential task is completed once you have reached the diameter required, I find it useful to carry on widening the recess until it is somewhere near what will be the finished inside diameter of the bowl. This is done so that the heavy shocks of the initial cut into the projecting burrs can be made while the block is still on its first heavy duty mounting.

When using the bowl gouge approach the tool is presented at 45 degrees to the lathe's axis with the handle down at about 15 degrees below the horizontal, flute pointing to about 2 o'clock.

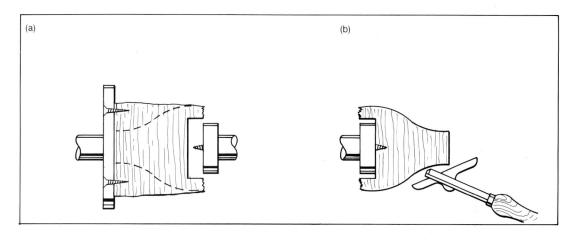

Mounting small waney edge blanks. (a) Make a recess in the top large enough to fit a screw chuck. Screw holes in the base. These are eventually cut away. (b) Remount and work outside, shaping the base with recess or spigot or foot for later remounting on jaw or other chuck.

The recess for the face plate is finished. It will provide a firm platform for the plate, and take four good holding screws. Here the recess has been cut to the plate size and not taken out to the finished dimensions.

The face plate is fixed into the recess and the bowl is now ready to have the outside turned and a dovetail cut into the base for later remounting.

The cuts are started about ½in (1.3cm) from the centre. Move towards the centre but advance into the blurred corona about ⅛in (3mm). The next cut starts 1in out and then 1½in until the outside diameter is reached. Again you work in a series of ⅛in-deep steps.

Once the recess has been completed, stop the lathe, remove the block, re-position the face plate (or a smaller one) on top, remount, and start to work on the outside to the required profile.

Complete the work on this mounting by cutting the dovetail recess for remounting on a combination chuck. Taking the insides out of bowls seems such a wasteful process. From a large blank what is in effect two or three smaller bowls end up as shavings on the workshop floor. I am afraid that today there is no easy way of avoiding this – unless you like segmented work!

In days gone past, the picture was different. Skilled turners would produce you a nest of bowls all cut out from the same single blank. They used long, curved hook tools and cranked parting tools. So why can't we? Indeed one supplier offers a cranked parting tool today, and a huge tommy-gun-shaped parting tool is available in America.

The answer is in the lathes we now use. Nests of bowls were made on pole or treadle lathes. Turning was done at relatively slow speeds, and often with green timber. If a tool jammed the lathe stopped instantly – there was not a massive inertia nor a powerful motor trying to push it on. It all happened much more slowly and there was time to react. Swarf was not allowed to build up in the groove, and the turner had both time and facility to keep removing it with a bit of bent wire. Some would take hours to remove the wood that we now take off in minutes. Having said that, some of the old chair bodgers working up in the Chiltern hills with their pole lathes turned

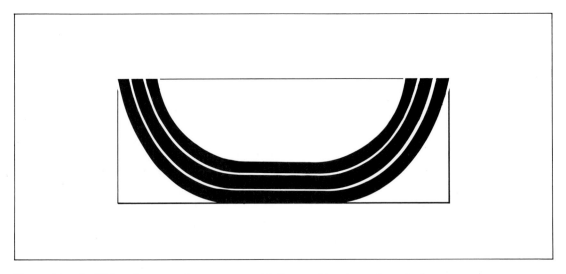

Nests of bowls. Using slow speed man-powered lathes and hooks and cranked parting tools, old time turners could produce nests of bowls from a single blank.

The bowl is now remounted on a dovetail collet chuck, the outside having been completely worked and sanded smooth.

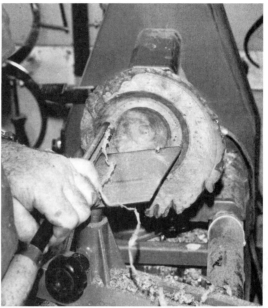

Hollowing out proceeds in a series of steps. In this flash picture the bowl's rotation has been 'stopped' and the jagged rim can be seen. To the human eye all that would be seen would be a two-inch deep blur.

out more chair legs in a day than today's turners do in a week. So although some things are easier today, there are costs; and the worst is waste.

Once the outside of the natural edged piece is finished, remount from the base. If you only went so far as to make a recess for a face plate the first time you worked the natural face, you now have to complete the working outwards to establish the interior margin of the rim and the wall size of the vessel. Do this before you start to hollow out the centre. Again it is the large diamond point and again the first cuts are made parallel to the lathe axis. You have to be even more careful now. In remounting off the finished base you have probably used a lighter mounting – a dovetail collet, or a face plate and shorter screws.

Your natural-edged bowl is now ready to have the centre hollowed out, but before you start this process let's just talk

about bringing a more normal sawn blank up to the same state.

With ordinary sawn faced blanks, the first job is to true up the face. This means tool rest across the face, ¼in (6mm) below centre (roughly), a cut or two from the outside in towards the centre with the bowl gouge handle down about 15 degrees and bevel rubbing, with the tool at about 45 degrees to the face. The flute is aimed in the direction of travel and inclined to about two o'clock. Make a couple of backhand passes with the tool rolled over so the flute is pointing towards you (at nine o'clock). Handle nearer the horizontal and tool at about 60 degrees to the face. On this backhand scraper pass, it is easy to feel the state of progress. Any unevenness is reflected in vibration in the

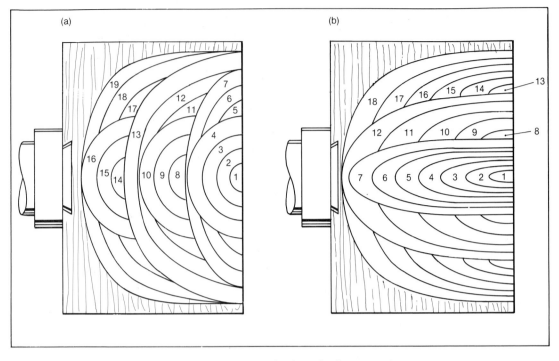

Sequence of cuts to hollow out bowls. (a) Step method gradually increasing depth by shallow steps. Uses broad bowl gouges with steeper bevel angles. (b) Depth method. Work down to the bottom then widen the hole outward. This is better done with smaller gauge bowl gouges with shallower bevel angles.

tool handle. At this stage, truing need only be approximate.

In the early days it is wise to mark the depth to which you will be working in hollowing out. This is done by drilling a hole down the centre with either a small spindle gouge or a wood auger. Mark the depth on the drilling tool with a ring of masking tape just as you did in marking the depth of the box. Remember to allow for the point of the auger or drill and for any dovetail or screws that you have recessed or driven into the base of the bowl.

The process of hollowing out is the same for both natural and turned edge work, except that in the former you have to beware of the jagged edges.

To hollow out, proceed in a series of scooping out steps, each increasing in depth. The first cut is made close to the centre and will of necessity be quite shallow. The second starts a little further out and goes a little deeper. After three or four cuts you will have reached a desirable depth for the first step, so succeeding cuts each start further out towards the rim and finish by sweeping in towards the centre. When the wall is reached, the first step is completed and a start is made on the second. Again this starts with a shallow cut at the centre. By the time you have taken five or six cuts of this step you should again have reached a target depth for the step. Further cuts continue to widen the hole towards the walls. Succeeding steps follow until the final depth is reached.

Not all turners use this approach. An alternative is to work in a series of steps

114

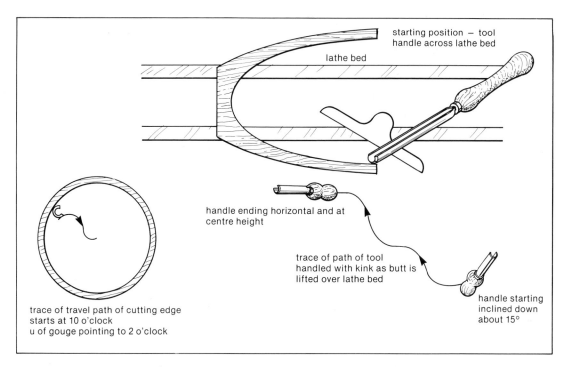

Labels in figure:
- starting position — tool handle across lathe bed
- lathe bed
- handle ending horizontal and at centre height
- trace of path of tool handled with kink as butt is lifted over lathe bed
- handle starting inclined down about 15°
- trace of travel path of cutting edge starts at 10 o'clock u of gouge pointing to 2 o'clock

Making a complete sweeping cut inside a near-finished bowl.

outwards, each one to almost the final depth of the finished bowl. The 'steps downwards' method does have one great advantage over the 'steps outwards' approach. Gradually increasing the depth across the full width enables you to make full, sweeping movements with each cut, and the result is that the wood cuts cleaner and you get a near-finished surface straight off the tool.

The actual cutting movement for a full sweeping cut is a complex one. The edge of the tool describes an arc. It starts high on the inside wall (at about ten o'clock) with the bevel on the nearside of the gouge, the rubbing on the wood of the side of the hollow. The U flute is up-pointing at about half-past one o'clock. This means that the handle is across the far side of the lathe bed and is at 15 to 20 degrees below the cutting edge.

The cut sweeps the tool edge into the bowl initially on a slight rising curve until it is half-way through its sweep, at about eleven o'clock from the centre axis. The blade has now rolled slightly, so that the flute is pointing to two o'clock.

Continue the sweep to bring the cutting edge to the point of the centre axis by which time the roll has taken the open flute to three o'clock.

This means that the hand on the tool handle (which started on the far side of the lathe bed and low to the right) has swept up towards the right chest. It has rolled slightly clockwise at the wrist throughout the sweep.

To steady the tool, use the underhand grip with the fingers wrapped back over the blade. This enables you to see what is going on.

Before you make the last few cuts, give the gouge a quick turn on the grind wheel. The cuts should be made continuously from rim to centre, in a full arc. Try to produce a finish that requires little further treatment and completely removes the last trace of the auger point of the depth mark. With average depth bowls or those with a smooth, even curve to the profile, that is all there is to it!

There are times however when we are working with more difficult shapes and we then need to use other cuts. The first variation comes where we want a wide, flat base that then suddenly sweeps up a steeply angled wall. Here it is useful to reverse cut the base from the centre outwards if you are using a conventionally-ground (45 degree) bowl gouge.

You do not need to move the tool rest for reverse cutting and all the normal rules apply. The gouge handle is on the far side of the lathe bed, it is angled down at about 15 to 20 degrees, the bevel is of course kept rubbing, and the flute points towards you at about eleven o'clock.

The lower segments of quite steepish walls may also be cut from the reverse side, working outwards from the base, but you may need a 50 to 60 degree bevel on the gouge.

Really deep vase-like vessels present another problem. The inside walls are likely to be near-vertical for some depth. You can start with a conventional bowl gouge with the bevel rubbing while working up near the rim, but in no time at all, as you cut down into the interior, the tool handle is against the far rim and bevel contact is lost (*see* the drawing right). If you try to reverse cut, you are working up the side of the flute and all bevel contact is lost. At this stage you may resort to a gouge where the sides have been ground back to give a bevel of 10 to 15 degrees with a long-pointed tip, and still work down from the top.

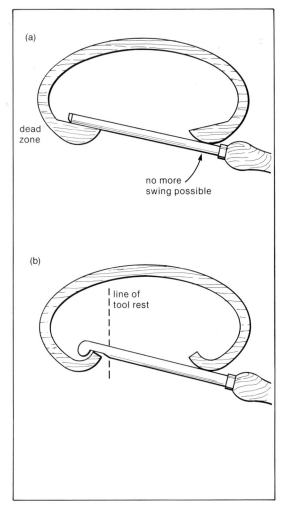

Undercutting bowl rims. (a) Limit of ability to undercut with a bowl gouge. (b) Side cutting round scraper used to get under the rim. The tool tends to twist and chatter, and fibre tearing is probable. Oiling the wood and taking the lightest cuts is the best solution.

There is another alternative that has been adopted by many professionals. It is worth experimenting with, but should really not be tried until you have had a year or two's experience working with the more conventional tools and methods, and have become fully skilled with these.

116

In recent years a number of turners have been experimenting with deep-fluted bowl gouges on which the shoulders have been ground back to give cutting edges along the top of the flute. Earlier mention was made of David Ellsworth's work with modified gouges. Liam O'Neill has developed a Sorby gouge by grinding the nose at about 70 degrees, rounding it into something of a fingernail and then taking the shoulders back for about 1½in.

The beauty of this gouge is that the 70 degree nose enables you to cut across the inside bottoms of deep vessels while the shoulder edge can be used for both pushing and pulling cuts. On pushing cuts the flute points away from you, and the tool is inverted so the flute points towards you on pulling cuts. In this way you can make shearing cuts up the inside walls of deep vessels. Indeed this is the only effective way of cutting up under overhanging rims. Mick O'Donnel also makes very effective use of a similarly ground gouge.

As was mentioned earlier, David has solved the problem of working deep inside narrow orifice vessels by using metalwork turning tool bits mounted on long handles. His skill is prodigious. He sits astride the lathe bed with his head set and his gaze straight down the lathe axis. From this vantage point, and looking at the angle of the tool handle outside the vessel, he can tell whereabouts inside the vessel the cutting tip is. He judges the thickness (or in his case the thinness) of the wall by the sound that the cutting action is making! There have to be frequent stops for the vacuum removal of swarf.

Mention was also made earlier of the hook tools developed by Ed Moulthrop and of the ring tools currently available in this country. In fact the Moulthrop hook is of a pattern much used by earlier turners working with slow-speed treadle-operated lathes. Hooks feature widely in the tool kits of all early Scandinavian turners, and their use is increasing again today. New versions are now being produced each year. One of the latest is called a drop gouge hook and it resembles a section of a bowl gouge with a side-mounted shank.

A standard set of turning tools supplied by Luna for use in their home markets now contains a hook and a ring tool in addition to the more conventional scrapers, skews and gouges. The ring tool is useful but it is really intended for end-grain work and it requires special techniques and skills. At first use it seems to have been specifically designed to produce gigantic dig-ins or make deep gouges. It is best used in green turning and is definitely less suitable for burrs and rough grain timbers. It comes into its own when used with special tool rests which have been drilled and fitted with pins against which the tool is 'stopped' and pivoted. This way it will cut away very fast, making long, fat shavings, and getting deep inside all sorts of shapes. Rings are now available from most UK manufacturers and those of the smaller diameter are the more readily controllable in novice hands.

It has long been said that the inside profile should reflect the exterior shape. Some turners like to go for an even wall thickness all the way from the top to the bottom. Others accept a gradual increase in thickness as you near the base. Very nice profiles can also be made where the wall is a little thicker nearer the rim, thins in the centre and then increases again towards the base. The one thing that

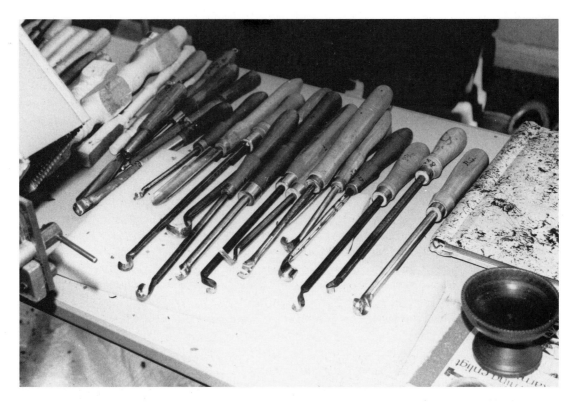

The standard tool kit of Bengt Gustafsson. Just out of view on the left are skews. There are two shallow gouges. The remainder are hooks of one pattern or another.

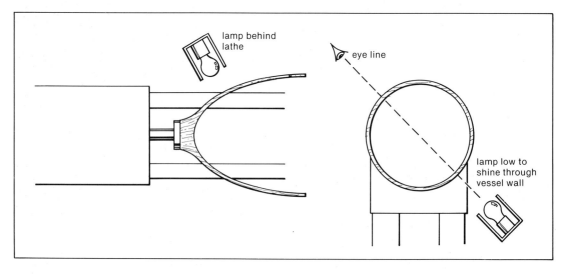

Position of light to show wall thickness on green turning.

should be avoided is ridges of thick and thin bits!

It is not always easy to judge the thickness of the walls, or just how much taper you have on them. At this stage a pair of large double-ended callipers can be very useful. Set the callipers for the thickest part and then see how much difference there is between this and the thinnest sections.

My own preference for thick-walled bowls has probably now become a bit of a bore, so let's spend a few moments thinking about thin wall turning.

Most really thin walled work is based upon the use of green timber. When there is so much sap still in the wood that it splashes the front of the smock, even runs down the gouge, the wood will cut very easily. In fact after a spell working on dry burrs where the turnings come off more as flakes and chippings, it is very refreshing to do some wet turning just to prove to yourself that you can get nice tool control and make continuous ribbons of swarf. In thin wall, green turning, the whole approach has to be one of delicacy, using finer tools, especially gouges, and keeping the edges very keen.

Green turning has to be thin. If you try to leave a slightly thicker base or lower wall, splitting is almost inevitable. But, of course, the thinner you go the more difficult it is to judge wall thickness; callipers are now altogether too crude. One means of overcoming this problem is to position a light on the far side of the workpiece – a 150-watt bulb in a smallish reflector

Cleaning the inside with fine scraper cuts. Note the angle of the tool rest and the use of a massive 2in (5cm) domed scraper. The end profile is close to that of the surface being cleaned.

Sanding the finished bowl. Both the bowl and the sanding drill are set at low speed. The sorbo on the pad allows the disc to follow the profile of the bowl.

The finished bowl: treated with colourless Danish Oil which was applied with the lathe stopped and then burnished in at slow speed.

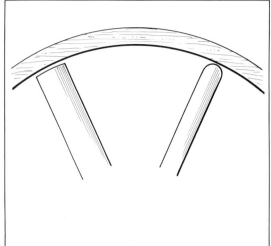

Scraping the inside – large v. small. Broad-domed scrapers of approximately the same curvature as the bowl help to produce clean, sweeping curves. Narrow, sharp radius scrapers take cleaner cuts but are difficult to use to get clean sweeps.

A much heavier block mounted on the Wadkin lathe. The block was too deep to fit under the band saw. The face plate was fixed to the back with long screws close to the rim – the screw holes will later be removed. On this mounting only a face plate recess will be cut and no attempt will be made to round the sides.

The face plate is now fixed so that the piece can be remounted for the outside to be worked.

holder is ideal. This is fixed so that it shines towards you through the wood. When the wall is thin enough you will see the glow of the light showing through. That is the time to stop – you haven't much left!

120

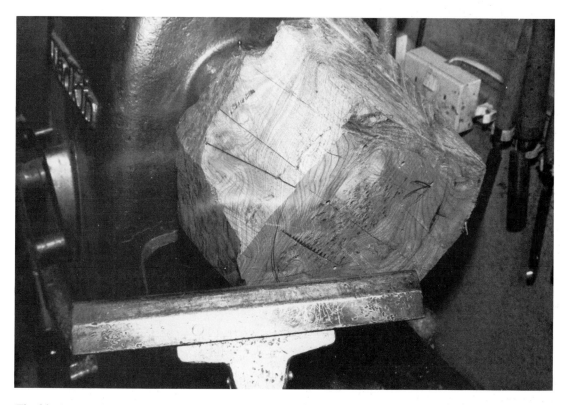

The block is ready for outside working. The rest is positioned across the corner and cutting will commence with a long and strong gouge working from the centre outwards.

Fortunately it is easy to get a good tool finish on green wood. This is vital, as it is difficult to sand. You will probably have to use wet or dry with liberal quantities of water, working right down to the finest grit. Because of the water you cannot get the wood to polish.

In general, good tool control can give you a good finish straight from the gouge. It is unlikely, however, that the gouge finish will be quite good enough, so just as you gave a final finish to the outside with a scraper, you will probably have to do the same inside. Indeed some turners take the final few shaping cuts in the bottom of all bowls using scrapers.

We considered in some depth the question of scrapers when discussing the hollowing-out of goblets. What was said then applies equally here, so at this point it may be worth turning back to pages 89–91 and reading it again.

Scrapers work best on even-grained woods — but then so do all tools. There can be a problem when scraping inside burrs, knotted or checked wood. Each change in the nature of the turning wood makes the blade of the tool bounce and vibrate, with an increased likelihood of a dig-in.

When scraping the inside of big bowls, a curved tool rest is almost essential. This is a device where the main arm can be positioned inside the bowl. Certainly, heavy-duty scrapers are required and the importance of cutting below centre on the vertical base and above centre on the side walls cannot be stressed too often.

You used a square-ended scraper for the finishing cuts on the outside of the bowl; you can never use them inside, not even to level off a flat base. Angled corner scrapers are used if you have a sharp corner to produce, otherwise everything inside is done with domed and rounded scrapers.

When scraping the insides of bowls take the lightest of cuts, trying to sweep the tool cleanly right across the face without break. On any curved surface choose the biggest tool with the radius that most closely resembles that of the profile being worked. This helps to achieve continuous, even curves.

One little tip. When you get down to the final scraping stage, wipe a little Danish oil over the surface. Now, using the lightest of touches with the scraper, delicately remove the oil-stained wood. This shows you where you have been, gives an indication of how deep you are cutting, and helps to lubricate the cutting process particularly when you are crossing end grain. On some of the fruit woods (apple and cherry) the fibres are very prone to tear away from their neighbours and the oil film seems to reduce this problem.

9 Finishing and Finishes

It has been said by some that you start finishing the moment that you first put a tool to the wood. It is true. Working with sharp tools, making long continuous cuts, ensuring that your stance allows flowing movements, keeping the bevel rubbing, and always presenting the edge at the correct angle, all help to produce a surface that requires little further treatment.

The more time and trouble you take in cutting the better. The absolute purist aims to get a perfect finish from the tool and to use no sandpaper at all. There is another school of turners. This is the 'knock it roughly into shape and then grind away the flaws with power grinders' brigade. Turners with a real pride in their craft eschew this approach – but there are limits. Practicality suggests that we do the best we can with tools and then finish with a little light sanding.

In the normal run of things there could be said to be four stages to finishing. First, as suggested above, there is careful tool work when making. Then there is the flatting down stage followed by fine smoothing. Finally there is the application of a 'finish' – oil, varnish, paint, polish, or whatever.

Flatting down has now been facilitated by the introduction of Sorbo-faced abrasive pads for use with power drills. These are available in 1, 2 and 3in diameters and are made so that abrasive discs can be either glued to the face or attached by Velcro. Certainly the latter is the more convenient as it enables discs of different grits to be used on a single pad. Actually I find that the 1in (2.5cm) pads have very limited application and on anything but the finest work the abrasive quickly pulls away from the felt backing. So for me it is 2in (5cm) for small work and 3in (7.5cm) for most bowls.

Discs are available in grit sizes from 60 to 400 but most turners find that 60, 120 and 240 provide a sound basis, the final finishing then being achieved with paper. The pads are used with the lathe and the power drill set to a low speed. Using higher speeds only increases the amount of heat generated and wears the abrasive away more quickly. Incidentally, domestically rated drills do not last long on this dusty job and the extra investment on an industrial quality machine is quickly repaid.

On the inside of bowls the best working zone is at four to five o'clock and on the outside about eight o'clock. After using the 60 grit to remove any remaining tool marks the 120 is used to really smooth it. Very soon at this grade the wood begins to polish and remaining blemishes can be seen as light, dust-filled marks. Stop the lathe and sand away the marks. You can use the 120 grit pad or hand-held paper as required. Start up again and finish the 120 sanding. Finally, give a quick run round with the 240 grit until the wood is clearly polishing. Stop again and see if there are still any circular score marks left by the coarse 60 grit. These must be polished out with the 240 pad.

The outside is finished and the piece is remounted on a dovetail collet. The rest is angled and cutting is being done by making backhand passes with the O'Neill/Sorby gouge. In this position wood is removed quite quickly.

There are times when drier pieces can now be taken straight through to the finishing stage by merely giving a final sanding with a 400 grit disc or paper. After this the piece is ready to have the finish applied.

Rotary discs can be used for flatting down wood that is in almost any condition – even green. However, if the sap is still at a very high level the problem is that of the grit clogging up and needing frequent clearing.

Against the huge advantage of speed and convenience, there are four problems with the rotary disc approach. First there is that of dust. Dust is generated in large quantities even from quite damp woods. All wood dusts are extremely hazardous to health. So rotary sanding should not be undertaken unless you have a dust collector *and* a face mask.

Secondly, starting with 60 grit it may be necessary to remove the deeper tool marks, but it can leave score marks that are the very devil to remove. Often in trying to sand them away with finer grit discs we run into the third problem – that of heat generation. It is not at all difficult to cause heat checking, even burn marks or changes of colour with medium and finer grit rotary discs.

There is also the problem of expense. The discs are not cheap and the cost of pads is exorbitant. In normal production the pads do not last long. There is one type where the bond between the drive shaft and the backing pad soon breaks down. If a disc does become detached it is only seconds before the Velcro wears away. Equally, on natural-edge work it is not difficult to catch the Sorbo and to tear this away in chunks. Despite the fact that

I have bought sheets of self-adhesive Velcro and constantly reface the pads, I still need four or more new pads a year.

Following the flattening down there are four basic approaches to finishing, and three to 'finishes'. The finishing styles are dry, wet, sealed, oiled, while the 'finishes' come down to: impregnating, skinning and hiding.

Let's start by looking at finishing. This is what is done before the final finish is applied. There is, however, some blurring between the two aspects in some cases.

FINISHING

Dry Sanding

Dry sanding is the cheapest and most widely used method. When turning is complete the workpiece is not treated in any way; it may not even have been given a rotary sanding, but is simply smoothed with sandpaper to the required finish. Various types of paper are used, from very ordinary glass paper to aluminous oxides and garnets. The cheaper the paper the shorter the time it lasts; and the big drawback with simple sanding is that it can take a long time to get a really good finish unless quality paper is used. The best grades of high quality, flexible backed wet or dry are ideal.

Sanding dry also requires some caution. Heat is generated – so much so that it can cause surface checking on many pieces. Equally you can blister your own fingers. The poorer the quality of the paper the quicker they wear smooth, and the greater the likelihood of heat.

Simply wearing gloves to prevent burns can tempt you to overdo the sanding and increase the heat build-up – and the checking. So frequent, short, sharp bursts are the answer. It also seems that holding the paper through a piece of genuine leather not only prevents the finger burn but it does, in some inexplicable way, appear to reduce the heating effect.

Wet

It was mentioned in an earlier chapter that green wood may have to be sanded wet using wet or dry with liberal applications of water, and a frequent rinsing of the paper to clear the clogged pores. Obviously, an object worked in this way will have to be dried before it can be oiled or lacquered. Often in drying it will distort to give shapes which some will think 'Interesting!' and others 'Reject!'

Sealed

Many turners adopt the sealed approach and it is at this stage that I part company. The traditional method is to use a sanding sealer, many of which consist of talc suspended in a spirit-dissolved shellac. They are intended to fill the pores in the wood with talc as well as impregnating the surface fibres with shellac. When dry this gives a harder surface for the final sanding which will now come to a silky smooth finish. I like to see the grain of the wood, and sanding sealers are specifically intended to fill that very grain.

The only time that I use shellac sealers is when I am trying to get a finish on particularly soft spalted beech or a very old piece of near-rotten elm. In this case liberal quantities of shellac are used to bind the timber together. Instead of GRP it is RWRS (Rotten Wood Reinforced Shellac)!

Oiled

I do about half of my finishing oiled. Most of my work ends up with an oiled finish – using either Danish oil, teak oil, or the pure mineral oil, pharmaceutical liquid paraffin. I find that a two-stage application of oil eliminates any need for sanding sealers.

There are occasions where I do want some grain filling, and this is where I sand oiled, using whatever type of oil that I intend to finish with. After an initial sanding dry with the rotary pads the whole surface is given a light rub with an oiled cloth. While the object is still wet it is then sanded with wet or dry paper held on a rubber sanding pad. Starting with 100 grit the paper picks up a lot of oiled dust which is then pushed back into any open pores as a paste. Finer grades of grit then smooth off the surface. Paper used in this way quickly clogs up and needs regular cleaning with a wire brush if it is to retain any cutting ability. It should not be necessary to start with a grade as coarse as 100 after the rotary sanding, but if you start finer the grit clogs up even more quickly. The 180 grit paper will also clog and need frequent cleaning but by the time the 240 grit is reached the bulk of the oil will have gone and dry dust will be collected on the paper. By now the surface will be very fine and some of the grain will be filled with a paste of the natural wood.

Whichever approach has been adopted up to this stage, in nine out of ten cases I will next finish off with oil.

My normal procedure is as follows. First the piece is turned against a pad of 400 grit wet or dry. After this, the lathe is stopped and the workpiece is given a rub of oil with a soft cloth. The lathe is then run and the oil is burnished-in, giving deep penetration of the surface. This raises any loose grain, and starts the sealing process. Once dry the piece is again spun and given a light rubbing with wire wool. After this a second coat of oil is applied and again burnished in. This completely waterproofs the surface, and the use of oil greatly enhances the natural colour of the wood, highlighting the contrast between light and dark figuring.

This treatment produces an interesting range of results. On close-grained woods such as ash and oak it gives a bright shine. On softer, open-grained woods such as elm a matt gleam, and on the very porous a complete matt which is still by no means lifeless. Even on porous woods repeated applications of oil can produce a shiny skin.

Danish oil and teak oil are broadly similar, but there are important differences. Both penetrate into the wood, changing its nature, thus sealing and waterproofing it. Teak is a cruder, coarser oil and is more likely to produce a surface film. It is also darker and darkens the wood.

It is believed that teak oil is toxic and that Danish oil is mildly so. A salad bowl should certainly not be finished with teak oil. Danish oil is widely used, but for complete safety a pure mineral oil is best. Many production wood turners have now gone over to using liquid paraffin (the laxative bought from the chemists). This can be used both for the oiled sanding and for the final finishing. It is completely odourless, tasteless (used in this way), and non-toxic. Being totally colourless it only brings out the natural colour of the wood without altering it in any way. It does not have quite the surface-sealing properties of Danish and teak oils so three coats are better than two.

FINISHES

Lacquers

Lacquers are very popular as finishes. They are applied with the lathe at rest but are then burnished with the lathe rotating. The best of these are pre-catalysed, dry very quickly, and the body can be either cellulose or melamine. Both give a good, hard finish which is water-proof, while the skin remains unbroken. They do, however, scratch through and you can then get staining under the finish.

For any turned object that may ever be wiped clean with a damp cloth, an oil finish is better than any lacquer. Most lacquer are applied by wiping a thin film all over the workpiece with a soft, lint-free cloth. This is done with the lathe stopped.

After a pause of about two minutes the lathe is started and the surface is burnished using the same (semi-damp) applicator cloth, forming a bright shine.

Do not try to put on a second coat immediately – this will only soften the first coat and produce ridges. The second application should, ideally, be made on the following day. Before application the surface should be lightly keyed by rotating against the finest grade of wire wool (0000 grade). The procedure for lacquering is then as with the first coat. After this you may care to finish off with a little Beeswax paste spun against a soft cloth.

The one advantage of the pre-catalysed lacquers is that they are absolutely colour-less and give a bright, sparkling finish to white woods such as figured Sycamore. Olive and salad oils can be used to finish salad bowls. Linseed oil is too crude, darkens with age, can give a sticky build-up and is best left to cricket bats!

Polyurethane lacquers are for boats! Having said that I have to admit that they do have a place in woodturning. If you are making a goblet or beaker (or a bowl, for that matter) that is going to be used to hold actual liquids (as distinct from wet salads) then two or three coats of two-pot polyurethane varnish on the inside could keep them watertight. I still prefer deep impregnation with multi-coats of oil.

Whatever the finish, wood should not be immersed in water to clean it. It can be sponged out with a damp cloth (no deter-gents) and should then be wiped dry. I did have one elm platter brought back that someone (not a child) had put into the dish washer!

French Polish gives a lovely finish but I find it so prone to damage or marking that it is best not used on turned work that is going to get regular usage.

Waxes

Another range of finishes, which are attractive but less practical, are waxes. Some turners apply wax straight on to the sanded wood, others apply burnished lacquer or oil which they let dry and then put a thick wax finish on top. Waxes can build up a deep, lustrous polish which on a piece of nice, dark elm does look extremely rich.

Beeswax is the most popular but it is the softest and if applied as a thick coating it marks very easily, particularly with water or alcohol. Carnauba, a vegetable wax, is harder, but can produce a film that is so brittle that it flakes off. There are proprietary blends of waxes, but you can make your own. Shred solid beeswax together with about 5 per cent of carnauba wax into a vessel. Work in just sufficient genuine turpentine to produce a paste of the consistency you like. Some people also add a trace of soft soap to improve plasticity. This is applied generously and is polished vigorously as the turpentine dries out. It takes a lot of elbow grease but a lovely patina can soon be built up. Again, however, it does mark easily with water splashes, so it should only ever be used on dry bowls.

While some of these finishes can be applied off the lathe, they all improve with the burnishing that can be given by holding a clean, dry cloth against the object while the lathe is turning. So this often means that you will apply the finish before you complete the last turning job.

FINAL TURNING

Everything now depends upon how you mounted the workpiece on the lathe. If it was screwed on to a face plate or a face plate ring, and provided you sanded down the base before mounting then all you now have to do is to remove the object from the lathe and fill the screw holes. The best materials to use for this are the shellac or wax 'stopping sticks'. These can be melted into the hole with a soldering iron and once cooled can be scraped to a flush finish. They do not subsequently shrink, crack or break away. Incidentally, if you must fill checks in the wood, then this is again the best material.

The problem that many turners now face was referred to earlier; it is that of the dovetail groove necessitated by the frequent use of collet chucks. These recesses are not particularly attractive and are quite likely to have a rough edge. One

way of getting rid of them is to cut the shoulders away with a carving gouge and then hand-smooth the contours.

You can speed up and generally improve the process by reverse chucking, and one method of doing this was referred to in Chapter 4. An alternative is to cut a groove in a wooden face plate such that the rim of the bowl fits snugly in the groove. It is possible to make this fit so closely that the bowl will now be held in by vacuum. However, do not risk this until you can do very accurate work. For safety use the tailstock. Put a blunt or rounded centre in the tailstock, extend the quill to a maximum and bring the pad up to hold the bowl in place on the face plate. Set the lathe to the slowest speed and position the tool rest so that you can cut away the shoulder of the dovetail with

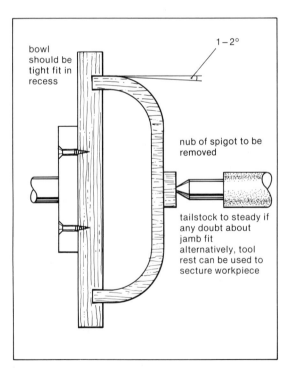

bowl should be tight fit in recess

1 – 2°

nub of spigot to be removed

tailstock to steady if any doubt about jamb fit alternatively, tool rest can be used to secure workpiece

Jamb fit chuck for cleaning bases.

Hammer finish achieved through differential contraction.

the small bowl gouge. You may even wish to scribe a couple of decorative grooves in the base with the long point of the skew.

A very popular way of finishing off the base, even of hiding screw holes from face plates, is to stick something on it. Coloured baize or self-adhesive cork rings already cut to size can be bought, or you can make up your own.

Many professionals do not like the use of 'cover-ups'. They always feel that you have something to hide, and that that something is poor workmanship. I must admit that there are times when I do use cork rings: not so much to hide screw holes but to provide a cushion or scratch preventer under a very big, heavy piece.

To cope with a wide range of different sized objects the self-adhesive coloured velours are ideal. The material is normally supplied in 18in (45.5cm)-wide lengths. From this cut a 9in (23cm) square. Mount a 10in (25.5cm)-plus diameter scrap wood disc on to a lathe face plate. Keep the protective backing on the adhesive of

the Fablon and stick this down on to the wooden face plate with a cross of double sided adhesive tape. Set the lathe to the slowest speed, and with the tool rest across the face and set at centre height, take a very sharp, pointed knife and hold this on edge on the rest. Cut a circle in the Fablon just inside the outer edges of the square. Move the knife in an inch and again cut a circle. You have made a 1in (2.5cm)-wide, 9in (23cm)-diameter ring ready to stick on the base of a large bowl. Keep cutting 1in (2.5cm) rings until you have a 2in (5cm) centre disc. Obviously you can cut rings of whatever size and width you require using this method.

SPECIAL FINISHES

Apart from what I would call the 'normal' methods of finishing, there is scope for huge areas of experimentation. Much of my work is with burr elm and I like to work with timber that has not dried right out. The piece is turned from beginning to end, including the final oil finish. It is then put on a shelf. This for two reasons; first I want to make quite sure that it is not going to split before I consider selling it to anybody; and second the burr marks will often contract slightly more than the plain timber and this gives an interesting 'ripple' or 'hammered' finish.

Jim Partridge colours wood. At one time I was violently against the concept of staining wood, but having seen both Jim's work and that of others who are prone to experiment (several in this country as well as America) I have become quite converted. Some of Jim's pieces are in oak which is then burnt black. To contrast this he then rubs ink-stained chalk into the pores.

Of course, woodworkers have for years been fuming oak to get that deep brown-black of Jacobean oak. This is done by enclosing the piece in an air-tight container together with a quantity of 880 ammonia. This is the highest concentration of ammonia available and to breath it in can be fatal, so it has to be handled with caution. It is available from suppliers who specialise in wood-finishing products. Others have bleached oak with lime or caustic soda.

The Norwegians specialise in painting wood. Beautiful hand-painted plates are often made of local birch or pine wood and are decorated in what is known as the 'rose painting' tradition.

There are also ideas which involve mixing turning and carving – flowers incised into the centre of plates; profile shapes cut into rims, and many more ideas.

Much of this leaves me with very mixed feelings. Wood is a magnificent material – it can have enormous character of its own without any applied decoration. Often it is the so-called 'faults' which give it its particular attraction. Burrs and spalting were once reasons for discarding timber. Knots and checks are a natural part of the material, so why hide them; aren't they its very character – true features? Leaving them unfilled, natural in colour, smooth, but oiled, makes wood what it *is*!

10 Design

Even deciding what the first words in a chapter on design should be is difficult. Design in terms of a plan, or what is intended is easy, but when we come to the dictionary definition of 'the artistic intention embodied in a piece of work', design becomes a barely definable concept. Of course there are some rules of good design, but then, as the saying goes, rules are made for the guidance of the wise and the obedience of fools. Acceptable design is very much a matter of taste and good design could be defined as that which appeals to those who should know. And then we get into the problem of defining who should know.

POPULAR DESIGN CONVENTIONS

Perhaps, then, we should start by looking at some of the design conventions that are current in wood-turning.

There has long been one cardinal rule, and that is that the internal profile of bowls should follow the external profile exactly, and that there should therefore be an even wall thickness from top to bottom. Why?

You will hear those who slavishly follow this rule criticising another's piece of work with a derogatory, 'You have two nice bowls there. It's a pity that they aren't separate pieces', referring, of course, to the different internal and external profiles.

When you probe this issue it often appears that the only real justification is the turner's own wish to demonstrate his skill in being able to achieve an even wall thickness, and not for any real artistic purpose. So why be hidebound by this so-called rule?

There is actually a justification for having differences in wall thickness! You look at the inside of a bowl from above – you see the plan view. As the object is a turned piece you are invariably looking at 'roundness' – so why should the inside not be rounded? Why should we have a flat bottom section on the interior just because the underside of the base has to be flat to support the vessel?

When you look at the outside of the object you are looking at a profile – at a section. Now it is the outside shape that matters; now it cannot be wholly round. It has to have a flat bottom to stand on, and, unless it is a lidded pot, it has to have a flat top to provide access to the inside. (We will forget for the moment the natural-edged or 'waney' tops.)

There is hardly one of the so-called rules of design that cannot be legitimately broken – provided it is done deliberately to create a particular, acceptable, effect. The rules say that bases should be smaller than the maximum diameter, but what about the Egyptian pyramids? We tend to think of bowls as having the widest diameter at the top – but think of the beautiful shapes created by the Byzantine craftsmen. Much of their work in ceramics, glass and basketwork featured the greatest diameter at one-third down from the top.

Good design must take into account a number of aspects. The first is that the design (the shape) must fit the intended purpose of the object. The second is that the object has to please the eye; and although beauty is in the eye of the beholder, there are some elements such as balance and proportion that most people recognise. The third parameter concerns the necessary relationship between the shape of the object and the intrinsic qualities of the material. The above could be considered the immutable basic rules. We could add to them, but then most of the additions would be those elements that we are most likely to vary from time to time.

Many consider that good design must be original – but then again, what about the enduring classic shapes of the Grecian and Byzantine periods? Good design may, too, exhibit the skills of the craftsman (as with even wall width) but then such demonstrations, if overdone, become mere ostentation. It can even be a hiding of those skills which is the ultimate demonstration of the craftsman's competence – for instance hidden double dovetail joints in furniture making. There, nobody but the craftsman ever knows just how beautifully perfect the actual joint is.

So, lets consider the three basic design elements of:

1   Purpose – use, utility and objective.
2   Shape and proportion – basic ground rules.
3   The intrinsic qualities of the material.

PURPOSE

The first consideration must be that of purpose because this must in the end transcend all else. Everything has a purpose. It may be to hold things, as in bowls; to dispense things, as in a jug or pepper mill; to fulfill a particular function, as in a door stop; or simply to provide aesthetic satisfaction (and fill space), as in a purely decorative item. It can even be legitimately done simply to demonstrate the craftsman's skills.

Of course we can, and usually do, have more than one objective. We may be making a pepper mill, the primary purpose of which is to dispense pepper; but at the same time we may wish to provide aesthetic satisfaction (and even demonstrate our turning prowess). The problems start to arise when we confuse ourselves by the emphasis we give to the different objectives, particularly when we subjugate purpose to novelty or aesthetic satisfaction.

A fundamental design mistake made by many craftsmen is to give undue weighting to a secondary objective. They are making a pepper mill, but get so carried away trying to demonstrate their skills at rounding beads, grooving, cutting coves and embellishments, that the resultant mill is fussy, difficult to operate and wholly over the top. Although the design should be interesting and balanced the object must still look and function as an efficient pepper mill.

I am sometimes challenged on this one. As stated earlier my speciality is using heavily figured English hardwoods; knots, warts and all. Several of my bowls, therefore, have holes in the walls. Some people ask me what the use of a bowl with a hole is. I am quite clear about the objective in this type of piece. I am making an object designed to fill space and provide aesthetic satisfaction – in other words it is intended as pure ornamentation and to be a statement about wood. If people want to put fruit or whatever in them, then that is up to them, they can always put masking tape over the hole! I am making them, and selling them, and most people buy them, as ornament. I am not, with these objects, catering for the 'Yes, but, what can I use it for?' market.

This of course means that the pieces have to be aesthetically satisfying. There does have to be something pleasing about the shape. The nature of the wood has to be highlighted and shown off – hence the grain is not filled, and they are not varnished to look like waterproof plastic. They may well have different internal and external profiles, because I am not trying to demonstrate how clever I am with a pair of callipers. Neither are they so thin-walled and fragile that at the first breath of wind they will split. They are intended to last for generations and I am particularly anxious that there should be examples of my work around long after both the last elm tree and I myself have disappeared!

No one gets offered a salad bowl in burr elm – the knots, pin holes and checks would be basically unhygienic; and a potential client who inquires of their suitability will be nudged towards clean-grain timber bowls. Salad bowls must be brought to a perfect smoothness and finish. With these, the internal and external profiles are more likely to be the same. You do not look down into an empty salad bowl (very often), and the turner is probably trying to provide the largest space/capacity that the outside form will allow.

Sticking for a moment with the specific purpose of 'decorative space filling' and the question of good design, there are still many aspects to consider.

Just think of a few of the different space-filling situations where people place pieces of turned wood. Probably the one where a substantial part of my work is aimed is as the centre-piece for a large dining table. Of course, the sizes of clients' dining tables vary, so we could be talking of bowls of anything between 12 and 30in (30–76cm) diameter. Items on a table are frequently looked down into – hence broader, shallower pieces with a satisfying top rim and internal shape feature strongly. People may want to put fruit in them on some occasions, so the shape has to be able to contain the fruit; but you generally see around the fruit and the removal of two or three items soon starts to expose the bowl's internal shape. So with big bowls the rim, internal shape, internal finish, figure and character of the wood are amongst my first considerations.

Few people ever notice the lower areas of the external profile so these are of slightly lesser importance on a table centre-piece.

A piece for an occasional table would have to be smaller, otherwise it would swamp most tables and look disproportionate. Also, occasional tables are not 'sat around'. We either sit back from such tables, plunged into easy chairs, or else the table is to one side. Now the piece is more likely to be seen in profile and the question of external shape takes precedence over internal form. Indeed the more closed-in forms, where the inside is virtually hidden, start to come into their own.

An item intended for a sideboard is seen almost wholly in profile; it needs to be larger, and to have some height. Now internal shape and figure are almost irrelevant.

Some turnings – my 'gallery' pieces, for instance – are of such a size and nature that they need to be given their own 'space'. No longer are they a decoration on a table; they may well stand alone (on some suitable support). Clearly these pieces, in their form, texture and material, have to be such as to make their own statement: 'I am a decoration. I am wood. I am magnificent (or delicate). I am here to add an element of aesthetic satisfaction to your life – appreciate me!'

You cannot make a major piece of decoration and then just hope that it will fit somewhere. You have to think where it is most likely to be placed – what decor it will have to compliment, what sort of clientele will see it in the gallery or shop where it is to be sold, and then make it accordingly.

Where might small lidded boxes go? Some are placed with others in a showcase collection. Others will be on mantle pieces, shelves, or room dividers. Some will find their place on a dressing table. The boudoir piece will be very different from the mantlepiece item. The latter has to stand out, while the dressing table item has to fit in. The box on the dressing table will probably be stroked, and it therefore needs to be smooth, sensuous in shape, delicate and beautiful.

The purpose of the piece is the first determinant design characteristic, and you must take great care not to swamp the primary objective with your personal secondary foibles. Showiness – of decoration or technique – is the first enemy of good design.

SHAPE AND PROPORTION

The ground rules of shape, proportion and balance are not easy to define. There is a school which believes that anything produced today should follow today's design trends and thus be contemporary. Certainly good contemporary work has a significant following. However, there is a very large buying public for items using classical shapes.

Probably the most widely used design principle is the rule of three (the crude approximation to the rule of golden section) and this is always a sound basis to work from. In practical terms it means that areas of emphasis should be placed at the one-third point rather than at the centre or edges. The Byzantine pot shape of which I am so fond has the greatest diameter one-third of the way down from the top. In a picture, having the main feature of interest in the centre is boring to the eye. Placed on the golden section it brings the whole thing to life.

In turned work curves are more generally pleasing than are angles; but moving from the round to the square and then back again can be pleasing, as on some table legs, banisters, spindles, and lamp columns. Continuous sweeping lines and flowing curves are more satisfying than are sudden turns – although again a sharp turn into a crown or base can frame nice, clean, sweeping walls.

Take an elliptical sphere. This is a very satisfying shape. It is complete, and the eye will first sweep right around the profile and then come to rest in the absolute centre – held in suspension, equidistant from all walls as it appreciates the whole. The impression is of lightness, an object floating free in space, of comfort and balance.

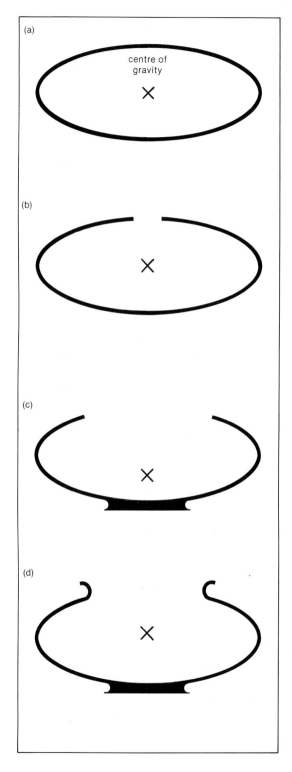

(a)

centre of gravity

×

(b)

×

(c)

×

(d)

×

To make this into a vessel we could cut a hole in the top, but to retain the sweep and symmetry it would need to be a small hole. If small enough the sweeping eye would move across the gap barely noticing it. But if larger, the gap becomes too big for the eye to jump across; the eye can no longer sweep right round but 'rocks' from the rim, round the base, and back up to the other rim. We now have an open-top bowl and the eye eventually comes to rest midway between the side walls, but has fallen to closer to the base. The vessel now has a heavier feeling and has to 'sit' on something.

Now let us lift the eye point. Put a return rim on the top of the vessel. Note that the curved rim has a similar profile to that of the main wall. The eye is lifted and the vessel opens out and is altogether more joyous. Repetition or the duplicating of curves in this way can be pleasing.

Where the curves repeat, as in 'a' (*see* diagram page 136), although of a smaller radius, this provides a much more satisfying line than those shown in 'b' where the smaller upper curve has a different arc to the lower. 'a' is complete while 'b' creates tension as the eye seeks to do something else as it reaches the top. The form in 'b' feels unfinished.

Take the sphere and make it into a lidded pot. The result is a squat, dumpy item. It looks like a lump of dough which has yet to rise into a crispy baked loaf.

Left: Moving the centre of gravity. (a) The centre of gravity is in the centre of the sphere. (b) A small top opening does not move it. (c) A larger top opening lowers the centre of gravity. Add a foot and it is brought down even further. (d) Putting a small return lip around the rim lifts the centre of gravity and gives the shape a joyous lift.

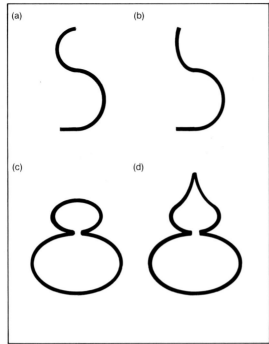

Mixing curves. (a) Repeating a curve in a different size gives flow. (b) Mixing the profiles is much less satisfying. But − (c) Duplicating shapes can be boring. To transform the lump-of-dough appearance we can add a different shape and a second curve. (d) The result is an 'aspiring', rising shape of a minaret.

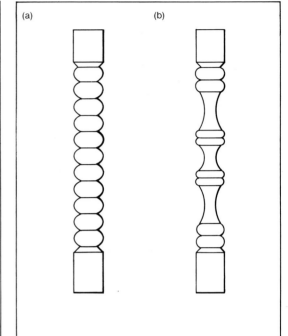

Mixing shapes. (a) A leg with a row of indentical beads looks deadly dull.
(b) Breaking the beads up with other shapes immediately adds interest.

Eastern designers added another shape to just such a profile. They put a pointed spire on top to cause the eye to soar upwards − they created the minaret with its spire aspiring towards the heavens.

In talking about multiple curves we should talk about repeat rather than repetition. Two curves of the same shape give emphasis to each other, three gives balance, but more create boredom. Table legs with a row of identical beads are deadly dull. Beads interrupted with long, tapering coves or other shapes are much more lively.

Now look again at the handle you produced earlier. How do the shapes fit together? Is there a continuous flow throughout? Does the variety appear overdone? Does the whole balance? There are two basic rules that are sometimes in conflict. One is that bases should be smaller (in diameter) than any other part of the item; but against that is the idea that if the base is too small the object looks unstable and top-heavy.

There is an interesting set of relationships between the profile shape and size of the base. According to the arrangement the piece can be made to apparently float off the table, rest on it, or take root in it.

A large, heavy base drags the eye down. Maybe the item is made of wood, but there is no need to make it look as though the whole tree is still rooted in the table! As a guide-line, a base that is greater than two-thirds of the maximum diameter is too big and heavy. One that is much less than one-third is unstable. 'So what?' you may ask. Well, this is (again) where the question of purpose comes in. If you are aiming for aesthetic satisfaction, beauty, appreciation and pleasure, then you have to ensure mental comfort. Too large a base and you have mental stodginess. Too small and you have the viewer anxiously sitting on the edge of a chair waiting for the object to fall over. If your purpose is to create tension in the mind, then go for extremes of thinness, tiny based instability, and unfinished curves.

Some bases act as a small pedestal and these give the floating-off-the-table effect. The pedestal may be fully visible from a normal viewing position or be hidden underneath. Sometimes the base is made deliberately visible and the shape is incorporated to be an integral part of the overall profile; in others it is so worked as to appear almost separate. Floating is achieved by holding the main shape above the table – at no point does the main profile intersect the surface of the table.

When the profile coincides with the table top the object appears to be clearly resting on the table. When the general profile, or the extension of the continuous curves of the wall, takes the eye into the table, then the object begins to take root. Extend this even further so that the extended curves go deeper into the supporting surface and the more firmly rooted and heavy the object will appear.

As I said a few moments ago, the greatest diameter (in a bowl) is often best not at the top but somewhere about one-third of the way down the wall. Take it lower and you again get heaviness; and

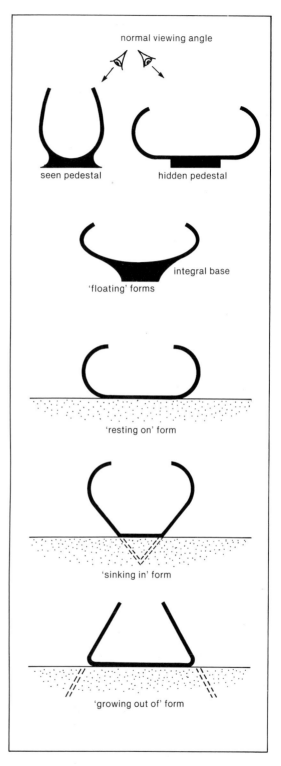

Forms of bowls.

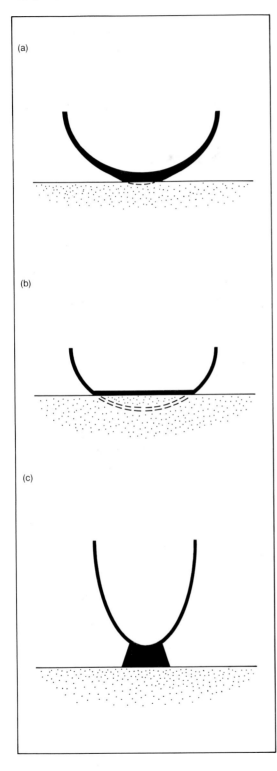

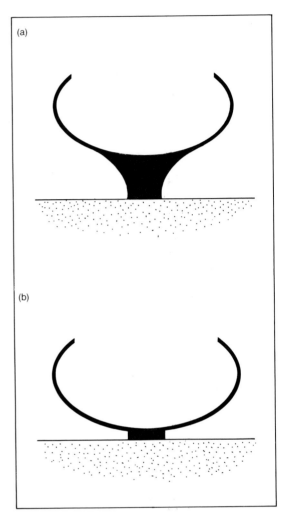

Above: Bases – don't make them too small. (a) The narrower the base the more unstable the piece appears (and often is). (b) The lower the centre of balance, the less unstable the piece appears (but it may actually still be unstable).

Left: Bases – keep them small. (a) The smaller the base the less the bowl seems to sink into the table. (b) A large base makes the object heavy and appear half-submerged. The angled corners and flat inside base add to the effect. (c) A small foot can look like an independent pedestal support to the main form.

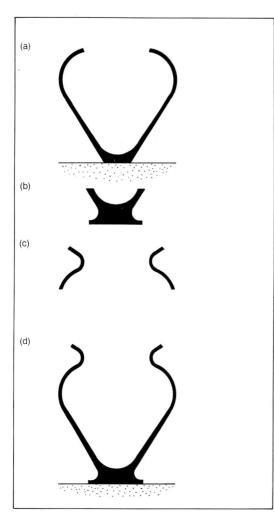

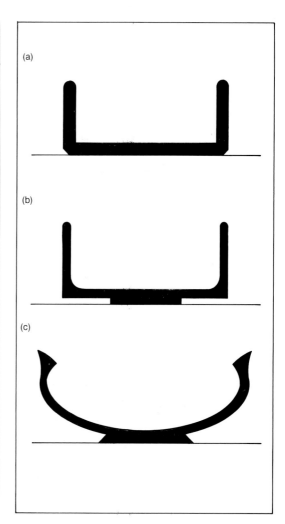

Bases – the ratio with tops. (a) Proportion is maintained by keeping the base diameter to less than a half but more than a third of the top opening diameter. (b) If we add a foot to give real stability to such a pot – even though it had the appearance of a pedestal – we have increased the effective diameter of the base and now need to increase the top aperture diameter. (c) Just opening the top would spoil the shape, but a flared rim would add lift. (d) The piece also uses another design device, that of sandwiching a different curve profile (the walls) between two similar ones (the foot and the lip).

Salad bowls. (a) A vertical-walled bowl has greatest capacity, but has awkward inside corners, and looks heavy and 'rooted' in the table. (b) The same bowl can be made thinner and with crisp external corners and a 'hidden' foot, to make it appear to 'float' on the table. (c) A functional but attractive salad bowl. The bowl has a reverse curve inside to contain the salad while tossing, and an insloping rim to catch drips. It has a substantial but near-hidden foot for stability. The whole form rises off the table and gives a pleasing external curved profile.

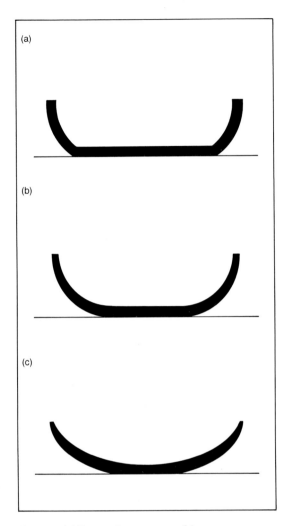

Curves. (a) Internal corners marking a change of direction are unnecessary.
(b) Longer radius curves are better, even though they still lead to a flat bottom.
(c) Continuous curves with no flat area are the most pleasing.

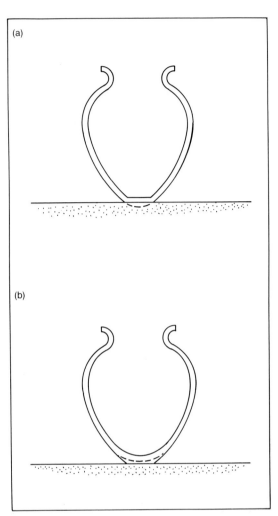

The importance of the internal profile. (a) The flat inside base gives this vessel a 'sinking into' form. (b) Here the rounded interior profile brings the vessel nearer to a 'sitting on' form.

bulges down towards the base are the ultimate in leaden stodginess.

The most deadly, dull shape of all is the vertical walled, flat bottomed bowl. So it may be useful – but you are producing simply a utilitarian piece with no thought for design or aesthetics.

The ultimate extension of this theme goes beyond 'taking root' and becomes a 'bedrock' issue. The pyramids hardly

appear to have been put there by man, but rather to having been created geologically by growing out of the desert sands or of being pinnacles of bedrock now exposed by surface erosion.

There are arrangements where it is right to have the greatest diameter at the top. This is where the form is that of the shallow dish with a smooth, continuously curving inner profile. There should, however, always be a relationship between the top diameter and the base diameter. If two pots have identical greatest diameters then the one with the bigger top opening has also to have the bigger diameter base. Hence the flared-mouth pot in the diagram needs a flared base to balance it, whereas the narrower mouthed, simpler pot, sits well on the narrower base.

So, as a basic principle, by keeping curves around the base we get a feeling of lightness. By taking them through and below the base we create an impression of stability and permanence – even of heaviness. At worst it creates lumpiness.

The importance of the internal profile now begins to come to the fore and this may be the most telling argument in favour of different internal and external forms. The general profile is the combination of the inner and the outer form. A flat internal base emphasises the external profile and the whole more clearly sinks into the table. A curved internal base can compensate for the flat bottom, and despite the downward sweep of the walls may still maintain the appearance of sitting on the top of the table. From this we can say that internal profiles should normally be curved, not flat bottomed.

A final point worth noting concerns pedestals. A pedestal may be considered to be a base so designed that it appears to be separate from the supported item. In general terms the simpler the pedestal the better, and from an aesthetic point of view

Right: More bases. (a) and (b) Sometimes we need to make the pedestal independent to maintain a true 'floating above' form. This way the base can be large and stable without appearing lumpy. (c) The massive lumpy base seen on some novice work.

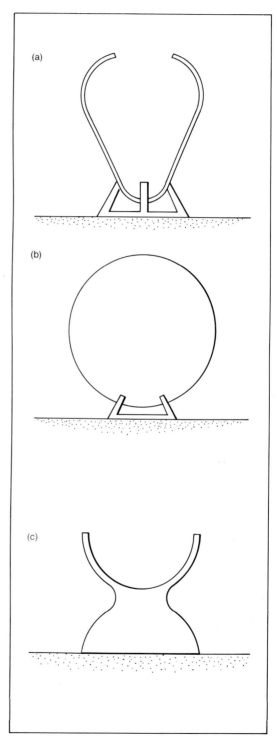

141

the smaller the better; but don't go over-board. There are times when you need a pedestal with a wider foot to give stability.

Thickness or thinness in bowl turning is also an important design criteria, but this is as much related to the intrinsic nature of the material as it is to anything else. There does, of course, have to be some relation-ship between the wall thickness and the overall size of the item both from a design and from a utility point of view.

If you are making a piece of grace and elegance (usually taken to mean a long/tall and slender piece) then it needs to be light and ephemeral. So it needs thinner walls. It probably also means using lighter coloured woods with more delicate figures.

To me, heavily grained and knotted woods shout 'ruggedness' and therefore demand substantial wall thickness. I personally find large objects with very thin walls made from dark burrs to be something of an anachronism. Yes, they are technically clever – maybe even supreme examples of the wood turner's craft, but possibly not of their art!

INTRINSIC QUALITIES OF WOOD

The third principle of design, that of the intrinsic qualities of the material, is broken by items such as some tall goblets with very thin, long stems. Trees do not grow that way, with match stick trunks supporting huge canopies. Wood was not intended to do such things, so these goblets are at cross-purposes with the intrinsic nature of the material. Perhaps, on this score, some criticism could be levelled against David Ellsworth for

making huge spheres with ⅛in (3mm) thick walls, but here we are in a different field. The overall size of his spheres, their unique character as fillers of space, and, of course, the absolutely supreme crafts-manship put them into a category of their own. Perhaps this is another example where the apparent breaking of rules achieves the highest art form.

Remember always that you are working with wood. Let it do the things that wood can do; do not try to force it to do those things that it can not. Let it be wood, let it look like wood. Make the most of its qualities, its colours, characteristics, patterns and nature.

The intrinsic qualities of wood which design should take into account are its:

Colour and colour variation.
Figure and grain patterns.
Defects, knots, shakes, burrs, spalts, worm holes.
Surface texture, pores, grain and fibrous nature.
Weight and density.
Living and 'vital' origins.
Strength, stability and permanence.
Workability.

How you interpret these qualities – the use that you make of each of them in your designs, the integrity with which you treat them, and how you integrate them with form and profile – will depend upon you as an individual. It is what you do here that differentiates between artist and craftsman. The good turner is both.

There is one design criteria that trans-cends all others. It is – KISS (Keep It Simple, Stupid)! There is a place for fine work of great intricacy and complexity, but in general, and particularly with the larger items, the more simple it is, the better. Simplicity is one of today's design norms. It is not only concerned with form, but has to take into account the whole package, including utility and the intrinsic qualities of the material.

No one should produce a delicately worked small box with multiple incised designs cut into a highly figured wood full of knots, worm holes and shakes. Each piece you make must have a primary focus – it may be concerned with the intrinsic nature of the wood, hence a natural-edged heavy burr bowl should be of simple shape. It could be a large, simple, open but beautifully finished piece in spalted beech. It may have tall elegance and line – a slender vase enhanced by the straight grain. Or it could be a thin-walled item in near-translucent holly. If it is fundamentally utilitarian it will not be so fragile or so ornamental that people will not want to use it for fear of damage.

If the emphasis is upon form and ornamentation as in a decorative spindle then we do not want to give the eye indigestion by adding a high element of figure. After all, who would make a nicely boiled egg then smother it with salt, pepper, butter, brown sauce, mint, tomato ketchup and custard? Remember – KISS!

Finally, and a little more practically, you can do a lot of interesting experimentation in design with a large piece of paper, a felt tipped pen, and a mirror. On the paper draw some profiles. Let the imagination run free and try various simple and compound curves. Now stand the mirror on edge so that it intersects one of the profiles and reflects the exposed section. By moving the mirror round you can test a wide variety of possible shapes and sizes. Each time you generate a shape that

Burr elm bowl finished with Danish oil.

you find pleasing, sketch it out in a notebook and keep it for future use.

On the subject of the notebook, wherever you are, wherever you are going, in one of your pockets should be a small sketching book of about 6 by 4in (15 by 10cm). When you see a shape that interests you, make a note of it. Make sketches of turned items that you would like to try. Walk around the pottery section of the local museum and again make sketches of shapes that appeal. When you are waiting for someone, fill in the time by doodling shapes. And when you wake up in the middle of the night with a brilliant idea, put the light on and make a note of it – if you don't it will be gone by morning.

You may not be the best artist in the world – that does not matter. What is important is that you start to think 'design' and you do not lose those flashes of inspiration that occur to all of us in the oddest of moments. The more sketches you make the more observant you will become, and the better will be your ideas.

11 Turning Wood

You can turn any and every type of wood – trunk, branch or root. Whether you want to or not is another matter! Obviously the type of turning that you are interested in will condition the varieties of wood you use. Most of my work tends to have a decorative bias so I am interested in heavily figured, strongly coloured woods.

There are times, though, when I am making chair legs that have to support weight, so the choice is then closer, straight grained timbers of a uniform colour. Maybe there is a mallet head to make and now the choice is restricted to a few strong, dense woods like *Lignum vitae*.

At one time or another I have used almost every type of wood available in this country, but I am now making it a policy not to use any tropical rain forest wood except in *very* special circumstances, such as the need for a particular hardness or density as with lignum.

In this chapter we are not going to spend time looking at the different species of wood, but more at the nature of wood, the factors influencing its character, the condition in which we get it, what we can do with it to make it useful to us, and, in Chapter 12, I will give a few points on buying timber.

TREE GROWTH AND STRUCTURE

First, think about how a tree grows. Obviously it is basically upwards and outwards! Consider the tree as a cone. Each year it puts another cone over the top of those already existing. The top of the tree, the crown, grows in height because the top of this year's cone is now sitting on the top of last year's. It also throws out branches and each of these becomes a sub-cone on the side.

When you cut through a tree you can see where each 'cone' has been built on the previous one's because in cross-section there are a number of concentric rings. Generally speaking, in the temperate and sub-arctic latitudes, each ring marks one year of growth. Hence if you cut through an upper branch and there will only be a few rings – that branch has only been there a few years. Down near the base of the trunk we get an indication of the tree's total age because there will be a ring for every year since birth (less a year or two germinating and developing underground). The branch which started life in the first year or two of the tree's life will have almost as many rings at its butt, as will the lower trunk.

Actually, each ring is in fact made up of two. There is the broader, lighter, softer part which represents the rapid spring growth when the sap was rising, and then the thin, darker, harder part which represents the slower summer growth during the drier months. Count the dark rings, which are easier to see.

Most of the 'life' of the tree is in the outermost cones; it is this area that is growing. It carries the sap, and is there-

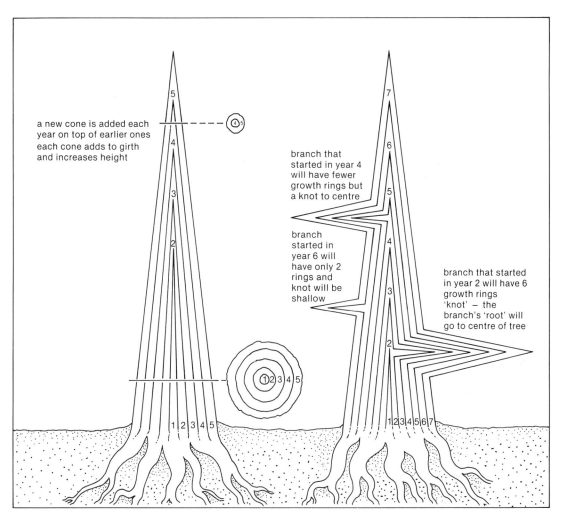

a new cone is added each year on top of earlier ones each cone adds to girth and increases height

branch that started in year 4 will have fewer growth rings but a knot to centre

branch started in year 6 will have only 2 rings and knot will be shallow

branch that started in year 2 will have 6 growth rings 'knot' – the branch's 'root' will go to centre of tree

Growth of a tree, branches and knots.

fore called the sap wood. In order to conduct the sap, often in considerable quantities, it has a wide, open pore structure. The fibre of the wood provides canals up which the sap travels.

If you remove enough of the bark the sap would evaporate away without getting up to the crown. Something else would also happen. Between the sap-wood and the bark is the cambium layer; this is a semi-liquid which creates cells which then divide. Some become sap-wood, some bark. It is the cambium layer which 'glues' the bark to the timber. So

again, in removing the bark the cambium dries out, growth is stopped, and death follows. In effect the bark is the tree's 'skin', both rain coat and sun shield.

It is the outermost rings that act as the main sap carriers. Each successive ring as you go towards the centre of the tree carries less. In essence the inner rings are dead, shrunk in size, and are filled with deposited mineral matter. We call these inner rings heartwood. Because their cells are no longer swollen out with sap and have shrunk, the wood has become more dense. In many trees a colouring process

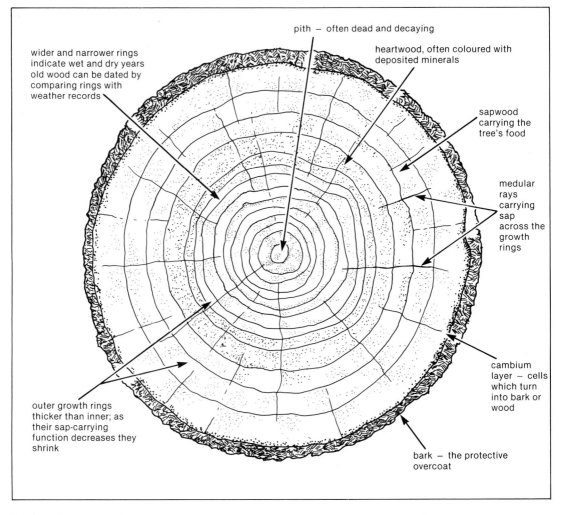

pith — often dead and decaying

heartwood, often coloured with deposited minerals

wider and narrower rings indicate wet and dry years old wood can be dated by comparing rings with weather records

sapwood carrying the tree's food

medular rays carrying sap across the growth rings

cambium layer — cells which turn into bark or wood

outer growth rings thicker than inner; as their sap-carrying function decreases they shrink

bark — the protective overcoat

Section of a tree trunk.

starts and you get a darker coloured heartwood and a light coloured sapwood. What is actually happening is that the heartwood cells are clogged with coloured waste material, usually of a mineral nature. Walnut is a good example, with a dark chocolate coloured heart and a white sapwood. African blackwood has a dense black heart and a creamy white sap. Padauk has a fawny white sap and a brick red heart.

Many of the colours are permanent. You can expose them to light for a hundred years and they stay much the same. Ebony always has the same level of blackness. Others react to light — the vivid red of Padauk slowly turns a dark brown, even near-black. Others only reach their full hue in light. Purpleheart when first cut looks like a generally uninteresting, even grained, mahogany of the poorest figure and colour. Within a week of exposure to light it turns bright purple and stays that way for years.

If you choose your piece carefully, very dramatic effects can be achieved by having a light blaze of sapwood on one part of the object while the rest is of dark heartwood. A bowl of African blackwood with a blaze of white on the side can be very attractive. Again you can get a thinner piece that is almost all light sap with only a centre slash of dark heart. But, if the timber is not fully dry there will be differential shrinking between heart and sap.

Some tree species grow much more rapidly than others. Trees that grow in temperate climates with both plenty of rain and summer warmth develop rapidly, and the annual rings are quite wide. Many trees from such regions also have a considerable depth of sapwood before the first heartwood ring is encountered. Arctic, desert, and Mediterranean trees have slower growth, small growth rings, and, a wild, contorted figure.

Trees from the tropics, where there are no clearly defined seasons, grow continuously and evenly throughout the year, and it is often difficult to see any annual rings. Some, such as ebony, are quite ringless to the untutored naked eye. Others have two annual growth rings, representing the two wet and two warmer seasons each year. In general, tropical hardwood trees have shallow depths of sapwood before the coloured heartwood. The tropical woods also have the more strongly coloured heartwoods.

Few native English trees have coloured hearts. One of the most dramatic found here is of course an immigrant, the laburnum, and has a thin layer of creamy white sap and a large, greeny-brown heart.

At the centre of a tree is the pith. This is a soft area that has already started to rot. Sometimes the process has proceeded so far that there is a hollow up the centre – the laburnum can be particularly troublesome in this respect, and as children many of us have stood in the hollow of an old oak tree. A hollow centre does not mean the whole tree is dying.

Running from the centre radially out to the sapwood are medular rays. These are rows of cells that carry some sap across the grain through both heart and sapwood. They may look like embryonic check marks but they do not in fact represent any weakness in the structure. They can be seen particularly in oak and appear in a piece of polished wood as dark bands running across the grain.

DRYING WOOD

The nature of the growth pattern of the tree has obvious implications for the woodworker. The first is that in the cone pattern of growth the series of canals that rise from the root to the crown form the grain, and therefore the grain runs up and down the tree, not across it. The second important point is that in drying out, as the canal tunnels collapse, the sapwood will contract more than will the already contracted heartwood. Also in drying, as the canal walls collapse, there is twice as much contraction at the circumference of a growth ring than across its width.

Hence, if the bark is removed from a felled log, or the limb of a tree, then as it dries out the outer rings of sapwood will dry first and will contract more than does the heart, and internal stress will be set up. In the end the fibres of the sapwood part, and splits, or 'checking', occurs from the outer surface to centre.

If on the other hand the bark is left on as a protective coat, then drying will take place from the ends of the log, and the drying effect will be greatest at the centre of the ends. Now the centre, though

147

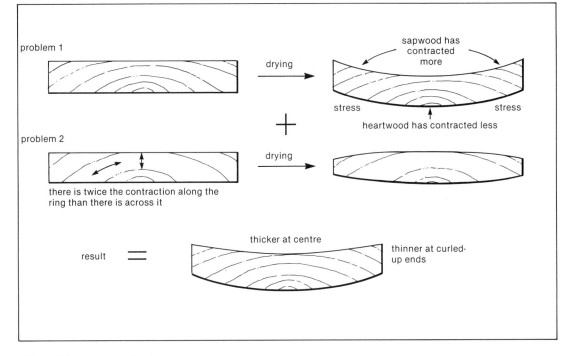

Effect of drying on a plank.

denser, contracts while the sapwood does not, and we get radial checking running outwards from the centre. This is much more marked on younger trees or on branches where the heartwood has not reached full, mature density.

When the log is sawn down its length into planks there are new hazards. A plank sawn from the centre could include pithwood and will usually split in drying. Any thick plank which includes the heart of the tree will check at some time.

The unwary can be caught out in this way. You want to make deep bowls, and there in the corner of the timber yard is a nice 5in (12.5cm)-thick plank of yew. It is being offered at a reasonable price. Check the ends! One look will tell you that it was cut from the heart. The plank, or items made from it, *will split*.

A plank sawn nearer the outside of the tree and parallel to the centre axis will have at its centre wood from deeper

annular rings, while at the two outside edges of the plank there will be zones of the more recent growth. The outer edges will contract more on drying and although the plank may not split it will curl up at the sides.

The most stable planks are those that are quarter sawn. Here the planks are sawn radially across the trunk with one edge pointing towards the centre of the tree, and the other out towards the bark.

Unfortunately, quarter sawn timber is more difficult for the mills to cut and is much more wasteful. Nor does it command a significantly higher price, despite the fact that it provides the most stable form of timber. Hence it is rarely on offer. Quarter sawing can give very attractive figuring patterns – from the ordinary-looking London plane it produces the beautiful lacewood. Some beech and straight-grained elm respond well to quarter sawing, as short medular rays are

148

revealed. To recognise quarter sawn timber look at the end of the plank: the growth rings are vertical between the two faces.

If we turn with wood that is not fully dried, then some contraction will occur as the finished object dries out. At worst this will mean a split. It could be a big one and go through at least a half of the object. At best it is likely to mean some distortion. What starts as a perfectly round bowl may take on a very interesting wobbly form. Certainly what started as a good, flat base is likely to result in a 'rocking' bowl!

It takes a long time for timber to dry out naturally. First the tree should be felled in the late autumn or during the winter months when the sap is at its lowest. It gives a new meaning to the American word fall, for autumn is when the sap is falling back. It should then be planked before the ends start splitting.

The term 'seasoned' usually means that it has been air dried for an appropriate length of time under the proper conditions. The proper conditions are easier to define than is the appropriate time. Ideally the timber, once planked, should have been kept dry – under cover; it should have been kept out of the sun – under cover; but there should have been the free passage of circulating air all around it to carry away the evaporating moisture – out in the open. The answer to the conundrum is storage in an open-sided Dutch barn, where the timber is exposed to wind but not rain or sun.

Under such conditions the 'rule of thumb' is that you should leave the timber a year for every inch of thickness. Unfortunately this calculation is not strictly linear. 1in (2.5cm) thick equals one year, but 4in (10cm) equals four years plus a bit (another two years?). One authority suggests that 2in (5cm) thickness may

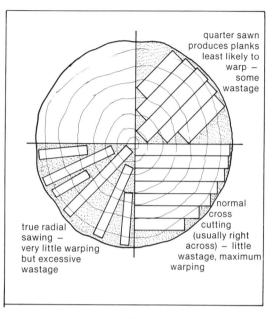

Quarter-sawn planks – the best compromise.

take four times as long to dry as does a 1in (2.5cm) plank.

Not all timbers behave in the same way – oak is particularly bad and here the seasoning time under ideal conditions is said to be four years for each inch of thickness.

One of the problems with the drying process is the variations in natural moisture content that can occur. When felled, most trees will have a moisture content in excess of 30 per cent of the timber weight. There are however extremes, and it is known that in some trees moisture adds 200 per cent to the weight of the wood fibre. We need to get the moisture content to below 15 per cent if we are to contain the possibility of significant drying movement and splitting.

Good air drying can only take the moisture down to equate with the normal humidity level of the area, and then only

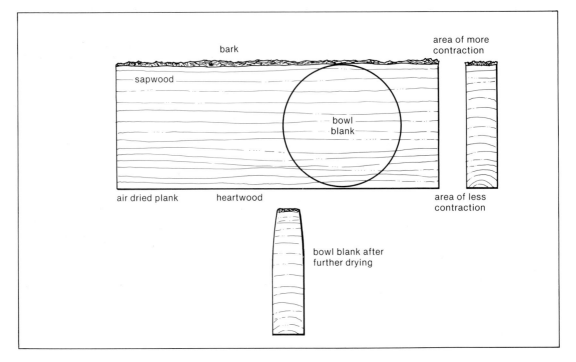

Movement in blanks after drying.

for relatively thin planks. In temperate countries this is likely to be about 17 per cent in the drier summer months, and 23 per cent in the autumn and winter.

Unfortunately up to 15 per cent is only good enough for garden furniture. If the finished piece is going into a room where there is regular, intermittent heating, you have to aim for a 12 per cent moisture content. For continuously heated environments this needs to be dropped by another 1½ per cent, while if the bowl is to be placed near a radiator or on a mantlepiece the target is 9 per cent moisture.

Pine, spruce, elm and sycamore are some of the better driers, then comes birch, followed by beech, cherry, apple and then the other fruit-woods. Oak tops the scale of drying difficulty amongst Britain's timbers.

I know less about seasoning tropical hardwoods, other than that they are said to be 'very difficult'. If I buy it at all I therefore just take a breath and buy kiln-dried. Sometimes I have bought part dried and have generally regretted it. One of the worst woods I know is olive – the sap is oily and it takes forever to dry.

The implication of all this is that we can rarely air dry timber in this country to a really safe level for turning and we may be forced to consider kiln drying.

Some professional turners now have their own small kilns. They are not difficult to make – components and designs can be found in the woodworking press.

One of the most satisfactory types of small quantity kilns is based upon the de-humidifying process. These develop a drying gradient that takes the moisture away very slowly, thus greatly reducing the amount of checking and wastage. Basically a dehumidifier kiln is an insulated box fitted with a low-level heater, air circulation system, and dehumidifier. The box may be as small as

150

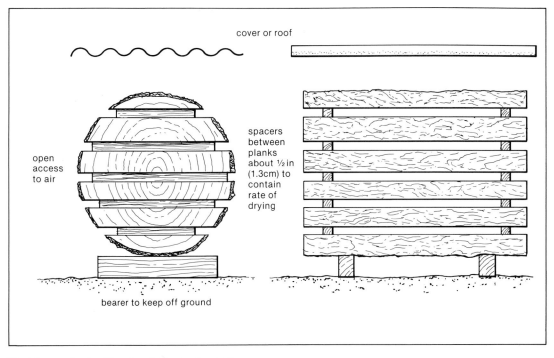

Stacking a planked log to allow air circulation.

a couple of tea chests, could be a small shed, or even the discarded body of a refrigeration lorry. Kilns are not expensive to build and the necessary equipment can be purchased for as little as £500 (1989). The running costs are minimal.

Obviously the savings in time can be enormous, but kilning can still take a while. Taking a 3in (7.5cm)-thick plank of oak from 50 per cent down to 10 per cent moisture requires something like 160 days in the kiln. There are some who say that you can never dry out the middle of planks of over 3in (7.5cm) thick. Even an already seasoned, air dried plank of these dimensions is likely to be at over 25% and will take about forty days in the kiln to get down to the required 10%.

Much depends upon the quantity of through-put. The hobbyist, turning only one or two pieces a week, could not justify the outlay on even the smallest of kilns. A local group of turners, however, might

consider a co-operative venture, and this is something being considered by some local chapters of the Association of Woodturners of Great Britain. I have now reached the stage where I am about to build a kiln of my own. It will be 8 × 6 × 4ft (2.5 × 1.8 × 1.2m) and will use a dehumidifier drier. The walls will be exterior ply with a sandwich of thick polystyrene.

Microwave Drying

There are other ways of dealing with the moisture problem. The first is to turn wet and just to accept the wobbly results (and a measurable proportion of totally split rejects). The second is to turn wet, and thin, and then dry in some way – possibly a microwave cooker.

Microwave drying is an interesting process. In essence the waves heat the material uniformly throughout, but as

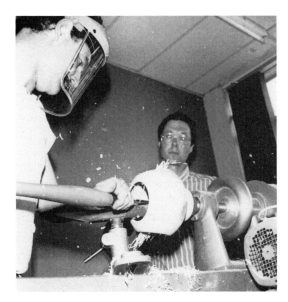

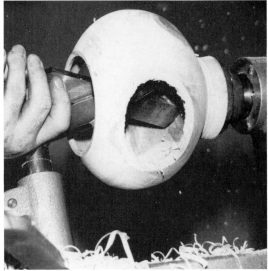

Liam O'Neill demonstrating hollowing out on a sphere. The wood is very green and the task has to be completed at one go. If left for more than a few minutes sufficient drying movement will occur for completion to be impossible.

Flashlight 'stops' the bowl to show a domed scraper being used to clean up the interior. Note the tool rest is angled into the sphere and the blade is tilted downwards.

wood is a good insulator, the heat generated in the middle is retained so that the temperature in the middle of the wood builds up to a much higher level than that at the surface. This means that the moisture is driven outwards and drying spreads from the inside out. In air drying, the surface is the first thing to dry and we get the differential contraction problem and surface checking. In the microwave the surface is the last thing to dry so the surface splitting problem is overcome.

There is, however, another side to this. If the heating is too great then the water in the middle of the wood is turned to steam, expands rapidly and the wood can split under the steam pressure.

The secret of microwave drying is careful control. The actual time in the oven will depend upon the overall size of the piece and only to a lesser extent upon the thickness. As a basis for experiment with thin wall bowls, try four minutes at full power. This should raise the internal temperature to the desired level, which appears to be about 80 degrees centigrade (180 degrees Fahrenheit). Once the piece has reached this temperature remove it from the oven and stand it to cool. It is at this stage that the moisture, heated from inside and driven out towards the surface, evaporates off. Then put the object back for another heating and cooling cycle. This is repeated until the object appears to be dry enough.

You can be a little more scientific and use a moisture meter – these cost between £60 and £150 (1989). Alternatively, a sample of the wood can be weighed as cut and then given a thorough drying for some hours in a conventional oven before weighing again. The weight loss will give an idea of the original moisture content. You can now weigh the workpiece before you start to microwave, calculate what the finished weight would be when the desired moisture level has been reached, and then go through the processing cycles until this weight has in fact been reached.

It has to be mentioned that one school of 'microwave driers' recommends the use of the 'defrost' setting for repeated longer periods rather than the short, sharp full power route.

There is a problem with the microwave approach. Differential contraction will still occur during drying; there is no way of modifying the different densities of heart and sapwood! There is also a stage in the microwaving process when the wood becomes semi-plastic. It can be deformed by hand into distinctly oval shapes. Microwave-dried pieces are often not perfectly symmetrical and sometimes the distortion is deliberately induced by squeezing the walls while in the semi-plastic state.

Rough Turning

The method that many turners use for coping with wet or part-dried woods is what is known as rough turning. Here the blank is mounted on the lathe and turned inside and out until it is an even thickness all round, 1in (2.5cm) thick for a bowl of up to 10in (25.5cm) in diameter. As a guide the wall thickness of a rough turned bowl should be at least 10 per cent and up to 15 per cent of the overall diameter. Hence an 18in (45.5cm) blank would be rough turned to a wall thickness of 2in (5cm). You may get away with thinner walls, but once in a while you will find that the piece has so deformed in drying that you can no longer get a round out of it when remounted on the lathe. It was when I encountered a substantial batch of deviant blanks that I started to hand-carve and hand-finish some bowls!

When rough turning the inside, the piece should be face plate, face plate ring, or glue chuck mounted. Dovetail recesses should be avoided as in the subsequent drying these will certainly lose shape and become unusable.

Once part-turned in this way the piece is put on a shelf for six months to allow to air dry. Again, stack it to allow circulation of air and avoid excessive heat. What can be useful is to leave it in a dry shed for three months then bring it in to a cooler part of the house for a month or two before finally taking it into a centrally heated room for a couple of months.

Actually I have developed an alternative which gives me a tolerable level of waste. Production rate increases throughout the year and builds to a peak in the rush pre-Christmas. Starting on Boxing Day I cut up the year's timber into blanks. These are then stacked in a large greenhouse which at this time of the year is empty and dry. The blanks are left there as I work through the stack rough turning them as time permits. The rough turnings go back into the greenhouse until seed sowing (late March) by which time the moisture content has reduced considerably. It is then on to racks in a dry shed or the standby shelves in the workshop. Small blanks I start turning by April and the larger ones by the summer. Splitting to the point of being useless is down to about one blank in fifteen to twenty. Last winter, though, the two that did split were the biggest – two 30in (75cm)-diameter pieces of heavily burred elm, split from centre right out to rim. It was a day for tears!

Bag Drying

If dealing only in small quantities, the initial drying process can be accelerated in a way that seems to avoid all checking problems. The blank is cut and is rough turned. It is then stored in a sealed plastic bag and the bag put into a warm place. Try the airing cupboard.

In the bag the timber sweats. Each day you take the wood out and turn the bag inside-out. Put the wood back and reseal. Yesterday's exuded moisture now evaporates from the outside of the bag, while sweating continues inside. When there is no more moisture build-up on the inside of the bag the wood is getting somewhere near dry enough.

Peg Drying

PEG is short for polyethylene glycol, a water-soluble, inert, wax-like substance. It is non-flammable (the flash point is 304°C/579°F), evaporates only slowly (over generations) so does not give off fumes, and is non-toxic. It is used in such a way that the wax fills all the pores in the wood, the moisture dries off but the sap canals in the wood cannot contract because of the wax stuffing.

It is the treatment that has been used to preserve salvaged Viking long boats, the body of the Cheshire Bog Man and, of course, the timbers of the *Mary Rose*. It is not, however, suitable for use on all woods, particularly the more dense hardwoods; and it can only be used effectively when the wood is green.

PEG is bought in slabs and has to be dissolved in water (a process greatly speeded by the use of heat) to make a solution of either 30 or 50 per cent. The strength is quite important and the best way of ensuring accuracy is to use a hydrometer to test the gravity of the solution. A long-scale beer making hydrometer can be used. A 30 per cent solution has a gravity of 1.05 at 16 degrees Centigrade (61 degrees Fahrenheit) while the 50 per cent solution is 1.093 gravity at this temperature.

The wood to be treated is immersed in the solution. The PEG permeates through the timber, replacing the sap by osmosis. Ultimately the wood can take up 25 to 30 per cent of its own weight of the wax. Naturally it takes time for full permeation to occur. A 2 to 3in (5 to 7.5cm)-thick, 9in (23cm)-diameter blank of walnut requires about two months soaking in a 30 per cent solution at normal room temperature or about one month in a 50 per cent solution. The absorption process can be greatly speeded up if the bath is kept heated, and again rough turning before immersion both speeds up the process and reduces the wastage of PEG wax. There appears to be no reason why a turn-finished thin wall piece should not be immersed to prevent any subsequent movement. Once soaking is complete the wood is put to dry.

The strength of the PEG solution is checked after each use and is made up to the right gravity ready for the next piece. The drying process can also be accelerated by heating but at normal room temperature a blank will take about six weeks. It can then be turned in the normal way right out to a full finish.

There is, however, a problem with finishing. The waxyness of the PEG does tend to clog the grit of sandpaper, and the surface does not take many of the popular finishes. I am afraid that the dreaded polyurethane is one of the most satisfactory; however, the dull waxyness of the untreated PEG surface is not unattractive. Of course, PEG is not a cheap approach, and to maintain a good level of throughput you may need several vats.

The bulk of Ed Moulthrop's big bowls are made from tulip wood, which he keeps until it is spalted. It is then rough turned and immersed in PEG vats. (Remember that some of Ed's bowls are 5ft (1.5m) tall and 2ft (0.6m) in diameter.) He has a 'tank farm' in the woods at the back of his workshop, containing something like three dozen tanks. Few would aspire to this size of work or levels of production.

So we can use wood in any condition. We can also use almost any kind of wood. Broadly, the denser the wood the cleaner it will turn and finish. Also, the more even the grain the easier it is to work. Some of the worst woods are the low density, long fibre grain woods such as poplar and willow. Larch is poor, as it splinters.

Some woods are a joy to work because they give off a perfume when being cut. Fruit-woods are nice, the rosewoods have that smell of damask roses, and who can resist the smell of cedar wood? Olive fills the workshop with an olive oil odour. Some are not so pleasant. Hydeua is bad and *Zebrano*, or zebra wood, smells like the floor of a zebra's stable – or worse.

There are woods whose dust is dangerous, ranging from being carcinogenic to merely irritant. Padauk gives some people a rash. There are woods which are toxic. Laburnum makes highly decorative pieces, but it should never be used for salad bowls – or for anything that might ever contain foodstuffs. Never allow small objects, particularly wooden eggs in laburnum, to go into a house where there are young children (who tend to put things into their mouths).

FIGURING PATTERNS

There are parts of the tree, or certain conditions of the tree, which make some woods more attractive than others. Branch wood is younger, will contract more on drying and is therefore more prone to split, but the crotchwood from the trunk where the even grain pattern is disturbed by the grain of a branch is usually beautifully figured. Crotch pieces should be cut so that the pith of both the main trunk and the branch are avoided, otherwise a split is inevitable.

Burrs, or as the Americans call them Burls, are my favourite. These are the wart-like growth that occur on the side of some trees. They were most common on elms, occur extensively on oak, may be found on plane, birch, black poplar and many more. They are caused when the tree reacts to some parasitic or other irritant. This stimulated extra growth which in turn resulted in blind branches. From the outside the surface looks like a relief model of a mountain range; inside, the straight grain has been replaced by a myriad of tiny whirls and circles. Cut along, the root of the 'blind' branch makes a long dark pattern not unlike a Medular ray.

The burr represents an area of great stress, but because it has no clear grain pattern it is often more stable in the green state than is clean timber. Some burrs do have small checks and defects, but these rarely open out, and they can in themselves add character to the timber. Unfortunately, oak burr has considerable and variable contraction on drying, and can check badly. Birch and acacia, woods which do not themselves have the greatest character, can provide burrs of some interest.

155

Stumpwood can be particularly lovely, again offering swirling and contorted figuring and a variety of colorations. The stumpwood of the redwood is sold as thuya burr and is one of the loveliest of all with a range of rich browns and blacks. Some of the most beautifully figured walnut burrs come from the stumpwood.

Very many people believe that rose-wood comes from large garden roses. Some think it is from the rose's root bowl. They do not realise that it comprises a whole genre of tropical trees.

Spaltered Wood

Another of my favourites is spaltered (or spalted, or splated) wood. This occurs naturally, but it may be stimulated artificially. It is caused by a fungus growth that gets into the wood. This can attack the living tree and is commonest in beech. As the fungus moves through the timber it kills it off. It leaves zones of colour and sometimes areas of white. Veining through are black lines which form no particular pattern, nor follow any feature or weakness in the timber's structure. In sycamore spalting sometimes produces little grey rings, while at other times it creates areas of yellow and of a pale purple. Tulip wood spalts nicely, giving purple and brown markings in what is otherwise a light cream wood.

A university team in Norway is current-ly studying spalting and has identified twenty-four different fungi that cause various effects. It seems that the spores are widely distributed and that the growth can be stimulated almost spontan-eously under ideal conditions. However, you can make sure by placing a piece of diseased wood in with the wood to be spaltered to infect it.

To generate spalting, the log has to be kept wet and at a reasonable temperature. A beech log wrapped in plastic, fed with water every so often and kept at 20 degrees centigrade (70 degrees Fahrenheit) will spalt very quickly. The research team claim complete penetration of a sizeable log within eighteen months.

As we said, however, spalting kills off the timber, and ultimately the tree; and dead wood rots. Hence those parts that spalt first will rot first and patches of soft rot are likely to be found adjacent to areas of usable spalt. Once affected, the timber loses its strength. The furniture industry uses a lot of beech for furniture carcasses, and in High Wycombe, the centre of the furniture trade, they call spalted beech 'doubty timber'.

The spalting stops when the timber is dry, but the spores remain and will regenerate if the wood is again wetted. It may be advisable to give spalted wood a dose of microwaving to try to dry off the spores before the bowl you make starts generating fungus on the client's dining room table! Perhaps the next piece of research should be on how to kill off spalting once it is there! There is currently some concern about the effect of breath-ing dust of spalted woods and getting the fungi down into the lungs.

Fiddleback

Another figuring pattern favoured by wood turners is known as 'fiddleback'. Here there are rays of a lighter colour that run across the wood, usually at right-angles to the main grain pattern. This is called fiddleback because it is a pattern widely used on the backs of better quality violins. It would appear to occur most frequently in ash, but can be found in most other woods. It is not normally seen in beech, but does sometimes become apparent when there are certain types of spalt which then emphasise it.

Fiddleback creates beautiful effects. Some ash I had was part olive-colour and overall fiddleback. It had the appearance of a fine-woven tartan. One plank of figured sycamore had the fiddleback lights, but these were diffuse and gave the whole the appearance of watered silk. Three dishes made from this plank have been hung on clients' walls as pure decoration.

What causes the fiddleback effect, nobody knows. One suggestion is that it is found where a tree growing in open parkland has developed in girth rather than height. Because the tree is in the open it is more subject to the wind, hence the rays are flex stress marks. Another suggestion is that it is compression stressing in larger trees. In fact it does represent a fundamental disturbance of the grain, as can be seen on the face of a sawn plank, but it does not affect the structural strength of the timber.

CUTTING A TREE

Finally, while we are discussing timber we need to address the question of how to cut up a tree.

There is no doubt that the most economical way is to have it planked into a number of planks of various thicknesses. It can then be stored by stacking the planks on top of each other, virtually reassembling the trunk, but putting small spacers between each plank to allow the circulation of air. This is known in the trade as cutting and sticking.

One of the thicker slabs should be that at the centre where you want to make sure that you have picked up most of the pith. Remember that this plank will ultimately split down the middle, but it may still give you two half-width, good planks.

You may also wish to have the outermost planks left fairly thick in case you want to do any natural edged work.

People who have portable chain-saw mills will come and plank a butt on site, but normally it is a case of doing a deal with a saw mill which will pick up the butt, take it to the mill and plank it for you. With smaller trees you will probably wish to cut it up on site into blocks and slabs with a chain-saw. Again the same basic principle applies. Cut out the heart wood.

In all cases the sooner you can reduce the tree down to planks or usable blocks, the better. It will start drying out and you are less likely to have unwelcome splits in particularly nice areas.

Once it becomes known that you are a wood turner, people will start offering you wood. Usually the tree has been felled and cut up into rings – often as little as 9in (23cm) thick. Sorry, but they are generally useless! If you have the chance, get them to leave the wood in long lengths, then get to it as quickly as possible. Make sure that the bark is left on and seal all ends and open surfaces with emulsified wax. The ends of smaller pieces can be dipped into molten paraffin wax. You should also wax the edges of cut blanks if you are going to store them.

A fall-back emergency treatment can be given with PVA emulsion – the poly-vinyl acetate glues that are available in large tins at most DIY stores. Once you have it all ends sealed, you can start thinking about cutting and moving it. You do at least have time to breathe before radial checking sets in.

12 Buying Wood

However diligent we are in our woodland searches, or lucky as we might be in being given wood, most of us still have to buy some materials from timber suppliers. The most frequent question that I am asked at craft fairs is, 'Where do you manage to find your wood?' – as if it just grew on trees!

TIMBER MERCHANTS

In order to get the quantities and quality of burr elm that I require, I now have to buy whole logs from timber merchants, who know my special requirements. The last two butts came from over 200 miles away.

I still buy single planks – either for a special purpose to meet a particular order, or because a particularly nice piece of figured wood is offered. I have (not without protest) had to buy the odd pre-cut blank or block when a client has asked for a particular type of wood.

What is fascinating is the trading that goes on between merchants. One small plank of plum that I bought off a stand at a woodworkers' show I later traced back through three merchants who had sold it to one, then to the other. It may be this multiple layer trading that accounts for the high prices now asked for wood.

There are also enormous variations in the prices charged by different merchants, and making a direct comparison is often made more difficult by the fact that each has their own way of expressing quantities and price. Some work on a price per square foot for planks of different thicknesses; others per cubic foot or metre regardless of thickness; and some on the weight in kilograms. Then, on top of that, we have the additional complication of moisture content. A considerable amount of the weight can be moisture. It can account for anything between 5 and 50 per cent of the bought weight.

Sometimes we are given a measured moisture content. More normally the timber is offered as 'kiln dried', 'part seasoned', 'air dried' or 'as sawn'.

Kiln Dried

Kiln dried is rarely available in thicker sections, and 4in (10cm) is the absolute maximum. If dried and then sealed (in a totally enclosing polythene skin) we can expect the moisture content to be about 12 per cent. However, kiln dried timber left in normal atmospheric conditions soon absorbs moisture from the air's humidity. In the wet months of the year the moisture content can climb back to over 20 per cent. For every 1 per cent increase in moisture over the basic 12 per cent we have to add 0.5 per cent to the weight for a given volume.

Air Dried

Air dried timber in thin section could be as low as 15 to 18 per cent moisture in the drier months, but it is more likely to be over the 20 per cent mark. The length of time that the wood was drying could be significant, but if dealing with thicker timbers (4in/10cm thick-plus) we could still expect over 30 per cent moisture in the centre.

Part Seasoned

Part seasoned has little meaning. To some timber yards it means as little as a month or two in stick. Other yards use the phrase to cover several months seasoning. The term is often applied to exotic woods, many of which are notoriously difficult to dry. In the case of olive I have known part seasoned to give well over 40 per cent moisture.

As Sawn

As sawn means only one thing – wet! Moisture will almost certainly be thrown out as you turn it. So you must calculate again for at least 35 per cent, and if the tree was felled and planked in the early summer you are likely to be in the 70 per cent-plus zone.

PRICING

To help you work through this jungle, I have devised some tables, which can be found with explanatory notes in the Appendix (page 186). These will assist you in the calculation of the amounts of timber you will require for a given job. It is worth mentioning that when you are pricing a turning job, a very crude rule of thumb is to set the selling price figure at a minimum of four times the price you paid for the wood itself.

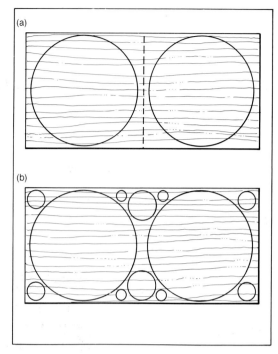

Cutting blanks from squares. (a) The blank has been cut from a square. 10 per cent wastage is allowed for saw cuts. (b) Cleaver cutting may give you the main blanks, some small bowl blanks, egg cups, and light pulls. The 'smalls' are profit.

If producing any quantity of work it certainly pays to buy the timber in quantity. A group of hobby turners should look closely at the idea of buying planks and sharing out the cost. The cheapest way to buy is undoubtedly to purchase whole logs and have them sawn to your specification and delivered to you. Wood bought in the plank and collected may cost double that which is cut and delivered if you buy it as a log – but you will have a lot of wastage.

If you do start to think on this scale you will need to know about another measure. Logs are usually sold on the basis of Hoppus measure. The Hoppus measure is the cubic footage volume based upon multiplying the length of the log by the quarter girth at the mid-point.

159

13 Choosing a Lathe

You should by now be familiar with at least one lathe. I emphasised at the beginning that you should do a little turning and get some idea of what sort of turning you want to do before you ever contemplate buying a lathe of your own. However, there will be some who will have picked up this book and turned straight to this chapter, so let's start by looking at what a lathe is.

Basically a lathe is a machine for rotating a piece of wood. It needs to be big enough to turn the largest pieces you want to turn. It needs to be strong enough to take the shocks of the roughest job that you are likely to want to do. It needs to be powerful enough to work under load. And it needs to be solid enough to do all this without whip or vibration.

It could be added that it needs to do it properly – and at the correct speed; and to be user-friendly – i.e. not have a heap of inconveniences, all of which points have to be borne in mind.

The basics are, first, the means of power. Today almost all lathes have an integral electric motor. A few turners do still use treadle lathes or rustic, pole lathes. One friend has a home-made machine driven off a half bicycle – he says it keeps him fit! As far as I can see all it does is generate a prodigous thirst. Secondly we need a headstock which holds the spindle, on to which is mounted the chuck. The wood is driven via the headstock, therefore this end of the lathe needs to have the greatest strength.

Some lathes consist only of a headstock unit. They are designed for the exclusive production of bowls. The tool rest for these may be on a massive, free-standing tripod, or be cantilevered off the headstock casting; but there is no bed or tailstock.

The more conventional lathes will have a bed. This has two functions. It supports the headstock and at the other end the tailstock which in turn steadies the outboard end of the workpiece. The bed also supports the tool carriage, into which is mounted the tool post, on top of which is the tool rest. The rest has to be strong and rigid as we need to provide a firm and steady base so that we can control the tools whilst absorbing the shocks and pressures of the turning wood.

SPEED

There needs to be a system for varying the speed at which the motor turns the spindle. The drive between the motor and the spindle is usually through a belt. Today this will be a vee-belt although on the older lathes (as with my 1951 Wadkin) it will be a flat, multi-ply, canvas or leather belt.

By having a stack of different-sized pulleys on the motor shaft and a similar but reverse stack on the lathe spindle, and by moving the belt from one pair to another, the speed of spindle rotation can be varied.

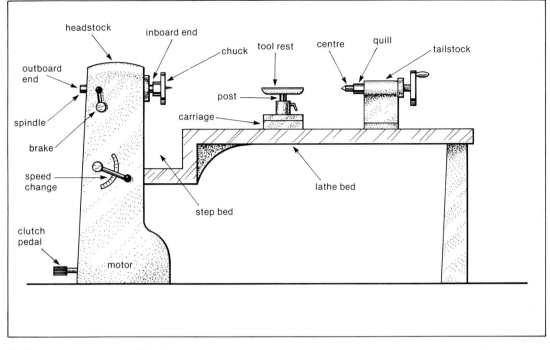

The basic arrangement of a lathe.

Three speeds is the minimum you are likely to encounter, and under no circumstance consider anything less. Five speed arrangements are common and some lathes offer more; a few even have a continuously variable speed drive.

The better lathes have external levers and a clutch or belt tensioning arrangement so that speeds can be changed without stopping. Most hobbyist machines have to be stopped, a door on the headstock opened and the drive belt lifted from one pulley to the next. The higher quality hand-change lathes have electrical interlocks so that the motor is automatically switched off the moment the trap door is opened. Certainly, external change systems which can be operated while the lathe is running are the most convenient, and those with infinitely variable speed drives are very nice. However, money is better spent on other features before investing in lathes with sophisticated speed changing mechanisms.

SPINDLE

When considering the loads put on to a lathe spindle it is clear that the spindle needs to be strong, replaceable, and be running in good, low friction bearings. Double-caged roller bearings are a feature of good lathes, plain metal bush bearings are a feature of the cheaper and some older models. Plain bearings do wear out and this is a problem as it is essential that the spindle not only runs free but also runs true with no trace of play or vibration.

It is useful to know if the spindle bearings are of a standard pattern that can be picked up at any bearing supplier's. Having to obtain replacements from the lathe manufacturer can be time consuming and expensive, and with some older models quite impossible.

HEADSTOCK

To give the rigidity to hold the spindle firmly, the headstock casing needs to be massive, heavy and thick, and of cast iron or machined cast steel construction. Fabricated (welded steel plate) or cast alloy headstocks are rarely adequate and are best avoided.

LATHE BED

The solidity of the whole lathe will depend first upon the overall weight, and the·construction of the support legs and then, and even more importantly, upon the lathe bed.

Many currently available cheap lathes have flimsy beds – sometimes made of alloy, sometimes of a single narrow-gauge steel tube. Avoid them like the plague! Light-gauge twin tubes are useless. There are, however, some lathes with single rail beds that are quite solid and are wholly satisfactory; no one could ever fault the Myford for rigidity.

Solid cast steel beds are the best, with steel girders second. They are very heavy and difficult to transport or move, but that helps to keep the lathe on the ground when turning out-of-balance pieces. Most important of all, a good, solid bed will ensure that the headstock, tailstock and tool rest are clamped as one and can not vibrate or move independently.

Many modern lathes have twin bed rails – some of girder construction, others of heavy gauge steel tube. Either can be very good if made sufficiently substantial.

Some do present a minor problem when the rails are widely spaced, as with these you are more likely to catch the tool handle while making a swinging, scooping cut on the inside of a bowl.

Good clearance under the bed is very useful, and here some of the modern high-mounted twin tube lathes really score. You have to work for a very long time before the build-up of swarf actually reaches the cutting area.

The tailstock is moved along the bed according to the length of work. It needs to match the robustness of the headstock, but it also has to be easy and convenient to move and to clamp. It is normal for the clamp to have a lever handle for tightening – a nut and bolt necessitating the use of spanners is a real pain as frequent movement or adjustment is required. Lathes where the levers are hidden in deep recesses are also aggravating.

TAILSTOCK

The simplest lathes have a fixed tailstock quill and centre. This means that the whole tailstock has to be repositioned each time you wish to take a firmer grip – something that you have to do frequently with a fixed centre.

A good lathe has a tailstock with a quill that can be moved in and out by turning a hand wheel on the tail. There will also be a clamp for locking the quill in a fixed position. The moving quill means that you can adjust up the tailstock point without moving the whole stock. This way you can easily retighten on the workpiece if it starts to become loose. This may occur frequently when turning between centres using a prong drive at the headstock end.

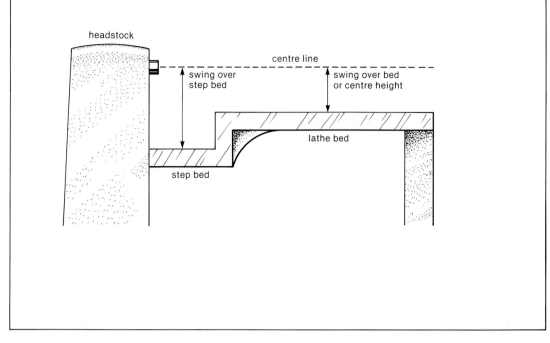

Lathe bed clearance. Warning — most manufacturers express 'swing over bed' as the height of the centre line above the bed, hence an 8in (20.5cm) swing could take a 15¾in (40cm) diameter round blank. A few, however, give the 'swing over bed' as the maximum turntable diameter, hence they show 15¾in (40cm) instead of the more correct 8in (20.5cm). You may then expect 30in (75cm) capacity.

A simple test which many new modern lathes fail is a check to see that the headstock and tailstock line up. Put either a point or a screw chuck in the headstock, and a point centre in the tail stock. Run the tail up to the head. Both points should meet *exactly*. If they do not, and many of today's lathes bought off the shelf do not, you may have to machine the base of the tailstock to get a perfect match. The best thing is not to accept any lathe that does not pass this test — let the manufacturers sort out their own quality problems!

The second main function of a moving quill is for drilling holes with a drill chuck mounted on the tailstock. This is an essential facility for getting holes central and vertical, as in candlesticks.

Obviously to be able to drill a reasonable depth you need a quill with a decent

Speed change lever on the Wadkin. A foot-operated clutch pedal lifts the motor table to take tension off the belts while changing gear.

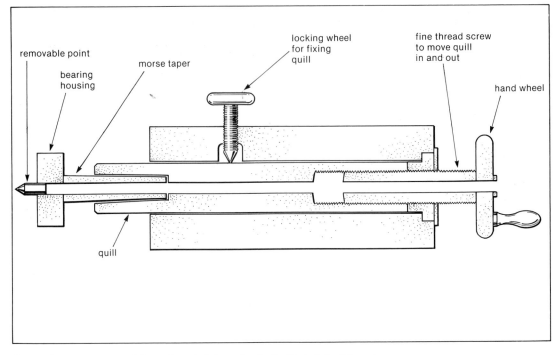

General arrangement of the tailstock (plan view). Quill, tailstock bearing, adjusting screw and hand wheel are all hollow to allow the feeding-through of a long hole-boring auger. The quill and thread need occasional lubrication.

amount of movement. Something like three inches should be regarded as being a minimum. When drilling deeper holes, as in bud vases, you can expect to have to move the tailstock up at least once.

Earlier I talked of the importance of having a 'live tailstock' – one in which the centre point revolves in its own bearings. On many lathes the centre point can be removed, in some cases with the bearing and in others without. This feature is usually coupled with a hollow quill. Such an arrangement means that a long hole-boring tool can be fed through the stock and down into the workpiece. This is used for drilling cableways through items such as standard lamp columns.

MORSE TAPER

There is a facility that I believe to be essential on all lathes, and there are many which do not offer it including several in the middle price range. This is what is known as a morse taper. Better lathes offer a morse taper facility on both headstock spindle and tailstock quill.

The morse taper is in fact a hollow centre which is drilled to precise dimensions with a fine taper to the walls of the hole. The taper is given a number according to its size. Number 1MT is the smallest, and 2MT or 3MT are commonplace and are ideal for lathe use. Accessories with a morse taper shaft are push-fitted into the hole and by friction alone will turn a considerable load.

Amongst the many accessories available with morse taper shafts are Jacobs

164

The Multico lathe on a working day! The bed consists of two very strong steel tubes and is very rigid. There is plenty of clearance to prevent swarf build up. The tool rest is substantial and the head and tail stocks are solid. The lathe suffers from a very light spindle, has morse taper (No. 3) on the tailstock only, and a totally inadequate screw chuck.

chucks (for drill bits), live tailstock centres with built-in bearings, a range of cup chucks, lace bobbin blank chucks, two- and four-pronged drive centres, machine drills and taps, and so on. The value of the morse taper is that fittings can be interchanged quickly and many are available as a standard (non-proprietary) component and do not have to be bought from any one lathe manufacturer. In fact many old morse taper bits can be picked up from scrap boxes on market stalls.

Some lathes offer morse tapers on the tailstock only – these are better than nothing; but to me a taper at both ends is an essential, on at least one of my lathes.

TOOL REST

Now we come to the last of the basic fitments – the tool rest, both the carriage and the rest itself. In two years I broke five carriages on my Elu lathe. They were made of a zinc alloy casting and were just not robust enough to match the lathe's apparent capacity and the type of work that I wanted to do. Strength and rigidity are essential. Even if you are not constantly turning huge blanks of difficult burrs, you will have dig-ins, or the tip of the rest will catch one of the jaws of a rotating jaw chuck. Tool rests do get banged, and they must be capable of withstanding such normal exigencies of day to day work.

CARRIAGE BODY

The carriage body must be of steel or cast iron. It must be inflexible! I have not yet seen one in any other material that I would consider to be satisfactory.

Obviously, the carriage also has to be easy to move and to adjust.

The post of the rest needs to be of substantial diameter, and this is especially so if you wish to use longer rests such as the curved bowl rests. A diameter of ¾in (0.4cm) is probably the minimum acceptable. The rest also needs to give a reasonable height – those available on some lathes will not rise above centre height and this makes skew planing difficult, and deep-wall interior scraping impossible.

We each have our own preference for rest profiles – I like my rests to have a sloping face, not be too wide, have a nice, rounded top lip, and be deep and thick enough to be strong. I also like a curved rest for getting down the inside walls of bowls. Some curved rests have broad, flat tops – these are ideal for scraping but present difficulties for gouge work. In other words, you will probably end up with two or more rests!

Should the working lip of the rest get damaged, and nicks do occur, then they should be cleaned with a file. It is essential that the top should be smooth so that you can slide the tool from side to side along the rest without snagging.

SPEED RANGE

A very important consideration in anybody's choice must be the speed range offered by the lathe. A lot of work done on short length, small diameter spindles really does require a top speed in the order of 2,500–3,000 r.p.m. but I see little point in going any higher than this. I find that many turners seem to be more interested in the high speed end of the range than the low when making a choice

of lathe; this is probably the opposite to what they should be thinking about!

A good slow speed range is very important, and the 700–800 r.p.m. minimum offered by many lathes is not slow enough for even moderately large diameter work. If really large bowls take your fancy then you are going to need speeds down to 200–400 r.p.m.

The ideal range would be something like 200–3,000 in about ten steps (or an infinitely variable arrangement between these two extremes).

BED LENGTH

Bed length will again be conditioned by your work focus. The 1,000mm of many modern continental lathes is quite useful. Some British machines go a bit longer (usually 48in/122cm). Lathes with longer beds than that tend to take up a lot of the workshop space for only very occasional use. If you want to make long standard lamps or four-poster beds, then you can always make the items from jointed sections!

Some turners never want length – they may even only ever turn bowls. Here the bowl turning heads or short bed lathes are ideal.

SWING/CLEARANCE

To me, swing over the bed (the height of the centre axis above the bed) is a critical factor. Anything less than 8in (20.5cm) cannot be considered even as a stand-by. On the older girder bed lathes there was often a bed section that could be removed at the headstock end. This was called a step bed and was designed to permit the turning of bigger diameter face plate mounted blanks. With the step removed on one of my lathes I can swing a 34in (86.5cm)-diameter piece.

On some lathes the headstock spindle projects out at both ends of the stock. The outboard end has a reverse thread so that even bigger face plates can be used with a free-standing heavy tool rest. Theoretically I could swing an 84in (215cm) bowl – if I did not have a wall or roof to the workshop! I heard recently of one turning shop that has a pit in the floor off the outboard end of the headstock. they can swing a 10ft (3m) diameter disc.

If you do wish to consider working off the outboard end, remember that the direction of rotation will be the reverse of what you are used to, and you will have to re-kit with reverse-handed scrapers and skews.

Some medium-priced lathes are made so that the headstock can be swung round through 90 degrees on the bed giving an 'off the front' turning capability. Again this facilitates the turning of larger diameters. It is fine for occasional use but it is so dependent upon the quality of the tool rest, and those offered by some manufacturers are sometimes relatively flimsy cantilevers which do flex. There is also the hassle of repositioning the head backward and forward. I really do like to do my big turning over the bed with a solid, bed supported, tool rest.

A word of warning. You may fancy the idea of turning larger bowls and be attracted to lathes with 8in (20.5cm) clearance (or more). Some of those available are fine – some, however, are not substantial enough for the loading that big work presents, particularly at the roughing stage. The Multico and clones are solid enough for the capacity offered,

Cleaning the top of the tool rest with a file. Ordinary mild steel (seen here) is not the best material as it marks too easily.

and on one of these machines I have, so far, touch wood, only bent rather than broken a tool rest.

FITTINGS

From here the choice of lathe is going to be governed by the fittings that you require, and that are available. It is worth looking at the cost and quality of those fittings and whether or not non-proprietary equivalents can be purchased. Some lathe manufacturers offer £30 to £40, 3 and 4 jaw chucks of their own that I would not look at, but as good chucks can be bought to fit any lathe from some tool suppliers then it does not matter. Centre or long work steadys are essential in long spindle work and these may only be available from the lathe supplier. Tyme, Myford and Coronet offer an extremely good range of fittings for their lathes and particularly in the case of Tyme and prices are very reasonable.

Items such as morse taper fittings, combination chucks and special rests are again available for most makes of lathe, from suppliers such as Axminster Power

Tool, John Boddy, and Craft Supplies; so you are not necessarily tied to those made by the lathe manufacturer.

Very few turners are interested in copy turning, but if your problem is turning large numbers of identical legs or spindles then a copying device will save much heartache. This greatly restricts the choice of lathe because very few offer anything at all, and some of those that are available are not particularly effective. I am reasonably happy with the one on the Multico, and it was really for the copier that I bought this particular lathe.

The basic principle of most copy devices is that they use a small cutting tool fixed to a spring-loaded carriage. This in turn is fixed to a finger which traces the outline from a pre-cut template pattern. The carriage is power driven on the larger machines and hand wheel moved on the smaller.

WEIGHT

One thing should have emerged through these notes is that weight is all-important. It usually denotes strength and it certainly does something to guarantee stability. In fact I would say that unless you intend to transport your lathe to give demonstrations (and that really is a fool's game!) then go for a machine that is as heavy as your floor will stand. There seems to be greater stability with a heavy lathe freestanding than there ever is with a lighter unit, however well bolted to the floor.

FREE-STANDING LATHES

Some lathes are complete and are freestanding. Others have bases as an optional extra. Many of the proprietary bases and stands are satisfactory. If, however, you do decide to make your own there are three points to take into account. First there should be a means of bolting the lathe to the stand. G-cramps are not adequate because they can shake loose just at the critical moment. Second, the stand should be heavy and rigid. Third, you should be able to bolt the stand to the floor if your lathe weighs anything less than 300lbs (136kg)!

Again, of course, it depends upon the type of turning that you are going to do. If your interest is in lace bobbins then you could probably make a suitable lathe for about £50 and use it unsecured on the kitchen table.

At the end of the day there are going to have to be compromises. The ideal lathe has never been made. I get closer to my ideal by looking at scrap machinery sales – old long bed metal work lathes sold off for £25! Second-hand lathes may be the way you can get what you want at a price you can afford, although I have seen DIY equipment sold at auction for more than its undiscounted retail price.

There are, then, a number of basic factors to take into account when choosing a lathe. You cannot just go to an expert and ask, 'What lathe would you recommend?' If they tell you, then they are not an expert! The two lathes that I have suit me very well and I could therefore recommend them to anyone. They would, however, be totally unsuitable for 95 per cent of other turners. The true expert knows that each turner will have specific requirements within a framework of basic factors. In the end your choice should depend entirely upon the type of work that you want to do, the particular facilities that *you* find essential, what is available to suit that type of work; and, of course, the depth of your pocket.

There is one bit of advice I could add. Try to make the right choice the first time because you do get used to a machine and its particular foibles. We do all change our ideas – you may start with the intention of turning bowls but end up being totally absorbed by fine spindle work. Try to think things through in advance. Wait, find what you want and then get that. If you do change your ideas, however, you will always be able to sell provided you did not buy one of the cheap, lightweight pieces of junk that are currently on offer. I had twelve responses to a 'lathe for sale' advertisement I placed in my local paper, and my price was fair but keen. Three telephone callers even offered to buy unseen.

Sometimes you strike lucky! A while ago, by asking around, I found one middle-quality lathe which had only done three hours' work; it had many accessories and tools and the deal was struck at one-third of the price of a new one.

Sometimes you are unlucky – I heard of two Wadkins in the West Country; nobody knew much about them and they were taken away at £25 each and had been scrapped before I heard about them.

14   The Workshop

The first thing you need is a building, and one thing is for sure – however big the one you have is, it will never be big enough! I started in a 10ft by 8ft (3 × 2.5m) shed, then moved to a garage, then two garages and a shed; and I am quite sure that the bits and pieces that I now have would, given reasonable space, fill a substantial-sized factory!

A lot will depend upon the sort of turning you propose to do. If you get into the massive stuff you will not only require substantial space for the lathe, but even more for the storage of timber and rough turned blanks. There can even come a time when you need a gantry hoist to lift blocks on to the lathe (as in Ed Moulthrop's workshop).

A wooden shed is quite adequate. It should be sited where there is plenty of light. Ideally the orientation should be such that the view across the lathe and out of the window is pleasant – there are times when the inspiration is necessary! And of course you will have to have access to a power source. If you do use a wooden shed, line the walls with poly-styrene and fibre boarding – turning with cold hands on a winter's day is the short cut to an accident.

DUST COLLECTOR

Now let us see what you have to cram into your shed. I know one professional woodturner who, when asked 'I am just taking up turning, what lathe should I buy?' countered with the question: 'Do you have a dust collector?' 'No!' 'Then buy one of those first!' He was right.

Since I installed mine I have slept better, need only a quick shower instead of a full bath after a day's work, can actually find tools previously hidden under layers of dust, and find that some tools actually keep better. It has trebled the life-between-overhauls of the power drill that I use for sanding. In fact I have already recovered the dust collector's costs in one way or the other.

Unfortunately dust collectors require space and they are not directly productive, so many turners do not put them high enough on the priority list.

There are quite neat wall-mounting collectors available for the smaller work-shop. Alternatively, a larger collector can be housed outside in a lean-to. This has other advantages. Collectors do create a fine dust on start-up and they add significantly to the ambient noise level in the workshop. It can become quite oppressive towards the end of a long day. So if it can be the other side of a wall, so much the better.

There is no need to have miles of flexible hosing. Very satisfactory ducting can be made from 4in (10cm) rainwater pipe. This will enable you to have an inlet over each of the machines and main work stations and to be able to take the ducting through the wall to the outside collector. Use curves rather than right-angled bends,

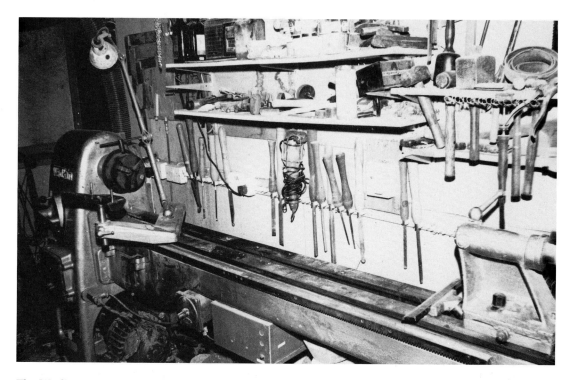

The Wadkin RS lathe. The motor is a 3 hp, three-phase unit but the small box under the lathe bed is a perfectly adequate phase converter that costs a little over £100. (The lamp is *not* fixed to the tool rest!)

and in order to maintain maximum suck you need to provide stoppers for all the inlets not immediately in use. The actual pick-up point at the lathe needs to be on a flexible mounting so that it can be positioned directly behind and close to the working zone. A bell- or hopper-shaped inlet properly positioned can take away not only the dust, but also a considerable quantity of the turnings.

Go for the biggest collector you can afford/accommodate. The bigger they are, the larger the particles that they will handle, and they make excellent vacuum cleaners for cleaning up the shop after a heavy day. The critical factors are the bag size and the volume of air that the unit draws, and only consider a machine with metal fans. 'Nasties' will occur and odd objects will get drawn in − it is interesting what they do to a lager can!

POSITIONING THE LATHE

Then we come to the lathe itself. We have already considered the choice of unit − let's now think about positioning it. If it is a big machine don't forget to think about floor loading! Beyond this there are two fundamental considerations − light and access. There is no doubt that abundant daylight flooding the working area and into the inside of turning bowls is the best possible arrangement. So the ideal siting is under a window that extends beyond the tailstock.

Lighting

You will also be frequently working outside the hours of daylight so you will need electric light and plenty of it. The base light can be a 6ft (1.8m) fluorescent tube

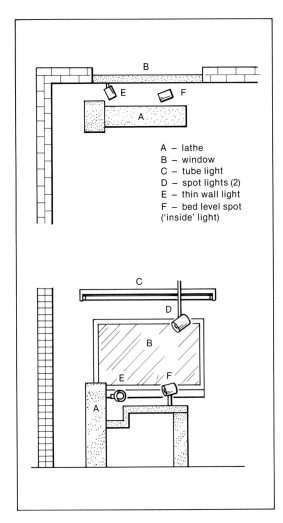

A – lathe
B – window
C – tube light
D – spot lights (2)
E – thin wall light
F – bed level spot ('inside' light)

Lighting the lathe.

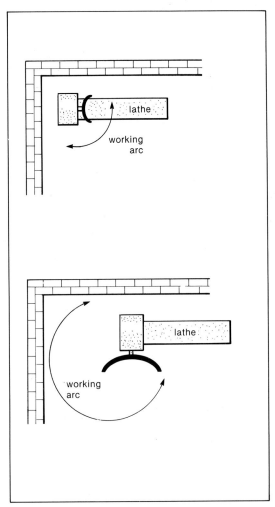

Lathe position for front face working. (a) A lathe for working over the bed – usually a step bed lathe can be positioned tight into the corner. (b) A lathe where larger work has to be turned off the front face requires more space.

mounted parallel to the lathe bed but over your head so that it shines on to the forward side of the workpiece. If directly over the lathe bed it can give a bad shadow.

On a separate switch and 1ft (0.3m) either side of the tube, I like two spots. These shine on to the face of platters and into shallow bowls as well as brightening up the whole work area when required. I also have a third spot positioned behind the tailstock and at lathe axis height. This will shine directly into deep vessels.

If you do a lot of thin wall turning you will find another light useful. This is mounted low behind the headstock pointing towards the workpiece and in such a position that it is directly behind a bowl when viewed from the normal working position. This is for thin wall turning and you only use the lamp when nearing the completion of turning so that

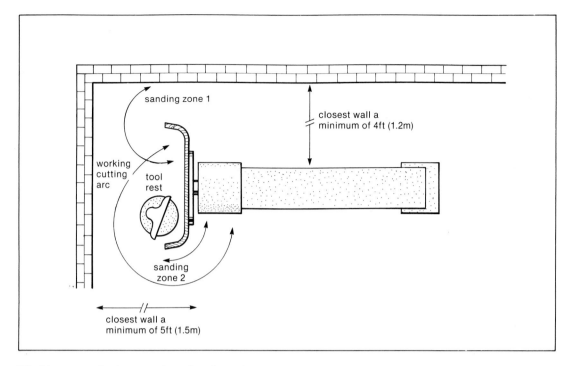

Working space for large outboard end turnings.

you can judge from the level of translucence just how thin the walls are becoming.

Access

The other basic aspect of lathe positioning concerns access. You need space! Just how much depends upon the type of turning you are going to do and the facilities offered by your lathe. An absolute minimum standing zone allows 4ft (1.2m) from the lathe bed to anything behind you. Preferably you want over 5ft (1.5m).

Several lathes have a relatively small swing capability directly over the bed and compensate for this by allowing the headstock to swivel so that larger diameter pieces can be turned off the front face of the lathe. If you envisage using this facility you will need even more space between the lathe and anything behind

you to allow the swing of longer handled tools. Front face turning also means that you cannot position the headstock up into a corner as there will be times when you are standing at the outboard end of the headstock in order to work on the outside of a large item.

The other arrangement met on many lathes is to allow turning off the outboard end of the headstock spindle. This means even more space. Not only do you now need room for a normal working arc but the arc tends to increase to over the 180 degrees, *and* you tend to turn bigger pieces!

Theoretically I could turn a wagon wheel off the end of my old Wadkin and therefore a full 'elbow room' working arc would mean having the lathe at least 6–7 feet (1.8–2.1m) from a rear wall with at least 5 feet (1.5m) from headstock to side wall.

So now there is a conflict. We need

173

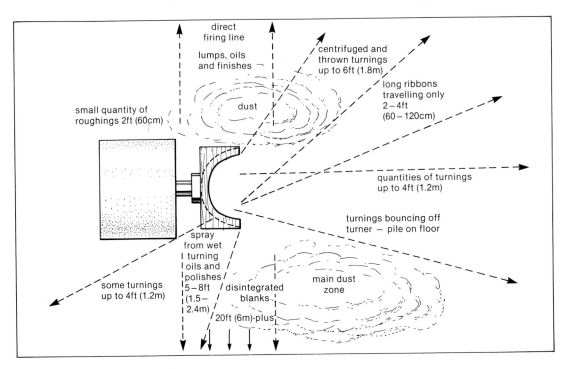

Floor clearing and firing line zones.

space around the lathe and yet we want it near a window for abundant daylight. If you have plenty of space the choice will probably be to have the lathe standing free – away from all walls, and then to hope that there is enough light. There are times when it can be quite useful to work from the far side of the lathe bed.

Where space is limited, then the position closer to the wall/window is to be preferred.

POSITIONING OTHER TOOLS AND EQUIPMENT

Behind the headstock will be the bell of the dust extractor on its movable mounting. Close to hand you need the grid wheel or tool sharpening device. Ideally this can be at the end of the lathe bed or just behind the main work zone so that all you have to do is to turn round to give an

edge a 'quick lick' (have the grinder switch on the unit itself). The more handy the unit is then the better will be the quality of finish on your work!

Equally, the tools that you use most frequently should be closest to hand – again arranged so that they can be reached without moving from the work stance. I use plastic water pipe clips screwed to a wooden board to hold the tools. This is mounted on the lower window frame directly behind the lathe bed and the most regularly used gouges are at the headstock end.

In general I find it preferable to have tools and accessories clipped or hung on wall boards. Each has its own position and that position is known. You can reach out instinctively without looking and bring to hand any item in regular use. Certainly there is no rummaging around in draws to find infrequently used gauges or wheel dressing tools.

Shelves anywhere near the main cutting zone are a snare and a delusion. They catch all the flying turnings and anything on them soon gets hidden or lost. Old kitchen cannisters make ideal containers for sanding discs, bits of wax and various knick-knacks. A biscuit tin will keep sheets of sandpaper dry even on the most clammy of winter days.

BAND SAW

Somewhere there needs to be another major piece of equipment – a band saw! It needs to be a substantial one. Buying ready-cut blanks is the short road to penury. Buying a small 3in (7.5cm) gape (depth of cut), light, hobbyist band saw (the three wheel type) is the next shortest road!

You do need a good, solid saw with at least a 6in (15cm) gape. The broader the width of cut (the 'throat') the better, but this dimension is rarely as critical as is that of 'gape'; particularly for bowl blanks.

With the saw you will need at least four blades – two narrow ones for cutting round tight radii and two broader ones for long, straight runs. In each width have a fine-cut blade for thinner work (probably 10 teeth per inch) and a coarse blade (usually 3 or 4 'skip' or teeth per inch) for thicker slabs of 2in (5cm) and over.

Manufacturers suggest a ½in (1.3cm)-wide blade will cut down to a 2½in (6.5cm) radius and a ³/₁₆th (4.5mm) blade down to 1¾in (4.5cm) radius. I must admit to going down to about 10in (25.5cm) diameter on ½in (1.3cm) blades, but do everything smaller with ¼in (6mm) width blades.

I have found it false economy to buy lengths of blade and make up my own,

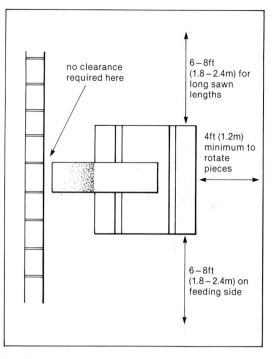

Working space for a band saw.

and even falser to try to resharpen worn blades. A supplier I know will make exactly what I want for my obsolete saw.

Unfortunately you cannot stick the band saw into a corner. You need room to swing boards outside the gape and you will, on occasions, wish to feed long lengths through, so you need clearance in front of and behind the machine (I have to work longer lengths through an open window!). And don't forget to have a dust collector inlet by the cutting zone. Band saws create a surprising amount of throat-tickling fine dust.

If you are fortunate enough to have a separate storage space for timber then the band saw could be sited there.

PLANER

Planers are useful but by no means essential. Where they do come in to their

175

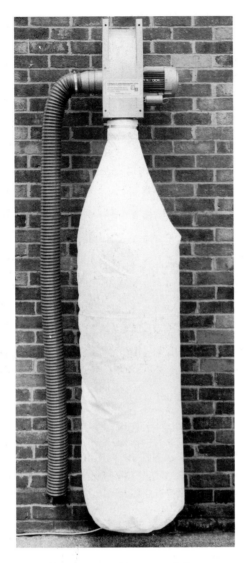

A small capacity wall-mounted dust collector. Quite suitable for a single lathe.

own is for producing a reasonably flat face on the top of a blank for mounting on to a face plate. They can also help in truing up lengths for spindle work. I find that I get by with a portable planer. Sometimes this poor tool is really abused, in that it is used to 'knock the corners off' the more massive blocks of chain-sawn wood that are too big to go through the band saw.

CHAIN-SAW

A chain-saw is a tool that I put in the essential category. I must admit to being greedy in having acquired several through auctions, gifts and the local newspaper.

First, with a chain-saw you can make the most of the many offers you will get of 'If you'd like to cut it up, you can take it away.' My most recent offer was of a dead oak tree. However, when I got to the house in question I found that it needed felling, and on one side was a glass conservatory whilst on the other was the neighbour's greenhouse. That gift horse I did look in the mouth!

Although petrol-driven saws are useful for really big jobs and work out in the field, I find that I now do most of my cutting up with the largest model of Black and Decker electric-powered domestic saws. This I find quite adequate for slabbing substantial trunks, as long as the chain is kept sharp. Sharpening takes only three minutes with the proper file.

WORK-BENCH

A work-bench is always needed – if only to rest blocks on while screwing on a face plate. It need not be too big, but it should be solid. Workmates are not adequate. A strong vice fitted to the bench is also needed. Of course most turners find themselves doing odd jobs with wood. The nature and size of those jobs is likely to place more specific requirements upon the size and shape of work-bench than is the turning itself.

A good bench will provide cupboard space and that is always at a premium. However, unless you use the work top

A work bench is needed – you must have somewhere to heap the junk!
Sometimes this one is cleared to give space for wood carving.

regularly, a large bench can be a real trap. You just use it to pile things on – part turned pieces, half used sandpaper, split items wanting glueing, tools for re-handling and so on. In no time at all there is no room left for working. Having a small bench makes you keep it clear!

A bench drill is required on occasions and is likely to assume greater significance if you have to start drilling angled holes, as for the fitting of inclined legs in stools.

Another near-essential is a bench sander – again with a dust extractor pick-up point. This will be used for smoothing bases, finishing some edges, squaring off, and a number of day-to-day tasks.

From here on the layout and equipment of the workshop will depend upon the particular focus that your work takes. If you move into the furniture end of wood-turning you will need glue pots, cramps and laying out space – and so on.

A circular saw table may be needed for some things. It has never had a role in my type of turning.

The one thing that I do find useful if workshop space allows, is some tall shelves. I said shelves are a snare, which they are if mounted anywhere near the lathe itself. However, a full-height set of office shelves is ideal for stacking small blocks, part turned work, and dry blanks.

The biggest problem that we all face is usually that of lack of space. The second is that of being squirrels! We are already short of room but we then fill every corner with unused equipment and off cuts of wood and metals that 'might come in useful one day'. For me to say don't do it! would probably be the ultimate piece of hypocrisy – but don't!

15 Health and Safety

Woodworking is one of the highest rated occupations in terms of insurance risks. Fortunately for turners the greatest number of accidents seem to be related to spindle routers, morticisers, and circular saws – the three machines that we do not use. There are, however, still substantial risks from the machinery that we do use, and getting insurance cover can be quite costly. It does not end there. There are other less obvious dangers; however, let's deal with the obvious ones first.

Loose clothing, long hair and ties are death traps anywhere near machinery, and sleeves with loose cuffs are a particular hazard in turning. For many reasons you will want to wear long-sleeved tops; so make sure that the cuffs grip the wrists tightly, can not come undone accidentally, and will not catch any rotating part. Equally a high, fasten-across neck cover prevents irritating bits from going down inside.

Never reach across the workpiece whilst it is rotating; again something could catch. Proper turning smocks are good. They fasten up the back, have proper cuffs, and come high up the neck. Overalls are the next-best thing.

The need to take care with the electrical installation is also obvious but it is easy to fail to notice that the cable of hand tools is getting too close to a working part. Loose or training cable runs should be kept to the minimum. Have a separate switched outlet for each unit and proper starters on the heavier duty machines. Make sure that there is an earth leakage trip somewhere in the main supply. Many people fail to take into account the loading that a number of machines can put on to a circuit, and particularly of the demands that some machines make upon start up. A 2hp dust collector draws about 14 amps for the first second or two.

It is advisable to have a direct line to the workshop from the main switchboard – don't just take a spur off the garage power point.

All portable tools should be fitted with rubber plugs – the plastic variety get broken very quickly in any normal workshop environment. Of course in commercial workshops and out on site, all portable equipment must be operating on 110 volts.

The drive belts to lathes should always be fully enclosed and all lathe doors or hatches should have micro switches that automatically shut the power down whenever a door is opened. Three and four jaw chucks are knuckle smashers. If it is at all possible have a guard over these.

We have said that a band saw is an essential tool in most turners' workshops. Good saw practice requires that the top feed guides should be close to the top of the work. The exposed length of the blade should always be guarded, and the wood being pushed through should always be fed with a pushing stick.

But as I said these are the obvious problems. There is another, almost as obvious, and that is the need to shield eyes from flying wood chips or from sparks when sharpening tools. Proper glasses, goggles or a face shield should always be worn. If you do any routing or chain-sawing, ear protectors are essential and most DIY stores stock very efficient ones. *Don't* just turn up the volume on your personal stereo to drown out the machinery noise!

In my workshop you need a hard hat! Out of balance, green wood blanks do sometimes fly off the lathe, and while most fly away from you (guided in that direction by the tool rest) they can still bounce back off the wall. It doesn't happen very often, but once can be enough.

Gloves have their place. When sanding, the heat build-up can be considerable — and very quick! If sanding inside a natural-edged piece thick gloves can reduce some savage bangs from a jagged edge.

The hidden dangers are worse. The dust from some timbers is actually carcinogenic. Iroko is highly suspect. Some woods such as pernambuco and padauk will cause a rash on the exposed wrists. The dust from all timbers will give respiratory problems. Rosewoods can prompt bouts of sneezing. There is currently some suspicion about spalted woods. It has been suggested that the fungi in the wood could breed in the warm, damp environment of human lungs. At one time all that I had to do was to sand down a couple of burr elm bowls to ensure a bad night's sleep, and the snoring used to wake the whole household. Small face masks with cotton pads do help, but not very much.

The complete respirator masks are strongly recommended. They are expensive, but then avoidance of lung

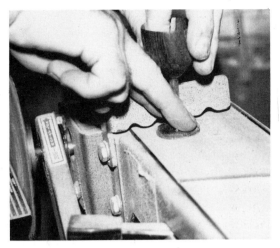

The bench sander used to clean up the base of an egg cup.

disease does not come cheap these days. Incidentally they can sometimes be bought at lower cost at agricultural wholesalers, as farmers use them a lot. Most professionals have a powerful dust collector and yet still wear a respirator mask.

Fine wood dust suspended in the air can produce an explosive mixture.

POSTURE AND STANCE

Included under the general heading of health and safety I would put posture and stance. Actually these have an even wider importance as they can effect the quality of your turning.

First you need to have the height of your lathe axis correct for you. I am 5ft 11in tall and I find that the axis needs to be about 44in (about 100cm) from floor level. If it is too high you cannot get over the top properly when planing with a skew chisel. If it is too low then the chances are that you will be working with your neck bent or shoulders stooped over. The first problem will be fibrositis, next osteo-

179

arthritis in the neck and permanent damage; several full-time turners suffer from this. Ray Key, Reg Sherwin and Richard Raffan and others have their lathes mounted on 6in (15cm) RSJ sections to give added height, and neither Ray nor Reg are that tall.

To help in aligning the tool inside deep spheres, one well-known turner sits astride the lathe bed and 'hangs' his head in a set position looking straight down the lathe axis. Already this held position is causing him quite severe neck problems with fused vertebrae.

Lifting techniques are important. Never try to lift heavy blocks of timber with the back bent – get down on your 'hunkers', with knees bent and back straight; the head should be up. To lift, straighten the legs.

Standing for long periods in one position on concrete floors is not good for the feet. A mat to stand on, or thermal insoles to the shoes, are really quite a sensible idea.

In terms of turning quality there are other aspects to the standing question. As a basic principle you should stand in such a position that you can sweep right through a single cut without moving the

The Racal Airstream dust mask. It has a battery-driven fan in the rear which draws in air through very efficient filters and blows clean air down across the face. They are comfortable, only mildly inconvenient, and incredibly effective. Note also heavy gloves being worn to hand-sand the natural edged bowl.

feet. The feet should be planted and the body should swing as the tool travels. In fact most of the movement should come from the body and not by moving the elbow.

Ideally, for many cuts, the tool will be held with the forearm making a straight line with the tool handle and the elbow locked against the side. As it is, the elbow takes a pounding – it is really acting as a cantilever arm shock absorber. Once after turning a 2ft (0.6m)-diameter bowl in solid burr elm the shock vibration set up a case of golfer's elbow that lasted over three months. The use of longer handled tools where the handle can be locked against the thigh can help to limit this problem.

Keeping the workshop dry and warm not only adds to personal comfort but does make it a safer place to work in. I have done more damage to my hands when they have been cold than at any other time.

Some people are very lucky. They have stoves in their workshops in which they can burn wood waste. Living in a smoke-less zone makes this impossible. It also makes the disposal of shavings and turnings very difficult. Digging some of the finer material into the garden helps to lighten up a clay soil, but after a few years' turning with a garden now 3ft (1m) higher than the surrounding countryside, I have a distinct waste disposal problem.

Waste must be disposed of, however, and not be allowed to build up under the feet. It certainly improves safety and considerably lessens the problem of find-ing dropped bits if the workshop floor is kept reasonably clear. At the end of each session a quick vacuuming with the hose of the dust collector keeps the floor visible.

FIRE

Fire is an ever-present hazard when working with wood, and I have been told that pieces of cloth that have been used for the application of Danish oil can dry out and ignite spontaneously. It has not happened to me – yet – but anything such as bits of rag, used wet or dry, bent screws, or whatever go straight into a lidded bin which is regularly emptied.

Overall, safety is a matter of common sense and constant vigilance. We all too quickly adopt short cuts, or try to do too many things at once and in no time at all we have a broken finger. So, just in case the worst does happen have a first-aid kit handy and make sure that you replace the plasters as they are used!

One final point, a little precaution that costs nothing. Have the tetanus injections – a two-part treatment which lasts ten years. You certainly can become infected from some timbers without immunisation.

16   A Small Return

We all have dreams. Wood turning starts as a hobby, and after a time you become relatively skilled – for some it may take five years or more, others may manage something quite significant in only two.

Friends, given a piece of your work for every birthday and Christmas are still complimentary and grateful. Your own house is full, and you even sell the odd piece to work-mates. The seeds have been sown – this is the way out of the rat race – certainly the way of 'retiring' early. You will take up turning for a living!

I can't say don't, can I? But think very hard. There are over 20,000 wood lathes in this country (one recent estimate suggests 30,000-plus). There are many turners who try to sell some or all of the items that they make. There are a few, a dozen or so, who make a reasonable living. There are many professionals who have to take on other work. Even the best will tell you that less than half of their time can be spent on making the things that they want to. The rest has to be spent on the repetitive bread-and-butter lines – banister rails, platters, standard pattern and sized salad bowls, etc. They also have to schedule in an amount of paid teaching and lecturing.

Regular 8am to 6pm days churning out platters and small bowls to order, at wholesale prices that are only practicable if you have a phenomenal speed of work, is just as dreary as is the commuting run into the office. And you have to have a volume of such work and have contracts with sales outlets which themselves turn over a good volume of turned goods. There is no turner in Britain who makes a good living producing only one-off, art pieces.

There are two mutually interacting problems. First, in Britain we do not have the widespread appreciation of wood that you find in some other countries. Yes, we recognise quality furniture, but very few accept wood as a medium for artistic expression. In the USA some turned pieces command ten even, thirty thousand dollars. In Britain if a piece sells at over £500 it is cause for a national holiday.

The second problem all turners suffer from is that of the turners who subsidise their customers. They charge so little for their work that they cannot be covering all their real costs and certainly not their time. I know some who will buy a piece of wood for £4, take almost an hour to make an item that they then sell for £5 and think that they have made a profit of a pound. The cost of the finishes, the sandpaper, the tools, the lathe, the supporting machines, the workshop, the power, the light, and a dozen more things have all been overlooked. And that £1 is all that they think that their time is worth! What they are doing is not only subsidising their customers, but they are also fundamentally devaluing wood in the eyes of the general public. It is this, not the competition, that worries many turners.

Go to any craft fair and you will see

wood turnery being 'given away'. In my first year of really trying to sell my work, although only a part timer, I sold £4,700 worth. There was even £800 surplus in the 'business' bank account at the end of the year. When the books were finally put together, however, I found that my 'cost of sales' (i.e. stall fees and travelling to fairs) added up to almost £2,800, and that by the time I had taken into account all the things that had been paid for out of pocket or from the family joint account (plus the cost of the timber that I had had in stock at the beginning of the year and had subsequently used), I had actually made a loss of over £600.

As a matter of interest a cross-section of turners who sell work through craft fairs identify that the costs of sales amounts to never less than a third and frequently as much as a half of the actual selling price.

So, with the cost of timber at a quarter of the selling price, cost of sales at between a third and a half, there is not much left to pay for the overheads let alone to pay any wages to the turner.

Certainly as your sales volume goes up things get better, but one of the best professional turners has said that in order to make an income of £10,000 he needs to sell £30,000 worth of goods per year (at his wholesale selling price, not allowing for the shops or galleries' mark-up). And that, in the British market, is a lot of turnery to sell.

It is now recognised by many part-time craftspeople who have used craft fairs as their principle sales outlet that this approach is not very good. They will also tell you (and I can bear this out) that their take is going down year by year at some fairs and that there are very few that are still reliable as money earners. There are more and more fairs, more and more organisers (many of whom who do not warrant the appellation 'organiser'), and there are more and more craftspeople trying to get on to the circuit. Many events are now little more than street markets and the quality buying public that once followed craft fairs has turned away. If you are selling bric-a-brac or volume domestic treen where you are competing directly with cheap imported woodware, craft fairs are fine, but that is about it.

Selling through craft fairs is a complex subject in its own right, but it is important because, despite all the difficulties it is where many craftspeople start until they have built up a more reliable trade elsewhere.

There are different types and qualities of fair, each of which requires a particular type and range of goods. At some fairs you can only sell light pulls, domestic treen, and tiles in wood surrounds. At others it is the natural edged and 'art' pieces. The average sale price for all stands at the former is about £4 whereas at the latter it could be £45. So you have to judge which fairs to use, what to take, where to set your prices, etc.

You cannot just walk into the better fairs. First they are expensive and you have to be sure that you are in the right arena. The stall may cost you £200-plus for three days, and on top of this you could have travel and accommodation. The organiser will want to see your work (not just photographs) and may then put you on the waiting list.

But even then you cannot guarantee success. You will certainly have competition to contend with (more on that in a minute). There will then be the weather, other attractions, swings on the stock market, time of the year (nobody spends money in September), and many other factors. This year I have done two fairs (one previously an average income event) at which my daily take was under £20, and I needed £120 to break even at both of these particular shows. I have recently done the fifth show at one venue where over the years my take has gone down progressively from £450 to £53 and you can actually see the difference in the type of person attending. Against all this there are local Saturday fairs where the table costs only £10 and the £250 sales are therefore very satisfactory.

Craft fairs may be pleasant, but they can be very unprofitable lost days, so they can not be relied upon to provide an income. Other outlets are needed. When you are just starting to sell, 'Turner-ware parties' are very useful. A friend books up a small round of them about Christmas time and sells £100–£300 on each evening.

Later, a studio at the workshop on a good tourist route can be a great asset, but you will still need contracts with retail outlets. It is not unusual to have to supply on a sale or return basis until you are known. The retailer will sell at your price but will expect 33⅓ per cent discount. Once you are established they will buy from you, but it will be at a margin often greater than one-third discount.

The greatest mistake we all make when we start to sell is that of under-pricing our work, and of thinking that we have to be cheaper than the competition. Some work is price-sensitive – it is run-of-the-mill, there are many others selling just the same sort of thing, and you have no special design or quality edge; here you have to be priced somewhere near the competition if you are to sell anything much. But in general, if people like what you are offering it almost does not matter what price you ask.

I have never been worried about competition. At a recent craft fair the organiser had put all five of us wood-turners together. I was twice as expensive as the next-highest priced and up to five times higher than what others were charging if you compared us purely upon type and size of object. My sales for the week-end were higher than the total of the other four put together. I was however worried about the prices that one of the cheaper was charging, not from a competition point of view but what it did for the overall image of wood. And I said so!

If you plan serious sales then there are many aspects of marketing that you will have to look into most carefully. After that you have to start costing out all the elements that have to be covered. When you do this you will quickly decide that you cannot 'afford' to produce at the sort of prices that some of the competition are charging. I succeed at some of the fairs that I still attend because my work is different and attention-grabbing and I do not make those items which everybody else makes and gives away.

In setting price I have already discussed the crude way of reaching a reasonable figure, and that is to take the cost of the timber as bought from a normal retail outlet and to multiply this by four. This is applying the rule of quarters. Of the retail price one-quarter is:

1 The cost of the wood.
2 The depreciation and maintenance on tools and equipment plus other workshop overheads.
3 The cost of sales (cards, letterheads, telephone, craft fair stalls, travelling, packaging, etc.).
4 Your time – the 'profit'.

One of my first craft fair stands. Price of the items on display range from £3 to £45.

If you were lucky enough to have been given the wood it does not matter – still work on the basis of what it would have cost you in a retail outlet; the gift piece will offset all those that went wrong (checked in the drying process or whatever).

The 'quarters' are interrelated. Often, wood bought more cheaply requires more preparation – hence higher machinery and time costs. If you buy your timber in bulk or as whole logs you need a higher multiplier to accommodate the additional primary working equipment and the higher wastage.

Many times, your cost of sales will exceed the quarter – what about the 33⅓ per cent discounts asked by retail outlets?

You have to spend more time making the quantities of smaller items that have low timber and raw materials costs, but the once-in-a-while nice big, premium priced item which was relatively quick to make can bring the whole equation back on track. But for all that, the 'quarters' idea still works as a rule of thumb.

At the end of the day selling woodturning comes round to 'getting on your bike' – seeing what other people make and what they charge and then working out something different; going round selling – not house-to-house touting your wares, but looking for commissions. Start with the bread-and-butter work doing turning for local builders, make items for antique restorers (their prices are very keen!) pick up commissions for sets of table ware, persuade gift shops to carry small lower priced trinket items, and hope that one day you will make it to the Harrods, Liberties and Bond Street Galleries of this world.

We all have dreams! I hope that yours are as sweet as mine.

Appendix: Timber Buying Tables

Table I gives the volume of timber required for a given size of blank. It assumes that a square block capable of producing the required diameter and thickness had to be purchased. Careful cutting, where smaller blanks were produced from the corners between the larger ones, has not been taken into account.

As a crude measure you should expect to pay at least twice the price for a round blank per cubic foot as you would for a plank of the same material. Some producers have a much higher mark-up, arguing that this is due to the wastage in cutting blanks. Their argument only holds good if you compare the blank price with the price per cube of a whole un-planked log. There can be an overall wastage of 60 per cent in converting from the log, but the table has already taken into account converting from the plank to the square, and then added a further 10 per cent cutting margin which should be more than generous enough.

Table II is a reference table of the more frequently encountered woods and shows the density or specific gravity of each. The figures are based upon kiln dried at 12 per cent moisture. It is used in conjunction with Table III to calculate volumes of timber bought by weight. It also shows the approximate weight per cubic foot of each.

The final two tables, Table III and Table IV, are more complex. They start with a set of typical specific gravities (at 12 per cent kiln dried) and then give the weight in kilograms per cubic metre and in pounds per cubic foot at that moisture content. The second section of Table III gives the volume of timber in a block of ten kilograms weight at the various stages of moisture content – kiln dried taken at 12 per cent, part seasoned as an average of 25 per cent, and as sawn is based upon 40 per cent moisture. In using the part seasoned figure it should be remembered that this can mean anything, and certainly as high as the 40 per cent shown in the 'as sawn' column. If in any doubt use the latter figure and err on the side of caution.

Table IV is a shortened table, showing the weight in kilograms of a given volume of kiln dried timber.

Thickness or depth								
	1in	**2in**	**3in**	**4in**	**5in**	**6in**	**7in**	**8in**
Blank Diameter								
6in	0.021	0.042	0.062	0.083	0.104	0.125	0.146	0.167
8in	0.037	0.074	0.111	0.148	0.185	0.222	0.259	0.296
10in	0.058	0.116	0.174	0.231	0.289	0.347	0.405	0.463
12in	0.083	0.167	0.25	0.333	0.417	0.5	0.583	0.667
14in	0.113	0.227	0.34	0.436	0.567	0.68	0.793	0.907
16in	0.148	0.296	0.444	0.592	0.74	0.889	1.037	1.185
18in	0.187	0.375	0.562	0.75	0.937	1.125	1.312	1.5

Table I   Volume of square timber required for given blanks.

Wood	Density (specific gravity)	Weight in lbs of one cubic foot at 12% moisture
African walnut	0.55	30–40 lb/ft^3
afromosia	0.69	39–49
agbu	0.52	32
alder	0.53	33
apple	0.71	43–45
ash, American	0.56	35
ash, English	0.51–0.71	32–51
aspen	0.45	28
balsa	0.16	2½–21
beech	0.72	45
birch	0.66	37–43
birch, yellow	0.71	44
blackbean	0.7	44
blackwood, African	1.2	75
blackwood, Australian	0.66	41
boxwood	0.91	52–71

Wood	Density (specific gravity)	Weight in lbs of one cubic foot at 12% moisture
brazilwood	1.2	75–80
bubinga	0.88	50–60
butternut	0.45	28
cedar	0.58	36
cedar of Lebanon	0.56	35
celery, top pine	0.64	40
cherry, American	0.58	36
cherry, European	0.61	38
chestnut, horse	0.51	31
chestnut, sweet	0.54	34
cocobolo	1.1	68
douglas fir	0.53	33
ebony, African	1.03	63–64
ebony, Macassar	1.09	68
elm	0.55	34
goncolo alves	0.95	59
greenheart	1.03	64
gum, American	0.56	35
gum, red river	0.82	51
hackberry	0.64	40
hemlock	0.50	31
hickory	0.82	51
holly	0.80	50
hornbeam	0.75	47
imbuia	0.66	41
iroko	0.64	40
ivory wood	0.90	56
jaccaranda	0.85	53
jarrah	0.80	43–65
jelutong	0.46	29
kingwood	1.2	75
larch	0.59	37
Lignum vitae	1.23	72–82
lime	0.54	34
mahogany	0.54–0.64	34–40
mahore	0.62	39
maple	0.66–0.69	41–43
meranti	0.55–0.67	34–48
mesquite	0.80	50
myrtle	0.85	53
oak, American red	0.77	48

Wood	Density (specific gravity)	Weight in lbs of one cubic foot at 12% moisture
oak, European	0.62–0.72	42–45
ogea	0.50	26–36
olive	0.89	55
ovangkol	0.80	50
padauk	0.72–0.77	40–50
parana pine	0.54	30–40
pear	0.70	44
pecan	0.75	46
pine		
pitch	0.67	41–43
ponderosa, Scots & redwood	0.51	32
Siberian	0.42	26
plane	0.62	39
poplar	0.45	28
purpleheart	0.86	50–63
ramin	0.66	41
rata	0.80	50
rosewood		
Brazilian	0.85	47–56
Honduras	0.96	58–68
Indian	0.85	53
sapele	0.62	35–43
satinwood	0.98	61
sequoia	0.42	26
snakewood	1.30	81
spruce, sitka	0.43	27
stinkwood	0.80	50
sycamore	0.61	38
teak	0.65	38–43
thuya, burr	0.67	40–43
tulipwood, Brazilian (Pao Rosa)	0.96	60
utile	0.66	34–47
walnut, European and American	0.64	40
wenge	0.88	55
willow	0.34	21–28
yew	0.67	42
zebrano	0.74	46

Table II   Density of frequently used wood.

GRAVITY AT 12% MOISTURE	kg/m³ at 12%	lbs/ft³ at 12%	Approx volume in cubic feet of 10 kilos of timber if purchased:		
			KILN DRIED 12% MC	PART SEASONED 25% MC	AS SAWN 40%+MC
0.16	160	9.6	2.30	2.15	1.99
0.34	340	20.4	1.08	1.01	0.93
0.35	350	21.0	1.05	0.98	0.91
0.42	420	25.2	0.87	0.82	0.76
0.43	430	25.8	0.85	0.80	0.74
0.45	450	27.0	0.82	0.76	0.71
0.46	460	27.6	0.80	0.75	0.69
0.48	480	28.8	0.77	0.72	0.66
0.50	500	30.0	0.73	0.69	0.64
0.51	510	30.6	0.72	0.67	0.62
0.52	520	31.2	0.71	0.66	0.61
0.53	530	31.8	0.69	0.65	0.60
0.54	540	32.4	0.68	0.64	0.59
0.55	550	33.0	0.67	0.62	0.58
0.56	560	33.6	0.66	0.61	0.57
0.58	580	34.8	0.63	0.59	0.55
0.59	590	35.4	0.62	0.58	0.54
0.61	610	36.6	0.60	0.56	0.52
0.62	620	37.2	0.59	0.55	0.51
0.64	640	38.4	0.57	0.54	0.50
0.65	650	39.0	0.56	0.53	0.49
0.66	660	39.6	0.56	0.52	0.48
0.67	670	40.2	0.55	0.51	0.47
0.68	680	40.8	0.54	0.51	0.47
0.69	690	41.4	0.53	0.50	0.46
0.70	700	42.0	0.52	0.49	0.45
0.71	710	42.6	0.52	0.48	0.45
0.72	720	43.2	0.51	0.48	0.44
0.74	740	44.4	0.50	0.46	0.43
0.75	750	45.0	0.49	0.46	0.42
0.80	800	48.0	0.46	0.43	0.40
0.82	820	49.2	0.45	0.42	0.39
0.85	850	51.0	0.43	0.40	0.37
0.86	860	51.6	0.43	0.40	0.37
0.88	880	52.8	0.42	0.39	0.36
0.89	890	53.4	0.41	0.39	0.36
0.90	900	54.0	0.41	0.38	0.35

GRAVITY AT 12% MOISTURE	kg/m^3 at 12%	lbs/ft^3 at 12%	Approx volume in cubic feet of 10 kilos of timber if purchased:		
			KILN DRIED 12% MC	PART SEASONED 25% MC	AS SAWN 40%+MC
0.91	910	54.6	0.40	0.38	0.35
0.95	950	57.0	0.39	0.36	0.33
0.96	960	57.6	0.38	0.36	0.33
0.98	980	58.8	0.37	0.35	0.32
0.99	990	59.4	0.37	0.34	0.32
1.03	1030	61.8	0.36	0.33	0.31
1.09	1090	65.4	0.34	0.32	0.29
1.10	1100	66.0	0.33	0.31	0.29
1.20	1200	72.0	0.31	0.29	0.26
1.23	1230	73.8	0.30	0.28	0.26
1.30	1300	78.0	0.28	0.26	0.24

Table III   Density, weights, volumes and moisture content.

Gravity at 12% moisture	Volumes (cu.ft)							
	0.25	0.05	0.10	0.25	0.50	0.75	1.0	1.5
0.16	0.11	0.22	0.44	1.09	2.18	3.27	4.35	6.53
0.35	0.24	0.48	0.95	2.38	4.76	7.14	9.52	14.29
0.45	0.31	0.61	1.22	3.06	6.12	9.18	12.24	18.37
0.50	0.34	0.68	1.36	3.40	6.80	10.20	13.60	20.41
0.55	0.37	0.75	1.50	3.74	7.48	11.22	14.97	22.45
0.59	0.40	0.80	1.60	3.21	8.03	12.04	16.06	24.09
0.65	0.44	0.88	1.77	4.42	8.85	13.27	17.69	26.54
0.69	0.47	0.94	1.88	4.69	9.39	14.08	18.78	28.17
0.72	0.49	0.98	1.96	3.92	9.89	14.70	19.60	29.39
0.75	0.51	1.02	2.04	5.10	10.20	15.31	20.41	30.62
0.80	0.54	1.09	2.18	5.44	10.89	16.33	21.77	32.66
0.85	0.58	1.16	2.31	5.78	11.57	17.35	23.13	34.70
0.90	0.61	1.22	2.45	6.12	12.25	18.37	24.49	36.74
0.96	0.65	1.31	2.61	6.53	13.06	19.60	26.13	39.19
1.03	0.70	1.40	2.80	7.01	14.02	21.02	28.03	42.05
1.10	0.75	1.50	2.99	7.48	14.97	22.45	29.93	44.91
1.23	0.84	1.67	3.35	8.37	16.74	25.11	33.48	50.21
1.30	0.88	1.77	3.54	8.85	17.69	26.54	35.38	53.07

Table IV   Weight in kilos of volumes in cubic feet.

INDEX